SHATTERED
BONDS

SHATTERED BONDS

CINDY BAND
and
JULIE MALEAR

Expanding
Horizons

Expanding Horizons
An imprint of New Horizon Press
Far Hills, New Jersey

Expanding Horizons books are published by

New Horizon Press
P.O. Box 669
Far Hills, NJ 07931

ISBN: 1-933893-02-8

First New Horizon Press Hardcover Printing: 2003
First Expanding Horizons Mass Market Printing: January 2007

10   9   8   7   6   5   4   3   2   1

Printed in the United States of America

Dear Reader,

Here is the latest addition to the true and often astonishing New Horizon Press crime series, in which ordinary people, who suddenly find themselves in terrifying and perilous circumstances, muster the courage within themselves to battle and vanquish evil. Told in the individuals' own words, these intimate accounts reach far beyond the headlines or nightly news broadcasts. They reveal in spellbinding detail what these true life heroes really felt and experienced as their lives spiraled from normal, everyday routines into extraordinary, incredible plights.

In her article, "Horror from the Headlines" (*Dayton Daily News,* January 2, 2002), Laura Dempsey highlights the true crime work of celebrated author Ann Rule and New Horizon Press. Regarding NHP true crime books, she writes that the story uncoils as someone close to the criminal sees the crime for what it is and decides to bring the perpetrator to justice, "involving numerous law enforcement personnel, prosecutor and defense attorneys, friends, relatives and coconspirators, plot twists, lucky breaks and strange coincidences that take believability right to the edge."

Through these real life tests of human resiliency and courage, we come to understand, as did those people who lived them, that in the darkest of times, amid horror, pain and cruelty, one can ultimately summon strength, call up courage and right wrongs. Most of all, by reading these true stories, we gain hope for the human condition as we see justice triumph and evil punished.

Shattered Bonds is the shocking true story of a young girl who comes home to find her mother lying dead at the bottom of the stairs only to begin to suspect that the killer is someone very close to her.

We hope you find *Shattered Bonds* both a spine tingling and illuminating read.

Joan S. Dunphy
Publisher

Dedication

We, the authors, dedicate this book to our departed loved ones—Cindy to her mother, the late Florence Band, and Julie to her husband Bennie, the late B.F. Cook Malear.

We also dedicate *Shattered Bonds* to two kind and intelligent lawmen, who not only helped and supported Cindy at a time when she most needed help, but who also delved into their files and their memories to help her and Julie write this true story—Nassau County, New York Assistant District Attorney William Dempsey III and Nassau County, New York Police Department Homicide Detective Jack Sharkey. Without their dedicated persistence, Florence Band might never have found justice.

Cindy Band and Julie Malear

Authors' Note

This book is based on the experiences of Cindy Band and reflects her perceptions of the past, present and future. The personalities, events, actions and conversations portrayed within the story have been taken from her memories, extensive court documents, interviews, testimony, research, letters, personal papers, press accounts and the memories of some participants.

In an effort to safeguard the privacy of certain people, some individuals' names and identifying characteristics have been altered. Events involving the characters happened as described. Only minor details have been changed.

Table of Contents

12   Contents

Acknowledgments

Thanks, first of all, to publisher Dr. Joan Dunphy of New Horizons Press for recognizing the potential of this story and for encouraging us from the beginning of our relationship to the book's final fulfillment. Thanks, also, to editor Lynda Hatch for her rapid and excellent toning of our manuscript, as well as to the rest of the talented staff at New Horizons Press.

But we are aware that we might never have reached Joan Dunphy and New Horizons Press had it not been for Richard Feit, who took an interest in the story and advised us to send it to Philip Schwartz at St. Martin's Press. Thank you both. And thanks to editor Charles Spicer, who phoned to tell us he was interested in the story and had sent it to Dr. Dunphy. We are very grateful.

Since this is a true crime story, we had help from lawmen. In addition to Detective Jack Sharkey and Assistant District Attorney Bill Dempsey to whom we have dedicated this book, we want to thank Officer Charles Hoeffer of the Riviera Beach Police Department for his technical help and longtime encouragement. We also thank Lantana Police Chief Richard Lincoln who was a sergeant in Delray Beach at the time of Howard Band's arrest and passed his memories along to us. We are grateful also for the cooperation of institutions such as Mohawk-Walsh Prison in New York; we give special thanks to Wanda Muncy there.

Many others helped us during our work on *Shattered Bonds*. We are grateful to Mike Kaplan, who attended Jericho High School in Cindy's class, and sent us information and pictures. Cindy and Julie are both grateful to A. Scott Cunningham for referring the two of us to each other for this book.

Among writer friends, Julie wants to thank author Ginger Curry who gave her constant encouragement as she wrote Cindy's story. Julie is grateful, too, for the "very helpful advice" of mystery writer Laura Belgrave, as well as that of science fiction and true crime writer Daniel Keyes. Julie also thanks the talented writers' group ANRALD (its name is an acronym for the disclaimer in novels: Absolutely No Resemblance to Anyone Living or Dead) for listening to and critiquing the book "as I wrote it." Included are writers Monika Conroy, Janet Le Clair, Ben Peck, Bob Kerpel, Lou Ruf, Bob and Loys Rafferty, Marlene Roberts, Adelaide Altman, Mariane Kulick, Diane Warner, Millicent Brady, Rayna Harris, Jim Cary, Tom Collins, Elizabeth Carmichael, David Drummond and Sandi Underwood. In addition, she thanks members of the Boca Branch of The National League of American Pen Women, Inc. for sharing their vast knowledge and abilities. To friend Erma Seymour, she gives special thanks for her constant encouragement and down-to-earth advice. She also thanks Kristie Breslin in New Zealand for her supporting e-mails. And last, but not least, she is grateful for the deep support of her four daughters of whom she is very proud: Marie Breslin, Donna Malear,

Laura Lindeman and Melody Pairo—along with their fine families.

Cindy wants to thank her loyal and beautiful friend, Tory Pierini, for her friendship and encouragement. "I would not be the gentle person I am if it were not for Tory's soft way. And I also want to thank her daughter Michelle for believing in me."

Cindy thanks *La Vieille Maison* and staff "for accepting me for whom I was," and to the owners Carolyn and Leonce Picot "for the strength of their convictions in me, for their trust in me and their concern for me, and allowing me to provide the best service I can in the best restaurant in the world and for believing in me unconditionally."

She thanks Joyce Fix for "her wisdom, beauty, intelligence, knowledge and class. I look up to her as someone who makes me feel good—an unending well of support."

Cindy considers *La Vieille Maison* staff as her "true family" and she is grateful for their constant encouragement.

Cindy is grateful to Walter Le Blanc, "whom I thank for his generosity and compassion towards me."

She gives thanks to Tony Thompson. "I thank him for coming to my side when I needed him and for being a wonderful encouragement always."

And she thanks Nancy Palilonis. "I thank her for being a pillar of friendship, someone I can go to who will never judge me and will always want what's best for me—a real friend."

Prologue

Cindy could see a number of silver and white police cars parked in her driveway. "The cops must be having coffee with my folks," she told her friends. "They do that around here sometimes."

"It's after midnight." Neil's face looked concerned.

A shiver of fear, so fleeting Cindy scarcely reacted, made her suddenly cold. Immediately she pushed the feeling away. *Nothing could possibly be wrong,* she thought. *It's just that Old Westbury is such a small, exclusive community that everyone knows each other, including the police. The cops are visiting, that's all!* "Or maybe," she said to Neil, "the burglar alarm went off by mistake. That's always happening, but they still check on us. Dad was doing some wiring on it this afternoon."

Climbing out of the car, Cindy stood by the driver's window for a moment looking around. There were five patrol cars there, one crime scene van and a number of unmarked vehicles. She saw a couple of Old Westbury policemen with their distinctive Canadian Mounties-type hats heading for the back door. Her thoughts were a jumble. Perhaps the vodka she accidentally drank at the party was fogging her brain, but nothing seemed to register except that in all the confusion, her parents might not notice she was late arriving home. And that was good. She still assumed the cops had responded to a faulty security alarm.

She called to her friends, "Goodnight, you guys. Thanks for the ride."

"Hey," Neil said, "We're going to wait right here!"

She waved and started up the long drive. It was then she noticed that all the lights were on in the back of the house, none in front. *So that's where everyone is.* As she hurried towards the light, she heard Storm, one of the family dogs—a huge, young German shepherd—barking in the dog run outside.

She scarcely noticed when Neil, who had jumped out of his car, hurried to her side and accompanied her to the rear of the house.

From the patio, Cindy could see about twenty heads through the French doors that opened into the kitchen. Thoughts ricocheted through her mind. *What a crowd. So many people inside, not just cops either. The alarm isn't ringing.* She opened the door.

She could see her father at the far end of the kitchen. He had on a silk robe, deep green and navy. As she moved closer, she saw it was tied loosely over his underwear. She felt slightly embarrassed for him, standing there with all those people and only half dressed. *Why isn't Dad looking at me? His expression is so blank,* she thought. *What is wrong? Where is Mom? What's going on here?*

When Cindy started into the kitchen she saw a neighbor, Leon Sultan, a physician, near the door. Before she could say a word he was beside her, his eyes locked on hers. When he didn't smile, she began to tremble. "What's going on?" Cindy said, her voice suddenly very small. Her lips were dry. She licked them, forcing herself to squelch the fear. She'd always considered the doctor to be a gentleman, very cultured, very sophisticated. *Why,* she thought, *is he looking at me so strangely?* She couldn't interpret it. He kept perfect eye contact, as if he could will whatever was happening away from Cindy. She felt edgy, but kept telling herself that it couldn't be anything bad.

"Cindy, let's sit down," Dr. Sultan said, motioning toward the butcher-block kitchen table. They both sat down, knee-to-knee, eye-to-eye. His familiar, kind face seemed terribly serious. "Cindy?"

"Yes?" Suddenly she knew she didn't want to hear whatever it was he was going to say. Her nails dug painfully into her palms as her hands clenched into tight fists.

"It's your mother, my dear. There's been a terrible accident."

Cindy didn't answer. Emotions were sweeping over her. Now she was trembling.

"I'm afraid your mother's dead, Cindy. She's had a fall. She's . . . she's at the bottom of the basement stairs."

She heard his words and felt numb. She looked up and saw her father off to her right. He still wasn't looking at her. He had a vacant, faraway stare in his eyes. In a flash, she lunged for the cellar steps.

The cops reacted like a shot. "Stop her!" They stood shoulder to shoulder to bar her way. One of them slammed the basement door shut. "Cindy," he said gently, "we have to move your mother's body."

Body? That's Mom he's talking about, she thought. *What good would that do? I just need to wake her up.*

She was in denial, rejecting what she'd just heard from the doctor.

Cindy felt the bang of the slammed basement door reverberate through her body and it seemed as if her whole soul was shattering. With the police officers barring the basement stairs to her, she suddenly whirled around and ran out the back door crossing the patio to the lawn. "Mommy! Mommy!" she shrieked over and over. Finally, she dropped down on the grass and beat her fists against the ground, sobbing and screaming. *If Mommy really were dead, they'd bury her.* And somehow Cindy thought that if she kept beating her fists into the earth, sooner or later her mother would hear them, like tom-toms, beating signals summoning her back.

Neil came from out of the darkness of the front lawn and threw his body against Cindy's, his lips next to her ear. "Shhh," he coaxed, trying desperately to calm her, stroking her hair, patting her shoulders. "Cindy, shhh, shhh."

Moments later, with everyone standing around, Cindy jumped to her feet and pulled away from Neil. She ran back in the house. "I have to get to Mommy! Why are you all keeping me from her?" she cried. Before anyone could stop her, Cindy pulled open the basement door and saw for a split second the crumpled form in the light blue nightgown lying at the bottom of the stairs. And then for the first time, she knew the awful truth.

Chapter 1

Young and Invincible

In the impressive English Tudor mansion at 9 Horseshoe Road on that steamy August afternoon, Cindy Band's parents were entertaining. At sixteen, Cindy couldn't get excited about her parents' friends coming over for a swim and dinner. After all, with a fantastic home, a live-in maid and plenty of luxuries and money, Howard and Florence Band often entertained. And, as always, the house looked fantastic. Before the housekeeper left for the weekend, she'd vacuumed the Oriental carpets, polished the ornate furniture, dusted the original oil paintings and shined the downstairs picture window.

Her parents' friends were okay. They were fine, in fact. No problem there. It was just that Cindy had more important things to think about. Her mind, as she seated herself at the butcher-block table in the kitchen, was on tonight's party at her friend Dina's house.

Yesterday morning, her mother had taken Cindy for a manicure at *Ambiance,* one of the poshest beauty salons around. The stylist had set her long hair in a really neat hairdo—a handful of her auburn locks pulled off to one side in a pony tail, which was accented with different-color bands and shiny ribbons hanging down. And Isla, who had her own exclusive brand of *Isla* cosmetics at the salon, had shown her how to apply the wonderfully subtle and soft makeup to her skin. Her mother always saw to it that Cindy had extra attention when getting ready for special occasions. There were times when Cindy felt overprotected, but she had to admit she enjoyed all the pampering. Her mother made her feel loved.

Today, Cindy was giving herself a pedicure at the kitchen table. She wondered, as she chose a matching polish for her toes, whether her friend Neil would be at the party. Neil Ferrick was a terrific guy, slight, with fair skin and blue eyes, whose curly, sandy-blond hair often looked wild and untamed, like a surfer's. Maybe she'd give him a call later on. He had a girlfriend, Shannon, but Cindy knew Neil was her friend, too.

Through the double doors that led from the kitchen to the patio, Cindy could see and hear her parents and the Robertsons laughing and splashing. The Robertsons' kids, Tara and Seth, were in the pool, too. It was clear that everybody was having fun. More power to them.

But tonight, Cindy would *not* stay and help clean up. For a minute, she forgot the housekeeper was off for the weekend. No matter. Mom and Ellen Robertson didn't mind cleaning up anyway. It gave them a chance to talk without the men horning in. After all, Mrs. Robertson was Mom's best friend. Being in education, they both liked to gab about school stuff and the advanced degrees on which they both were working.

The second her best friend Carol arrived, Cindy intended to split. Oh, she'd be nice to the Robertsons and their children. She'd been raised to be polite. She might even join them for a short while in the pool, after she changed into her new black bikini. She realized her folks were very generous; they gave her and her sister Paula whatever they wanted and she was grateful. It was just that there were so many more important things to do than make boring small talk about things that didn't even interest her. It was always the same: "Cindy, you've grown so," etc., etc. Still, she didn't want to be rude. She'd do a lap or two in the pool to make her parents happy.

"Cindy, come out here this minute!" Her father's booming voice startled her. "Cindy, don't you ever hear me call?" She turned to see her father entering the kitchen, the paunch he lately sported hanging over the top of his swimsuit, dripping water on the kitchen floor. He hadn't bothered to wrap a towel around himself. "Cindy Band, I'm talking to you!"

"What do you want, Dad? I'm busy!" She noted his frown, his reddening face.

"I want you to be halfway civil. We're having company, you understand me?" His voice showed his exasperation. He was flailing his arms, a habit he had. "Why aren't you swimming in the pool with our friends?"

"I was just coming." Not wanting to meet his eyes, Cindy turned back to fixing her toenails. "Besides, Paula doesn't have to cater to your friends. You let her go off camping. Your precious Paula doesn't ever have to do anything she doesn't want to do. You never criticize her like you do me all the time."

She heard him suck in his breath. *Uh-oh, shouldn't have said that,* she thought. She'd gone over the line. Her father could be simply terrible when he got angry. She still remembered the smacks she'd gotten when she was younger just for asking too many questions— like "Are we there yet?" when they were on a trip.

Quickly, she screwed the lid on her polish, placing it and the nail file in her manicure kit. He was standing close to her with his hands balled into fists. She wondered what he was going to do. She supposed all fathers acted this way. *And then parents wonder why their kids rebel,* she mused.

They both turned when Florence Band opened the patio door. Her reddish blond hair was covered with a cap. Looking at her mother, Cindy thought, *Mommy is really nice looking for a woman of forty-two.* Right now, a beach robe hid her lush curves. Nobody could ever say Florence Band wasn't a lady. She was always modest.

Florence spoke in her usual soft voice. "My goodness, you're both in here. Why don't you come on out to the pool, dear?" She patted Cindy's cheek with cool fingers.

"Okay, Mommy, sure. I'll go get my suit."

"And don't wear that bikini in front of the Robertsons," her father said, raising his voice again. "You look like a tramp!"

Gritting her teeth and glad to escape a confrontation, Cindy grabbed her belongings and rushed from the room. Then the quarreling started. She could hear her parents as she started up the stairs.

"You're ruining her self-esteem. She's a nice girl; she gets As and Bs in school. Couldn't you be a little less critical? She's a really good kid."

"It's you—you spoil the hell out of her! She needs discipline and I'm the only one who gives it, so don't tell me what to do. I'm the one who makes the rules here."

Cindy could picture her father waving his arms around. She was aware that many women found him good-looking, but he was a short man with a short man's complex. He had to be the boss. When he was upset or angry, he always raised his voice and waved his arms.

"Please, Howard, our guests—they'll hear you. Please keep your voice down!"

"Don't tell me what to do, Florence! Sit down. Just remember who pays the bills around here."

"I didn't mean to . . ."

He broke in. "Oh yeah? Then how come you were out there bragging about your father's success again? You make me sick. Always lording it over me. I've told you before and I'll tell you again: Do you know what you and the kids would have, if I weren't working my ass off for your father? You'd have nothing."

"I'd have *what*, Howard?" Florence's voice sounded upset. "Don't start in on me again. Remember, my father took you into the business when you desperately needed a job."

Cindy knew this was a sore point between them. She knew that her grandfather—her mother's father—had taken Howard Band into the business and given him a great job. Sure, Cindy's dad had built the company up until they were millionaires, but Cindy knew from hearing her mother and father argue about it so many times, that it was Cindy's grandfather's original business, his inventions.

"Oh just forget it! Get back out there and shut up."

A loud crash followed and Cindy considered running back down to see what was happening, but she assumed her dad had knocked over a chair or broken a vase in a fit of temper. He'd broken a lot of things lately. Years of childhood self-preservation, however, caused her to run up to her room and put the angry sounds out of her mind as she always had.

Cindy's bedroom was her haven, a beautiful, custom

designed affair with drapes of burgundy, tan and teal and a swan design that matched the coverlet on her bed. The drapes' reverse side matched the chair and wallpaper. She and Paula shared a big bathroom between their two rooms and each had giant walk-in closets. Kids at school referred to them as the "rich kids."

It was true, she and Paula had a luxurious life, Cindy told herself as she stepped out of her clothes. Her mother and father spoiled them. They gave them any material things they wanted. But there were times, like now, that Cindy would have given anything to have had a happy family. Since that was impossible or so it seemed, she just wanted to get away, get out of the house. All the tension around made her feel sick to her stomach. She felt like flaring out at both of them to stop, *just stop*. But, as always, Cindy only ran from the loud voices.

She wanted them to be a normal family, to get along with each other. Dad had always been hotheaded, but the family used to have so much fun. Trips to Grandma's, amusement parks—so many good times. Cruises to Mexico, Spain and Cape Cod. Such joy. She hated seeing and hearing her folks quarreling all the time.

She couldn't wait to get away! That's what she needed: to be with her friends and calm down. She never drank more than an occasional beer, but after this latest tirade between her parents, she was feeling shaky. Maybe at the party she'd have two.

Cindy dressed hurriedly for the pool, choosing an older, more conservative, one-piece swimsuit rather than the new bikini. *No need to make Daddy angry. He gets angry enough without a reason,* she thought.

It was after she'd come downstairs and joined her parents and their friends, that she heard the doorbell ring. Her father was napping in a lounge chair. He was always after her about being rude. Wasn't it a rude thing for him to nod off in front of company? Cindy bit her lip. Quickly, she climbed out of the pool to answer the door. To her surprise, before she could even grab a towel, her father jumped up and went to the door. He was back a moment later.

"Hey, Florence," he called. "Some strange woman's car has broken down out in front of our driveway. Listen, I'll go see if I can give her a hand, okay?"

Before her mother could respond, he left. Cindy heard the front door slam. Since by now she had toweled off sufficiently to enter the house, she ran over to the dining room window to check on the "strange woman" with the broken down car. Outside she saw a Cadillac with its hood up. Leaning against the car was her father. He appeared to be speaking animatedly to the woman. From that distance, Cindy couldn't see her very clearly except to notice that her hair was long and blonde.

"There's something familiar about that woman talking to Dad," Cindy murmured to herself. When nothing came to mind, she tucked the thought away and went back out to the pool.

After dinner that evening, her friend Carol came to the house. The two teens skipped upstairs to Cindy's bedroom to finish getting ready for the party.

"I'm so full!" Cindy told Carol as she wriggled into new jeans, which fit her body like a second skin. "Mom's a gourmet cook, you know. Her spaghetti *Bolognese* is the best! And we've been snacking all day—like on veggies, finger sandwiches, blueberries, cheese—even caviar. Wow, I'm totally stuffed!"

"You're lucky you're naturally petite and slim. You don't ever have to count calories, do you?" Carol observed.

Some time after eight o'clock, Cindy picked up her telephone and dialed her good pal Neil to tell him about the arrangements for that evening while Carol sat on the bed beside her.

"Yeah, Neil, the party's at Dina's." She laughed and said, "It's going to be a blast. Everybody will be there. You'll come? Cool! Do you think I can get a ride home with you afterwards, please? Great, Thanks! Yeah, Carol's here right now, but she gets to stay out later than me, you know, so I definitely need an early ride home. Billy Kelly is going to take us there. Okay, see ya. Bye."

"Well, are he and Shannon coming to the party?" Carol asked. When Cindy nodded, the two girls high-fived, their hands making a clapping sound.

Catching sight of the jewelry her friend was wearing, Cindy opened her velvet jewel box and held up a Gucci necklace of stunning beads. "Should I wear this?" she asked.

Carol agreed, her eyes wide, and then helped Cindy fasten the clasp, as well as the clasp on a gold chain bracelet with diamonds. Cindy decided to add hoop earrings, her own custom designed pair, which sported sparkling, diamond chips. She went to the full-length mirror, studying the effect for several seconds.

A car horn honked. Carol rushed to the window and waved. "Billy's here!" The girls picked up their purses and were set to leave when Cindy's mother came into the room.

"Great food, Mom. Thanks," Cindy said. "Listen, Mom, Carol and I are ready to take off now."

"Do you have to, hon?" She took the girl's hand. "Maybe you could stay home this one time, Cindy?" Florence's big brown eyes bore a pleading look.

Cindy *knew* her mother wanted her to stay. But at sixteen years of age, Cindy was a typical teenager, a little selfish, a little self-centered. Impatient, she pulled back and said, "No, Mom, I just *can't*. We're going to the most important party of the summer. Everybody will be there! We have to go—Billy's waiting for us down at the end of the driveway, so we've got to hurry."

Cindy took Carol's arm to steer her out the door, but Florence, who'd dashed to her bedroom, returned with two boxes.

"Look, Cindy, I've got some new clothes for you, honey. Maybe Carol would like to see them, too." Florence Band laid the boxes on Cindy's bed and opened the lids on them both. She held up a dainty apricot pantsuit trimmed in aqua embroidery. "Look, hon, here's one that . . ."

"Mo-o-m, please. I just can't look now! Cut me some slack! We don't have time. Later, okay?" Cindy gave her mother a quick peck, skimming her hair.

Florence Band looked so sad that her daughter stopped. "You know I love you, don't you, Mom? I'll call you later from the party."

"We'll be home all night, Cindy. Don't forget to call," her mother replied, resignation in her voice.

"You know I love you, don't you Mom?" she repeated.

Her mother smiled and nodded.

Cindy and Carol ran out the bedroom door and down the staircase. At the foot of the stairs, Cindy looked back up at her mother, who'd followed the girls into the hall, and waved. Cindy smiled, throwing her mother a kiss.

As they walked away, she said to Carol, "I am *really* proud of her. Really. In just two more months, my mom will be Dr. Florence Band. Can you believe it? And guess what? She's so modest, she doesn't want to be called 'doctor' at all."

"That's awesome! And your mom does a lot of charity work, too. I've heard how she . . ."

"Yeah, she's always helping people." *Carol is right. Mommy is super,* she thought. And her mother should understand. She had to realize that parties were a teen's lifeblood and Cindy had to go.

From the top of the stairs, Florence called out, "All right, then, dear. You girls have a good time. I love you, Cindy."

"Love-you-too." *Poor Mom,* Cindy thought, feeling a pang of regret, of compassion. Her mother was so good. She lived for the family—Cindy, her sister Paula and their father. But much as she hated to acknowledge it, Cindy felt her father didn't appreciate Florence Band. Otherwise, why did they fight so much? Or did all married couples do that?

Then, squaring her shoulders, Cindy shook away such thoughts, anxious to be off with her friends, to leave this big, unhappy house with its tension and quarreling. "You know," she said, turning to Carol as they walked through the living room, "my mom is really great, but sometimes I think she doesn't want me to grow up. And sometimes I don't want to either." Cindy sighed, then giggled. "But one of those times isn't tonight. Come on, let's run. Billy will get tired of waiting for us."

The two girls, dressed similarly in designer jeans and tees, left by the front door. They laughed in sheer exhilaration as they ran down the long driveway and climbed into their friend's car.

"What took you guys so long? We're going to be late," Billy complained.

"Sorry," Cindy said, shrugging her shoulders. "I had to give my mom some extra TLC."

Billy smiled. "I know how that is," he said.

He was a good guy, Cindy decided, as the car took off with a little lurch. They were soon gaily cruising down Horseshoe Road in Old Westbury, their faces flushed with the excitement of being free, of having lots of friends, of simply being young—a time of invincibility. Or so they thought.

Chapter 2

An Ominous Sunday

The sports car with the three teens inside sped between large, lavish houses with carefully landscaped lawns, each estate more expansive and beautiful than its neighbor. This was the stomping ground of such society elite as the Vanderbilts and Whitneys. Everything in the Band home was custom made. Howard Band had hired a well-known architect and a builder and paid them handsomely. Their neighbors embraced them. After all, when a family lived in this neighborhood in superwealthy Old Westbury, they were "the elite." And they tended to stick together. But at this moment, on this gorgeous summer night, none of that mattered to Cindy and her friends.

They arrived to find the party a blast, fifty kids or so whooping it up. There were no adults in sight, but plenty of loud music and liquor. Cindy wasn't into hard liquor or drugs, maybe just an occasional beer or glass of wine. But tonight, one of the kids, whose name she wasn't sure of, gave her some quaaludes. "Ludes" were all the rage this year. Not wanting to look like a nerd, Cindy slipped them into the pocket of her jeans and then forgot them.

The music was ear-splitting and wonderful! It took you out of yourself, somehow. For a while, somebody kept playing Pink Floyd music over and over. It was great.

"Hey, Cindy," one of the guys yelled. "What's your fave? Pick an album."

She picked two and listened as her friend played them. At first, she was having fun. They were all so loud and happy. Then she noticed a lot of the kids were acting like they were drunk. Someone had set up a few glasses with ice and slices of lime on the table. *Probably the parent touch,* she thought and smiled. She took a sip of what she thought was water and nearly spit it out. "Geez, what *is* this?" she asked one of the guys she knew standing by the table.

"Vodka," he answered. "Try it for once, Cindy. Don't be such a party-pooper." She sipped again. She'd never tried vodka before. It made her feel strange, as if she were losing control. Still, it made her family and its problems seem far away. She was really enjoying herself, at least until about ten. Then suddenly, she had the strangest little ping of worry. Well, not worry exactly. It was more of a feeling that someone was sending her a message, and that message was: *Call home.*

"May I please use your phone?" she asked Dina, the hostess.

"Why not?" The girl smiled and pointed towards the den.

Cindy went in and phoned her parents' number, letting it ring and ring. *Strange,* she thought, *they're supposed to be home. Why don't they pick up? Are they outside? Have they gone somewhere? No, not likely.* The little "ping" she'd felt turned into a giant trip hammer. She put down the receiver and left the den.

"Everything okay, Cindy?" Jay Weber, another of the kids, asked. She guessed he could see by her face that she was upset.

"My folks were supposed to be staying home tonight, but they didn't answer the phone."

"They probably went for a walk. Come on, I know what'll fix you up." He elbowed through the mass of kids towards the kitchen and handed her a beer.

She took it, mumbled thanks, but didn't open the beer can. She set it back on the counter when Jay left the kitchen.

She went back to the den. She had to keep trying. She thought of times in the past when she hadn't called on time or had gotten home a minute late and her father had yelled at her mother that she was bringing up a tramp. Howard Band was a rich, powerful man, but lately his temper would just explode at the least thing. And then he took his frustrations out on his wife, sometimes raging for hours.

Now, with the telephone receiver pressed against her ear, Cindy could hear ringing over and over. She found herself digging long polished nails into the palm of her hand. *Why do I feel so nervous, so unsettled?* she asked herself.

Suddenly, Carol appeared beside her in the den. "What are you doing, Cindy? You're missing all the fun!"

"I promised my mom I'd call. I want to see if I can stay past my curfew. C'mon, please answer!" This time Cindy wasn't giving up. She let the telephone ring on and on. They had to be there. Maybe they were outside on the patio, but why didn't they hear the telephone and come back in?

Sensing her friend was upset, Carol reached over to Cindy and hugged her as she sat at the desk, the phone still ringing. "Geez, Cindy. Is your dad going off the deep end again?"

"No, he's okay, I guess. They still aren't answering. C'mon, c'mon. Won't somebody *please* answer this phone!"

At last, her father answered. "Yes?" He seemed out of breath and somewhat annoyed.

"Dad, it's Cindy."

"Cindy, you had better get home on time tonight."

Cindy felt a relief so tremendous she wanted to cry. "Dad, I want to talk to Mommy, okay?"

She heard him inhale and exhale a breath with a swishing sound. Finally he said, "She can't come to the phone right now."

"Why? I want to talk to her, Dad. Put her on, please."

"Well, she can't talk to you. And you'd better get home on time. Or else!"

Dad is being stubborn, but at least Mom is there and he's not raging at her, just raging at me about my curfew. Everything is okay, Cindy thought in a rush.

The dial tone buzzed. Her father had hung up. She shook her head, stunned, the receiver heavy in her hand. She thought it strange her mother hadn't come to the phone after she had asked Cindy to call.

Oh well, she thought. *Obviously he's in a bad mood. So what else is new?* Cindy realized she could have asked for an extension of her curfew while she still had her father on the line, but she was upset about not speaking to her mother. And then, of course, he had hung up on her! She was supposed to be home by midnight. She hadn't even seen her friend Neil yet. How was she going to make it? Her dad had already warned her not to be late. He'd take it out on both her and her mother.

"Come on, Cindy," Carol said, "They've got some fantastic tapes. Let's check it out, girl!"

Pushing her concerns about home out of her mind, Cindy followed her friend back into the living room where some of the kids were hanging around, drinks in hand. The music was getting louder and people were laughing, joking and clapping in pace with the beat. It was wonderful.

At that moment, she saw Neil, his girlfriend Shannon and another girl come in. Well, at least they were here, but no way could she ask Neil to take her home now, right after they'd arrived. *Well, Daddy would just have to be angry,* she thought, *because I'm going to be late.* She'd wait a while and then ask Neil, after he and Shannon had had some fun.

"Who's that other girl with them?" Carol asked.

"Molly somebody, a friend of Shannon's. He said he'd be bringing them both. Guess you'll be staying here later than I can, won't you, Carol? You're so lucky you don't have a curfew. I don't see why my parents make me come home so early. They ought to cut me some slack! School hasn't even started yet."

"I know," Carol sympathized. "Well, at least have fun while you can, Cindy."

And that she did. For awhile, Cindy partied—talking, eating and enjoying herself thoroughly. Finally, remembering her curfew with a sudden, aching feeling in her stomach, Cindy pushed through the swarm of kids to find Neil. She spotted him, at last, through the open patio doors. He was with Shannon, swaying dreamily to the music. George and Billy were sitting nearby, illuminated by the moonlight and a string of party lights. Beers in their hands, they looked sleepy. Vaguely, Cindy wondered if they'd taken some pills of choice. She didn't think Neil ever did drugs.

When the music stopped for a moment, Cindy went up to the couple, hating to make them leave the party so soon, but beginning to feel nervous again about being late.

"Sure, Cindy, no problem. I promised I'd take you

home," Neil answered her request. "We've been here long enough anyway, haven't we Shannon? We'll be just a minute, Cindy. We've got to round up Shannon's friend first, okay?"

When they didn't come back right away, Cindy began to really feel sick to her stomach; nervousness filled her. Overwhelmed at the prospect of being late and having to face her father's anger, she ran out the front door and onto the lawn to get some fresh air. *Oh, I feel awful. I'm going to barf! Oh, geez, oh, please no! How embarrassing!* she thought. Although it was a warm night, a small breeze blew which calmed her stomach a little. Clutching a maple tree in the front yard, she took deep breaths until her nausea was under control and she could reenter the house.

By the time Neil and Shannon found Molly and the four of them said their thank yous and good-byes to hostess and guests, Cindy estimated that at least fifteen minutes had passed. *Dad will kill me for sure!*

They climbed into Neil's car. Cindy sat in the back seat trying not to notice that the hands of her watch were already at twelve. She groaned softly, hating to say anything.

"We'll get you there quickly," Neil told her cheerfully as he started the car.

But when they passed a drive-in theatre in Westbury, Shannon and Molly said, "Oh, let's stop there for a minute." It was a chick flick, the kind teenaged girls loved. Glancing at Cindy, who said nothing, Neil pulled over.

Geez, I might as well give up, she thought. *I'm already late now.* To combat the anxiety building up in her throat, Cindy shut her eyes and tried to fall asleep.

A little later, Neil looked back at her and said to the others, "I think we'd better get Cindy home, girls. She's got an early curfew, you know. We've been here fifteen minutes. That's long enough for a taste of this junk." Starting the car, he laughed and drove towards Old Westbury.

Cindy roused as they pulled in her driveway. "What's going on?" Cindy asked innocently, unaware that her whole world was about to change forever.

Cindy could see a number of silver and white police cars sitting in her driveway. "The cops must be having coffee with my folks," she told her friends. "They do that around here sometimes."

"It's after midnight." Neil's face looked concerned.

A shiver of fear, so fleeting Cindy scarcely reacted, made her suddenly cold. Immediately she pushed the feeling away. *Nothing could possibly be wrong*, she thought. *It's just that Old Westbury is such a small, exclusive community that everyone knows each other, including the police. The cops are visiting, that's all!* "Maybe," she said to Neil, "the burglar alarm went off by mistake. That's always happening, but they still check on us. Dad was doing work on the alarm's wiring this afternoon."

Climbing out of the car, Cindy stood by the driver's window for a moment looking around. There were five patrol cars there, one crime scene van and a number of unmarked vehicles. She saw a couple of Old Westbury policemen with their distinctive Canadian Mounties-type hats heading for the back door. Her thoughts were a jumble. Perhaps the vodka she accidentally drank at the party was fogging her brain, but nothing seemed to register except that in all the confusion, her parents might not notice she was late arriving home. And that was good. She still assumed the cops had responded to a faulty security alarm.

She called to her friends, "Goodnight, you guys. Thanks for the ride."

"Hey," Neil said, "We're going to wait right here!"

She waved and started up the long drive. It was then she noticed that all the lights were on in the back of the house, none in front. *So that's where everyone is.* As she hurried towards the light, she heard Storm, one of the family dogs—a huge, young German shepherd— barking in the dog run outside.

She scarcely noticed when Neil, who had jumped out of his car, hurried to her side and accompanied her to the rear of the house.

From the patio, Cindy could see about twenty heads through the French doors that opened into the kitchen. Thoughts ricocheted through her mind. *What a crowd. So many people inside, not just cops either. The alarm isn't ringing.* She opened the door.

She could see her father at the far end of the kitchen. He had on a silk robe, deep green and navy. As she moved closer, she saw it was tied loosely over his underwear. She felt slightly embarrassed for him, standing there with all those people and only half dressed. *Why isn't Dad looking at me? His expression is so blank,* she thought. *What is wrong? Where is Mom? What's going on here?*

When Cindy started into the kitchen she saw a neighbor, Leon Sultan, a physician, near the door. Before she could say a word he was beside her, his eyes locked on hers. When he didn't smile, she began to tremble. "What's going on?" Cindy said, her voice suddenly very small. Her lips were dry. She licked them, forcing herself to squelch the fear. She'd always considered the doctor to be a gentleman, very cultured, very sophisticated. *Why,* she thought, *is he looking at me so strangely?* She couldn't interpret it. He kept perfect eye contact, as if he could will whatever was happening away from Cindy. She felt edgy, but kept telling herself that it couldn't be anything bad.

"Cindy, let's sit down," Dr. Sultan said, motioning

toward the butcher-block kitchen table. They both sat down, knee-to-knee, eye-to-eye. His familiar, kind face seemed terribly serious. "Cindy?"

"Yes?" Suddenly she knew she didn't want to hear whatever it was he was going to say. Her nails dug painfully into her palms as her hands clenched into tight fists.

"It's your mother, my dear. There's been a terrible accident."

Cindy didn't answer. Emotions were sweeping over her. Now she was trembling.

"I'm afraid your mother's dead, Cindy. She's had a fall. She's . . . she's at the bottom of the basement stairs."

She heard his words and felt numb. She looked up and saw her father off to her right. He still wasn't looking at her. He had a vacant, faraway stare in his eyes. In a flash, she lunged for the cellar steps.

The cops reacted like a shot. "Stop her!" They stood shoulder to shoulder to bar her way. One of them slammed the basement door shut. "Cindy," he said gently, "we have to move your mother's body."

Body? That's Mom he's talking about, she thought. *What good would that do? I just need to wake her up.*

She was in denial, rejecting what she'd just heard from the doctor.

Cindy felt the bang of the slammed basement door reverberate through her body and it seemed as if her whole soul was shattering. With the police officers barring the basement stairs to her, she suddenly whirled around and ran out the back door crossing the patio to the lawn. "Mommy! Mommy!" she shrieked over and over. Finally, she dropped down on the grass and beat her fists against the ground, sobbing and screaming. *If Mommy really were dead, they'd bury her.* And somehow Cindy thought that if she kept beating her fists into the earth, sooner or later her mother would hear the fists, like tom-toms, beating signals summoning her back.

Neil came from out of the darkness of the front lawn and threw his body against Cindy's, his lips next to her ear. "Shhh," he coaxed, trying desperately to calm her, stroking her hair, patting her shoulders. "Cindy, shhh, shhh."

Moments later, with everyone standing around, Cindy jumped to her feet and pulled away from Neil. She ran back in the house. "I have to get to Mommy! Why are you all keeping me from her?" she cried. Before anyone could stop her, Cindy pulled open the basement door and saw for a split second the crumpled form in the light blue nightgown lying at the bottom of the stairs.

A garbled cry rose in Cindy's throat as she stared at her mother's lifeless body below. Before anyone could stop her, Cindy turned and ran from the kitchen, through the foyer and up the polished, walnut steps to her bedroom. She slammed the door, pulled from her pocket one of the quaaludes she'd been given at the party and swallowed it. She couldn't stop shaking. Maybe this would calm her. She had to calm down! Kids took ludes all the time. She didn't want to overdose, she just wanted the pain to stop. She couldn't stand it. *Oh, man, this can't be happening. I have to calm down. I have to!*

She waited out ten minutes by the clock on her night table. Then she took a deep breath and concentrated on only one thing: *I must reach Mommy.* Quietly, she opened her bedroom door and slipped into the hall. Stopping, she listened, then tiptoed down the hall. Everyone was talking to each other downstairs, mostly in the kitchen. No one seemed to hear her. She leaned over the balcony railing and stared at the tan leather couch in the living room below. *It's a long way down, but I won't be hurt. I must jump. I must get to Mommy,* she thought. "Mommy," she called at the top of her lungs, "I'm coming to wake you up!"

"Stop her." The voices were like a choir, everyone saying the same thing at the same time. A wave of people rushed towards her. Cindy saw her aunt, her father's sister, racing up the stairs in high-heeled shoes, her eyes wide behind her dark, tortoise-shell glasses. Running with her was a sea of police officers.

What happened next took place in seconds but seemed like an eternity. As they approached, Cindy turned to go back to her room. It was a nightmare. It was like a dream where you are running but not getting anywhere. It was all slow motion. Seeing the mass of people coming towards her, Cindy began trembling. Her teeth chattered, clicking against each other so hard they sounded as if they must surely break. All she could think of was her mother lying at the bottom of the stairs. *How could this have happened? Was it an accident or . . . ? I have to wake Mommy up!*

"I have to get to my mother," she cried. "I have to wake her up! I have to talk to her!"

"She's going into shock," a voice said.

"Get a blanket."

"Hurry, hurry."

Suddenly limp as a rag doll, Cindy felt herself being wrapped in a soft blanket like a mummy. One of the town policemen swooped her up as if she weighed nothing, carried her downstairs and out the front door.

"Get her to the hospital," someone said. "Right now."

"Put her in my car," said a voice Cindy recognized as her aunt's. The hum of voices was a cacophony in her ears. She felt herself being placed in the backseat of a car. "That's it, gently, gently," Cindy's aunt said.

A male voice said, "We'll notify the hospital. Go to the ER. Good luck."

Cindy felt the car start up and move down the driveway, heard her aunt telling her, "Everything will be all right." But Cindy knew it wouldn't. Things would never be all right again.

They were at the emergency room before long. People were there to help get her inside. A private doctor someone had called strode up to them.

Sobbing now, with her aunt holding her hand, Cindy was led into a private office. At the doctor's nod, her aunt went outside to wait. The doctor, a man with an assuring manner in his thirties, told her to sit down. "Cindy," the doctor told her, his hand touching her shoulder. "I know how hard this is for you, but you have to calm down. Now, I'm going to give you one hour. If you calm down, you can go home. If not, I'll have to admit you and put you on the psychiatric floor for observation."

The doctor looked closely at Cindy. He took a small flashlight out of his pocket and shone it in her eyes. "Cindy," he said quietly, "if you have ingested any substances—any drugs—we'll have to pump your stomach."

Now Cindy knew what she would have to do in order to go home and she needed to be home to wake up her mother. She knew she would have to quiet down.

When the doctor returned, Cindy was sitting there dry-eyed, staring at some invisible spot on the ceiling. "Are you alright, now?" he asked.

Cindy nodded, not trusting her voice.

After the doctor released her, Cindy's aunt drove her back to Horseshoe Road. They didn't talk. Once at home, Cindy went straight up to her bedroom with her aunt following closely behind. Cindy looked at the clock. It was 3:20 A.M. She was very, very tired.

"You go to sleep now, Cindy. You need the rest," her

aunt said, her tall form silhouetted against the light from the hallway.

Cindy laid down on her bed. To keep calm she closed her eyes and brought to mind trivial thoughts, anything not to think of what had happened earlier that night. Her aunt was the president of ORT; she hadn't finished her summer reading assignments; the capital of New York was Albany; Mommy would have been forty-two . . . Finally, her aunt left and closed the door. She was alone.

Now she let herself remember and her thoughts churned. She had to call someone. She couldn't go to sleep. She thought of her good friend, Carol, who lived nearby. Carol had a private line. She wouldn't mind being called in the middle of the night. Kids did stuff like that all the time. And she *had* to talk to someone! She would die if she didn't. Cindy reached for her telephone on the night table and dialed, but either the line was busy or the receiver was off the hook.

She tried two or three times more, then dialed the number of another friend, Frances. When a sleepy voice answered, Cindy blurted out, "Fran, my mother's dead. They say she fell down the stairs, but I'm not sure what happened. She's dead! I wish I were, too. It would be better for everyone." It was impossible to keep back the tears now. Cindy sobbed into the phone, swiping at her eyes with the back of one hand.

"Omigod, Cindy! Oh no. Listen, I'll be over as soon as I can. Oh, Cindy!"

"No, Frannie, don't bother. In fact, I just can't talk anymore." Cindy put down the phone. She put her head down on the pillow and tried to stop crying. Where was her mother? Cindy thought of planets. *Is Mommy out there somewhere? She can't be dead. Mommy couldn't just have fallen down the stairs and why would anyone have pushed her? What is going to become of me and*

Paula? Who will love me now? It was too painful to think about. Cindy didn't want to think anymore.

Finally, too tired to cry anymore, too tired to think, Cindy lay back and the blackness of sleep overtook her.

Chapter 3

Of Accidents and Crimes

A round 1:00 A.M., a persistent ringing burst through Detective John Joseph Sharkey's dreams like repeated gunfire. Muttering, he reached for the phone.

"Detective Sharkey? This is Dispatch Communications Supervisor at Nassau County Police Department. You're on call, right? The Westbury Police have radioed us there's been a suspicious death in Old Westbury and . . ." the voice droned on, filling him in on the details.

Sharkey grunted a few times in answer, listened more intently, made some notes on the bedside phone pad, then hung up.

True to his discipline, he jumped up and headed for the shower. The adrenaline kicked in as he dressed, quickly donning a coat and tie. The entire process took only a few minutes. Then he kissed Jeanette, his wife, and his two young daughters asleep in their own beds, and took off in the dark as he'd done so many times before.

About forty minutes later he arrived in the Village of Old Westbury and headed for Horseshoe Road, which, he noted from the phone instructions he'd received, was in an estate section called Stone Arches.

Upon arriving at the edge of Stone Arches, Jack Sharkey saw nothing but darkness, nothing was visible. He was glad when within moments, amber fog lights split the blackness. A cruiser marked *Old Westbury Police Department* pulled up near his car. The driver rolled down the window as Sharkey did the same and called out, "You Detective Sharkey?" At Sharkey's nod, he said, "Okay, follow me. The others are waiting just ahead."

Glad for the help, Jack followed. Ahead, he recognized the car of Detective Sergeant Tom Mangan, who was to be his sergeant for whatever this case turned out to be.

A little farther down the road, Jack spotted an automobile parked off the side of the road. Suspicious, Jack braked just long enough to write down the license. One never knew. Being observant could make or break a case.

When the caravan finally arrived at 9 Horseshoe Road, Sharkey saw the huge English Tudor mansion at the end was built on a crest. The house was on the right, set back about 125 feet off the road. The driveway was long—maybe 200 feet—and paved with cobblestones, from what he could make out in the dark. A big wrought iron fence, backed by stone pillars that held two big lanterns, guarded the entrance. There were no streetlights.

A damp fog hovered over the road. He couldn't remember seeing denser fog anywhere. Weird. Although used to all sorts of hard-to-handle situations, the dark scene, illuminated mostly by the police cars' flashing lights, gave him an extremely creepy feeling. He took a deep breath, parked and climbed out of his car. A shiver ran down his spine in spite of himself.

Looking over at the parked cars and others that were still arriving, Sharkey saw that he and Sergeant Mangan were far from the only ones there. The place was crawling with police vehicles. One civilian car had a "press" sticker on the windshield.

Sharkey greeted the other men, listened to the scoop, then he and the rest of the new arrivals entered the house through the French doors off the patio. The house held a mix of lawmen and, apparently, friends of the family. Detective Arthur French was there from the third squad of the Williston Park precinct. In Nassau County, there are eight different precincts that each contain eight different homicide squads. Jack Sharkey, being from a special homicide squad at headquarters, had jurisdiction over the Band case.

"The Band house is an impressive looking place," he murmured to Mangan as they stood in the kitchen. Through the wide doorway, he could see cathedral ceilings, a leather couch that seemed to be twenty feet long or so, museum-quality pieces, a grand piano, a maroon brick circular sitting area. It all was tastefully and expensively decorated, even he, no connoisseur, could tell. There was no time to sightsee, however. He glanced at his watch. Past 2:30 A.M. He was here to work. His brain was keyed up, ready to start solving this challenge.

Sharkey could see a man, no doubt the husband, Howard Band, which the other officers had told him about, talking with one of the Westbury policemen. He observed that the guy was jumping around like a lion in a cage. Well, he would speak with Mr. Band later, after he'd checked out the scene and made some observations on his own.

Sharkey followed Detective Arthur "Artie" French to the basement door, where Artie filled him in briefly on what was already known. Artie told him that Old Westbury Police Officer Dennis McCavera had been first to arrive at the scene and, accompanied by a neighbor who was already there—a Dr. Leon Sultan—attested that the wife was dead. At first, Detective French told Sharkey, Mr. Band wouldn't talk to the officer—just wailed and carried on, but finally, in his bedroom, the man told the officer that his wife had "gone down to the basement" to put leftovers in the fridge. "She must have slipped and fell, killing herself."

After taking a few notes, Sharkey went down the stairs, too, careful not to step on some spilled food that was at the bottom. He glanced around the area, noting a refrigerator, a freezer; as well as boxes, a bucket, pail, and suitcase—each in an upright position. And, of course, there was the victim, like a pale blue broken butterfly, stretched out at the bottom of the stairs.

No matter how a person steeled himself, there was always that one first moment of seeing a dead body that grabbed the viewer by the throat. That moment was now. Lying on her back with her face up, was a woman, early forties, light chestnut hair—Florence Band. Her left hand was extended out onto the concrete. Her left wrist wore a watch, its dial face down.

Sharkey noted that she was wearing a light blue nightgown, no slippers, no robe. Oddly, a BX cable with a light fixture at one end was draped over her right ankle. He knelt to examine her further. There were various pieces of rope underneath the body. There were indentations on both wrists and ankles. *Rope marks? This was supposed to be an accident. Had this lady been tied up? If so, when?*

The detective noticed another peculiar thing. The nightgown. It was completely free of wrinkles. It looked like it had been pulled down to just below, or even with, the woman's kneecaps. *Had somebody smoothed her clothes after she fell or was she placed here and never fell at all? Otherwise, wouldn't the gown be twisted or mussed or maybe even up over her head?*

Off to the left of Florence Band's head, perhaps two or three feet away, was a metal roasting pan containing an object wrapped in tin foil. Observing the object more closely, he saw that it was a turkey carcass with some meat left on it. The gravy was still coagulated around the carcass in the pan.

Above it and to the right was a plastic container, upright. He stared at it more closely. The container was approximately three-quarters full of what looked like a rich tomato and meat sauce. On the floor nearby was a pile of spaghetti sitting in a puddle of the dark red sauce, in the middle of which was the container's lid. Carefully picking up the lid by its edge, he observed a clear liquid on it. *The condensation shows this container has been refrigerated.*

Sharkey walked over to the refrigerator and freezer, which were diagonally off to his left against the back wall, fifteen, maybe twenty feet from the body. Opening each of the doors in turn, he saw that they were almost completely filled to capacity. *Why would the victim have tried to crowd more stuff inside when she had a refrigerator upstairs in the kitchen?*

As if the body could tell him the answer, Detective Sharkey went back to Florence Band. Kneeling, he picked up her left arm and turned the watch—a ladies' Movado with a blue face—so that he could examine it. The dial said "3:10." He looked at his own. Also "3:10." *Okay, then, so her watch is still running and accurately. Wouldn't a fall that was hard enough to kill a healthy woman also be hard enough to stop a watch?* he thought. Was he being paranoid or was something wrong with this "accident."

As he mused, Sharkey became aware of Crime Scene officers taking pictures around him. He walked

up the stairs to the kitchen and began to search for his
sergeant, Tom Mangan. There was plenty of activity in
the living room, but he saw neither Tom nor the de-
ceased's husband. As Sharkey walked down a short
hall, he opened a door. A laundry room. A deep growl
made him quickly shut the door. *So the Bands have a
dog. Did it bark? Had there been an intruder?* Ominous questions crowded Sharkey's mind as he stood
thinking about Florence Band's death and the scene before him.

It was, he decided, time to observe the other members of the household. First, he wanted to find Mangan.

Walking upstairs, Sharkey saw Howard Band through
the open doorway of the master bedroom.

"I'm looking for Sergeant Mangan," he said. "Have
you seen him, sir?"

"Inside," Mr. Band replied, indicating his bedroom.

"Thanks. Whose rooms are these?" He pointed to
one on the left and one beyond that.

"My daughter Paula, who's eighteen, and my daughter Cindy. She's sixteen. Paula's away camping and we
were going to join her in the morning. They just brought
Cindy back from the hospital. She became hysterical.
She . . . evidently she took something . . . some kind of
pill. My sister said she's finally sleeping." Mr. Band's
voice was low, but the man acted twitchy, putting weight
first on one leg then the other.

"Is that so, sir? And that room?" Sharkey walked
over to a closed door beyond the master bedroom.

"That's just a room we use for a sewing room."
Swinging open the door, Band pointed out clothes
hanging on a rack and a pile of laundry.

Excusing himself, Sharkey said, "I need to check on
a few things, Mr. Band. Why don't you go downstairs?"

Howard Band nodded but said nothing.

Sharkey went back to the master bedroom and entered. It was a luxurious suite with generous windows and tasteful furnishings. Sharkey saw his sergeant taking notes as he examined the sheets on the king-sized bed. "How's it going, Tom?"

"Hey, Jack. Let me show you something." Sergeant Mangan led the way into a vestibule where he indicated an open closet. Inside were pieces of cord.

"All right. They look like they'd match what's in the basement! The closet door was open, wasn't it, Tom? No need for a warrant?"

"No sweat. It was open. Think we should interview the husband?"

"Definitely."

As they stepped into the hall, the two lawmen saw that Howard Band had gone downstairs. They followed, heading towards the kitchen where they saw him talking to neighbors. Before they reached him, however, Detective Artie French stopped them.

"Hey, fellows, I learned that one of the younger daughter's friends—a girl named Fran—came to the gate a little while ago and told officers that the daughter is distraught and might try to kill herself. The friend was really worried. We sent her away, but we'd better check it out."

"Okay," Sharkey said, "Artie, you come with me up to her room on the double."

The two men hurried back up the stairs and knocked on Cindy's door. There was no answer. Fearing the worst, they turned the knob. It wasn't locked and they stepped inside.

It was a typical teenager's room, but there were traces of the child she had been. A light scent of cologne. A shelf full of little glass figurines. A multitude of furry, plush animals. A dim light revealed a pretty teenager lying on the bed, deeply asleep. The kid, who they'd said was sixteen, looked even younger to Sharkey. He thought of his own thirteen and nine-year-old girls. How would they face it if something happened to Jeanette? He shook the morbid thought off; his job was to figure out whether a crime had been committed, not to get emotionally involved with the victim. And victim this girl was, just as much as was her mother.

At that moment, the girl on the bed opened her eyes. "She's waking up, Jack," Artie said. They both bent over her.

For a moment, drenched with sleep, Cindy looked like any other just-awakened teenager. Then her hazel eyes opened wide with terror.

Sharkey rushed to calm her. "Hello, Cindy. I'm Detective Jack Sharkey of the Nassau County Police Homicide Office. This is Detective Artie French."

Cindy flinched. *Policemen. They are still here,* she thought. *Why? Mommy's death was an accident, wasn't it?*

Sharkey bent down. "Your friend Fran was worried about you," he said gently.

"What? Where is she? Is Fran here?" An edge of panic honed her words.

"It's okay, Cindy, it's okay. We told Fran to go home and we'd take care of you."

Cindy's voice was strained. "Tell me something, please. Is my mother really dead?"

"Yes, she is."

"Was it an accident?"

Sharkey exchanged glances with Artie French. "It's alright, Cindy. Try not to think about it for now."

"No, I need to know about my mother. Please!" The girl's pain was reflected in her eyes. Sharkey felt a terrible sense of urgency emanating from her.

Then her gaze suddenly focused on the phone cord

trailing across the room into the drawer. "My phone? Where's my phone? I always keep it beside my bed!" To the detective, her voice sounded nearly hysterical.

"It's over there." Sharkey kept his own voice calm. "Cindy, you have to try to stay calm so you can handle the next few days. It's okay. Come on now, Cindy, it's going to be fine." *It won't be fine, of course; not for a long, long time,* the detective thought.

"Do you have any more of those pills?" Sharkey asked quietly.

Cindy glanced fearfully at the men. If ever a girl needed her mother, it was now. Were they going to bust her on a drug charge?

"If I give them to you," she asked, "will you throw them away, please? Will you flush them down the toilet? Or will you guys get me in trouble?"

"No, I'm not going to get you in trouble for that. You've got enough on your plate right now. Don't worry about the pills. Just get them for us, please."

Cindy looked at him and Artie for a long moment, then climbed out of bed. Self-conscious about being seen in her pajamas, she rushed to her closet. From the pocket of her jeans, she retrieved the pills she'd been given at the party. "I only took one," she said, handing them over. "Okay, this is all I have."

"Thank you, Cindy." Sharkey realized that she was watching as he put the pills in his pocket.

Her shoulders slumped and she sighed. "I thought you were going to throw them away?"

"Now, Cindy, you know we can't do that. But don't worry, I meant it when I said you won't get into trouble over them." Firming his voice, he added, "Will you please put on a robe and try to pull yourself together? We need your help if we're going to find out what happened to your mother." He watched Cindy take a deep breath and knew his words had their desired effect. "Detective French will come back and talk to you in a little while."

The two men shut Cindy's door and headed towards the stairway. "No need to have her come downstairs into all this confusion. Give her a little time to get dressed, Artie, then just go up and take her statement. She wasn't even here when Mrs. Band fell—or was pushed—into the basement. But I can tell she was close to her mother. Still, we'll want to double check her alibi and talk to the kids she was with. Meanwhile, I'll try to interview the husband."

Sharkey hoped this *was* an accident, as much for the teenager in the room upstairs who reminded him of one of his own daughters as for himself. Still, he had an uneasy feeling in his gut about this woman's death. Either way, it would be pretty rough for Cindy. Poor kid, teetering on the verge of adulthood and coming home to find her mother dead. That kind of hurt wouldn't fade away.

Chapter 4

Disturbing Questions

As Detectives Sharkey and French pushed through the crowd in the living room, Jack Sharkey wondered about the victim's husband. He could see the guy gesturing wildly as he talked to a group of people. Sharkey wanted to talk to Mr. Band and get his account of what had happened. If there was a possibility this wasn't an accident, the husband might know something. He could even be the guilty party. Basically, Sharkey reminded himself, everyone is a suspect in a homicide. Detectives have to keep their minds open. There was no way to be sure if this was an accident or a murder except to have an autopsy performed, ask questions, check all the leads, then weigh the evidence. At present, they really knew very little.

It was hot, even at this hour of the morning. Or maybe it was just all the injustices in the world giving off heat. Sharkey patted at his brow with a clean handkerchief and mentally thanked his wife, who always kept him tidy even for these middle-of-the-night duties they both hated. He wondered if an intruder could have gotten into the Band home or if it could be the husband. How could a guy possibly kill his wife? To Sharkey, it was inconceivable, but, of course, it happened too often. As much as he and the other officers would like to be sympathetic, they had to consider Howard Band a possible suspect if his wife's death was not ruled an accident.

Sergeant Mangan entered the living room from the kitchen. Coming up to the two men, he asked if Sharkey was ready to speak with the husband. Artie French, who had been at the house since just after 1:00 A.M., was now in charge of the scene and other operations necessary in the home. He clapped the two men on their arms and walked away to check with one of the officers who had newly arrived.

"Howard Band is difficult to pin down, Jack." Sergeant Mangan shook his head. "He's got all these people around him."

"Yeah, I can see that. Of course, Tom, we have to hear everybody's story before we can even begin to think of who might be the bad guy. We all hate to treat family members with suspicion," he remarked in a low voice to the sergeant, "but that's the way it is so much of the time. Look at him. Did you ever see a guy trying harder to cry? Man, he should get an Oscar. But we've got to hear his side of the story. We've got to ask him about the events leading up to the death from his viewpoint. And hey, we can't talk to him here, that's for sure. Way too many people."

The other detective, a touch of gray in his hair, a little taller and thinner than Sharkey, looked around at the crowd who milled throughout the Band house. "I talked to the husband earlier, but it's getting so every time one of us says something to him, somebody comes up and 'Oh, Howards' him and off he goes to tell the story to one more group. How are we going to get him alone, Jack?"

"Come on," Sharkey said, throwing back his shoulders and stifling a wee-hours urge to yawn. "Let's look around for a place that's quiet." He walked to the stairs with the sergeant following.

At the upper level, they looked for an empty room, somewhere they could talk without interruption. "Didn't get much sleep, huh? Me either," Mangan said.

Sharkey shrugged. "We asked for it when we signed up, didn't we? The wife and I hit the sack about midnight. I remember saying, 'I'm on duty, but, man, I hope no cases come in tonight.' I guess I'd been in bed about an hour when the call came."

Sergeant Mangan nodded his head. "And was it dark out. Never saw an area so dark. Or foggy. I thought on the way in, the perp could have been anybody. Somebody could have come in here to rob the house and he could have hidden back in those woody areas behind the houses. All those huge places. Man, this place just reeks of money, doesn't it?"

"Yeah."

"Tell me, Jack," Mangan asked, "did you notice a car parked just off the road a way down? I thought that car might have somehow been involved, parked askew like that. I took its number."

"Is that right, Tom? Now, that's something!" Sharkey answered quietly. "Just shows how our minds work. I took down the plate number, too. You never know. I called it in to headquarters in case anything turns up later. If there's no innocent explanation for the car being there, then it *could* be an outsider that did it. But then why would the perp leave his car and take off on foot?" He opened another door and saw an officer interviewing a neighbor.

Looking over the balcony, Sergeant Mangan spotted Howard Band in the hall. "There's the husband, Jack. For a minute, it looks like he's alone."

"Okay, let's see what Mr. Band has to say about this evening's events, Tom." The two men went back downstairs, but by the time they reached the hall, Band had gone. They tried to catch up with him as he kept moving through the house.

Finally, they caught sight of him. Sharkey led the way over to the stocky, middle-aged man who was carrying a half-full cup of coffee and was once again surrounded by people.

"Mr. Band," the detective interrupted with a nod to the men and women extending their sympathies, "I'm Detective Jack Sharkey of Nassau County Homicide. I'm very sorry about your loss, sir. We're here to investigate. Since the cause of your wife's death hasn't been ascertained yet, we need to talk to you about the events leading up to her accident. Let's sit down in the den where it's quiet so we can discuss this tragedy."

Howard Band kept pacing back and forth, back and forth, as if he hadn't heard a word. Detective Sharkey repeated his request about moving into the den and sitting down. Then the phone rang and Band darted into the other room, saying, "It's probably for me. It's probably my daughter, Paula, calling from Lake George." Sharkey followed him and when the call proved to be for one of the Old Westbury police officers, Sharkey tried to get him into the den. At last, the three men, Mangan, Band and Sharkey went into the empty room.

Taking a seat beside Howard Band, Sharkey began to ask again what had happened. Detective Mangan was in a chair close by. At that point, someone called, "A phone call in the kitchen for Detective Sharkey." By the time he came back after answering a brief call from headquarters, the husband was up, pacing again. Then a handful of well-meaning friends entered the den.

"Mr. Band," Sharkey asked, managing to keep his frustration under control, "Is there any place where we can be alone and talk?" There was no way he and Tom could conduct an interview here.

"Oh, yes, of course. The upstairs bedroom . . ."

"Sorry, sir," Mangan said, "two of the other officers are interviewing people up there."

Among the crowd of people gathered around them listening, one man made a suggestion: "Say, what about the Village Hall? It houses the Old Westbury Police Department. You guys could talk there."

"The local police department?" Sharkey asked.

"Oh, certainly," Band said, suddenly quite accommodating. "I go there all the time, know the cops. I go there to use their Xerox machines. And I go hunting with some of the officers sometimes."

"Is that so?" said Sharkey politely.

"Yes, they even gave me a little medal. Sure, we can go there."

Band accompanied the two lawmen to the Village Hall about a mile away. They drove in Detective Sharkey's car and reached the building in three or four minutes. Sharkey looked around and saw the darkness lifting. It was getting close to dawn.

Once inside, they went through the police station, where the officer on duty led them to a room where they could interview Howard Band. They were directed to "the sergeant's room," a large interior office with a desk, a number of chairs and a telephone. Immediately, Band seated himself behind the desk. Sergeant Mangan sat at his right, but soon got up to find the coffee machine. Detective Sharkey sat in front of him and, after inquiring whether Mr. Band wanted coffee, began to ask about his activities the previous day and evening leading up to the point at which he found his wife dead.

"Mr. Band," Sharkey asked, "Can you start with

your afternoon activities? Please tell us what occurred?"

"We had a pool party," Band began. "It started about two in the afternoon. My wife, Florence, and I entertained the Robertsons, along with their two children." Band added that they ate "my wife's special spaghetti *Bolognese*" out on the patio around 6:45 or 7:00 P.M.

At the detectives' urging, Band continued to talk, saying that the friends left around 8:15 P.M. "Then I cleaned up with my wife. I put out the garbage, picked up the napkins while she was in the kitchen putting some things into the dishwasher."

"I see. And then what took place, Mr. Band?"

Band answered, "Well, about nine o'clock, I went up to our bedroom. I changed out of my swim trunks— they were dry by then—into some jockey shorts." He added that when he came out of the bathroom, he turned on the television and lay down on the bed.

"You remember what you watched, Mr. Band?"

"Uh, I think it was that special about the White House. Yes, that was it. And then my wife came up and said she had a headache, to please lower the sound on the television and I did."

"Then what, sir?"

Band mentioned that he began to have indigestion and his wife asked what was wrong. Blaming the problem on the dinner he'd eaten, he asked her to go to the medicine cabinet and get him some Pepto Bismol. She checked but found none. She told him Lafayette Drugstore might be open and she offered to go. He told her that he'd go, because she had a headache. She told him that Lafayette closed at 10:30. "My watch said approximately quarter after ten or twenty minutes after ten." Band said he knew he'd have to rush. Hurriedly, he dressed, got into his car and got onto the Long Island

Expressway, which was crowded. Lafayette Drugstore was closed by the time he got there so he went to Swenson's Ice Cream Parlor, which also was closed.

"So I phoned my wife from a pay phone in the *Crepe* restaurant and said, 'Florence, Lafayette is closed. Screw the Bromo, I'm coming home.' "

"What time was that, Mr. Band?"

"About ten minutes to eleven." Then, Band told them, he drove home, came into the kitchen through the garage, at which time he went over to the refrigerator and took out a bottle of Perrier water. He drank that and went back upstairs. Entering, he saw that his wife was in bed, lying on the right side. He undressed and got into bed. She asked how he was feeling and he answered, "I'll survive."

After a few more questions, Band continued the story, telling the detectives that his wife said she had "to get up and go downstairs and put some food into the freezer."

Edgy, the man interrupted himself at that point saying he needed to use the phone. He went up to the front desk where Detective Sharkey knew there was a pay phone. Band had mentioned he was anxious about his daughter Paula's coming home and not finding him there. A few minutes later, he came back to the interview room and resumed his story.

"After ten or so minutes," Band went on, "I was concerned that she hadn't come back." He went to look for Florence. Seeing that the kitchen door leading to the basement was "partially ajar," he looked down the stairs and saw his wife lying there. He went to her, stepping in the leftover *Bolognese* sauce on the way. He put his hand underneath her neck to cradle it, crying "Florence, Florence." Then he ran up the stairs, into the garage, got into his car and drove across the street to Dr. Leon Sultan's house. He pounded on the door, screaming, "It's Florence, it's Florence!"

The two men drove back to the Band house. After Dr. Sultan went down and looked at his wife, Band told the lawmen, the doctor quickly came back up, shaking his head as if there were "no use."

Having told his story, Mr. Band then excused himself to use the bathroom. When he returned and took his seat opposite Detective Sharkey, Sergeant Mangan brought in freshly made coffee and poured each of them a cup. They each took a few sips, then the interview continued.

"I just want to get it straight in my mind," Sharkey explained. "Would you please go over it again, one more time, Mr. Band?"

The husband, appearing very agitated, related the story again. As he was saying how he made the phone call from a pay phone in *Le Crepe* Restaurant, Sharkey interrupted him. "Why would you call your home to speak to your wife when, in fact, she knew where you were and you were such a short distance from the house?"

Although Sharkey waited for a reply, none came. *Why is this man refusing to answer?* he asked himself. "I'm familiar with the area, Mr. Band. Why didn't you just go to the *Landmark Diner* and get a Bromo? It's open all night." But Band again gave no reply.

"When you first discovered your wife, Mr. Band, how were you dressed?" Sharkey found it difficult to maintain eye contact with the man he was questioning. That always gave him a bad feeling. He leaned in closer to Band to scrutinize him better.

"Dressed just the way I am now. Blue socks, blue pants, shirt and these crepe-soled shoes," Band said.

"May I look at your shoes, please, Mr. Band?" asked

Sharkey. Band raised his feet for the detective's inspection. *No remnants of the thick, deep red pasta sauce,* Sharkey thought. *None at all.* The detective then asked him about the door leading to the basement. "How did you find it?"

"It was closed."

"I thought you said it was ajar."

"Well, it was ajar. I opened it further." Band was fidgeting in his seat.

"Why didn't you just call 911 instead of driving over to Dr. Sultan's? There are phones all over your house."

Band paused a minute before answering. "I did call 911, but when I got on the line I became hysterical and I gave the phone over to Dr. Sultan."

Detective Sharkey then asked specifically if Band had heard any strange noises while he was up in bed. "Did you hear your wife scream or cry out? Or hear the sound of someone falling down stairs?"

"No," the husband replied.

"Mr. Band, why, while you were lying up in bed and you went to go looking for your wife, why would you get dressed? Why would you put your shoes, socks, pants and shirt on to go downstairs to the kitchen to look for your wife?"

"I hadn't taken them off yet. These are the clothes I went out in to find the Bromo." Band's face was slowly turning beet red. "Are you trying to say that I had something to do with this? That I killed my wife? Is that what you're implying?"

"By no means! I'm just trying to get the facts."

"Am I under arrest?"

"No, you're not under arrest. We're trying to ascertain whether or not your wife's death was an accident."

"Of course it was an accident. What else would it be?" Fuming now, Band shouted, "That's it! I'm leaving." He jumped up abruptly and strode out of the police station.

Jack Sharkey didn't wait. He slipped out a back door, jumped in his car and stopped on the driveway opposite Howard Band. He slowly opened the car door.

"Mr. Band, there's no need for you to walk," Sharkey said quietly as he stepped onto the pavement beside the agitated man. "I'll give you a ride back to your house, sir. Please get in the car."

Moments later, Sergeant Mangan came out of the Village Hall and all three climbed into the lead detective's car. They rode in silence. As they reached the Band residence and turned into the long driveway, Sharkey checked his watch. It was 5:45 A.M.

Chapter 5

Wearing Black

After Sharkey and French left her room, Cindy lay there awhile. She thought it strange that the detectives and police officers were still hovering about. She decided to get dressed and the thought crept into her head that she should find something black to wear. She got up and after several minutes of staring blankly into her closet managed to find black pants and a black knit, v-necked shirt. Slowly, she put them on and stuck her feet into a pair of black sandals.

But try as she might, Cindy couldn't think clearly. Everything seemed to get mixed up inside her head and made her feel dizzy. When she sat down at her dressing table to pull her long hair into a ponytail, she felt as dazed as if she'd been hit on the head and hadn't quite regained consciousness.

She walked back to her bed and plopped down. A sudden weariness overcame her and she lay back on the bed, her head resting on a pillow. *Just for a minute,* she told herself. By the time she reopened her eyes, however, the sun was streaming orange rays through the skylight over her bed, bathing her cheeks in comforting warmth. The comfort faded quickly as she remembered what had happened. She knew she should get up, but she lay there as visions of the night before crowded her mind.

As though from a great distance, she heard someone knocking on her door. Getting up, Cindy opened the door to see Detective French, the one who'd been in her room earlier with Detective Sharkey. *They're still here,* she thought, shuddering.

Artie French, his reddish-blond hair thinning on top, wore a tan tweed jacket and a white shirt. "Cindy, I need to take a brief statement from you," he said gently. "We'll just do it here. No need for you to have to brave that crowd downstairs."

"Thanks," she said, looking away. She clasped her hands together to disguise how shaky she was. "I guess I should have gone downstairs, but I just couldn't make myself."

"That's okay, Cindy," he assured her. "It's better we do it up here, anyway. Too many distractions down there. Now Cindy, I need you to tell me about last night."

She nodded and pushed at the corners of her mind, trying to make herself remember everything that had happened. The sensation was sickening.

"I feel sick," she said. She sat back down on her bed as the detective took a chair nearby. Her stomach ached terribly all the while Detective French interviewed her.

"I'm sorry. I have to ask," he repeated more than once. The questions were brief: Whose house had the party been at? How had she gotten home? Who could confirm that she'd been there? How had her mother seemed before she left? and so on . . . They were easy to answer, but still the questions hurt. She knew he was trying to be kind.

Tears clouded Cindy's eyes as she told the detective about coming home and learning her mother was dead.

Suddenly she was sobbing again as the detective awkwardly patted her shoulder. Cindy was relieved the detective had come to her room. She wouldn't want all the people downstairs to see her so out of control. Too, she didn't want her father to see her being interviewed. Cindy watched as the detective jotted down his notes on a yellow tablet. His face looked sympathetic, but she knew the detective couldn't say how he felt; he had to stay professional.

At his probing, she tried to describe her mother. *It helps, a little, to talk about Mommy,* she thought. Cindy recalled a school paper she'd written awhile back about her mother. "She was just a good, good person," Cindy told the detective. "Always there for me. As far back as I can remember, she always worked. Sometimes when I was off from school, I'd go to work with her. I guess I was about eight or nine. She was a remedial reading teacher. I'd help tutor her students. She actually developed her own examination that's used across the country today. It's called the *Rally* exam. I illustrated the text. Everybody just adored my mother—her colleagues and all. And she was really dedicated to the Portuguese community in Mineola. My mom established an annual multi-cultural evening. At one of the schools, the children would dress and perform their native dances and they made food from their native countries. She was honored for the good things she did. She made home-baked goods with me to compete in school bake-offs. We won some prizes and . . ."

Remembering how her mother so often expressed her love by hugging or kissing Cindy and by always making time for her despite studying at night, entertaining and working so hard, Cindy choked up and couldn't go on.

Detective French got up from his chair. "Thank you,

Cindy. No more questions right now. We'll talk to you again later. You take care of yourself."

After the detective left, Cindy made up her mind to face the crowd. Quietly, she eased down the curved stairway and forced herself to enter the group of friends and relatives milling through the house. Neighbors began talking to her immediately, but their words were a jumble, their pitying faces a blur. She couldn't focus on anything. She felt a hollowness inside that made her want to whimper like a baby. The ache in her stomach throbbed. The pain hurt so much it was hard to breathe. For a moment, without thinking, she scanned the crowd for her mother, then, realizing what she was doing, she gasped and ran outside. She had to get some air.

Frances, the friend whom Cindy had called in the middle of the night, was standing there, her face pale. Cindy ran to her and they hugged. "I'm so sorry, Cindy. So sorry. I woke my parents and told them right after you called. You know what my Dad said?"

"No."

"You know how, sometimes, your parents and mine got together to eat dinner or swim or whatever? Well, sometimes my folks saw your Dad picking on your Mom and all. Dad said that it must have been your dad that did it."

Hearing her friend put her own fears into words shocked Cindy. *It isn't true, is it? Dad couldn't. He couldn't kill Mommy.* Her heart pounded as the dark thoughts ran through her mind. *Could he? No! But who then? If it was a burglar, why hadn't Daddy heard him? Oh, what am I going to do?* She clung to Frances, not knowing what to say, what to do.

Tears were on Fran's cheeks as she turned away, saying she'd be back, telling Cindy to hang in. Lifting her chin, Cindy walked stiffly into the house. She didn't see her father, nor did she see the detectives who'd been in her room earlier.

Through a haze, she saw her grandfather, her mother's father, come in on the arm of his second wife and another relative. He could hardly walk. Just shuffling along, crying, his head down, holding on as if he'd fall. Cindy's heart went out to him. Her mother was his only daughter; he loved her so much. Al Saffer was distraught. His sorrow was almost too much for him to bear. His pride and joy was dead.

A neighbor walked up and gently said, "Paula's here," nodding towards the kitchen where Cindy could see her older sister sitting at the table, her almond-shaped eyes accentuated by harlequin-style glasses. She sat talking to a couple of police officers, from time to time waving her hands to emphasize a point, a tissue clutched between her fingers. Paula was taller and more athletically built than Cindy. A T-shirt with "Union College" stamped in bright colors across her buxom chest topped her jean skirt. Her lovely brown hair was so thick it often made others envious.

Cindy turned to her neighbor. "How did my sister know to come home? We were going up there in the morning to pick her up and go on vacation."

The woman led Cindy towards a couch and they sat down. "Last night, they called Lake George where she was camping and whoever took the call went to her tent and told her. Her boyfriend brought her home. It took about four hours, I guess. How about you, Cindy? Can I get you anything? Are you alright, dear?"

Cindy felt the tears building again. She nodded, not trusting herself to speak. She saw people with cameras. News people. *Oh no, are we going to be in the papers?* she wondered. *I can't handle that now. I need to get away.* Making her apologies, she rose from the couch and went upstairs to the linen closet. She'd cover the mirrors.

Things have to be done right, she thought. *I have to follow tradition, because Mommy would have wanted that. Not that we're all that religious, I suppose. We don't go to temple and I know very little about the Jewish faith. Besides, Daddy always says he's an atheist, that there is no God, because if there were, there wouldn't be wars. But I want to do what Mommy would have wanted. I must cover the mirrors,* she told herself.

Cindy snatched up a handful of dark brown towels and began covering the mirrors upstairs. *And what else needs to be done?* She wracked her brain to recall what she'd heard about the etiquette of death in Jewish households. They must sit shiva—thirty days of mourning. She wished she knew more about it. All she could remember was that families who had just lost a loved one would sit on low brown boxes during the period called sitting shiva. But no candle burning—it was too close to Yom Kippur. With hot tears searing her eyes, Cindy searched for other dark materials to cover the mirror in the sewing room. It felt better to be busy.

She wasn't sure what had happened to her; her thoughts raced back and forth. *Did Daddy have something to do with Mommy's accident? Did he . . . did he do it? How can I ever look him in the face again?* Suddenly, she felt more alone than she'd ever felt in her life. There was so much she'd wanted to know from her mother—things about life. She wished she and Paula were closer. But they were so different. As a child, she had truly worshiped her big sister, but lately, they hadn't communicated about anything meaningful.

Cindy went into her bedroom, shut the door and entered her closet. Tears, stupid, useless tears kept blinding her. She took a long time searching through the rows of her clothes. She was looking for a perfect black dress. Nothing really satisfied her. *It has to be just right for Mommy's funeral,* Cindy thought.

One dress slipped off its hanger and fell onto her shoulder. Something about it cascading onto her in that manner triggered a memory, long repressed but now so strong it could not be ignored. She sank to the carpeted floor. With the dress still draped over her shoulder, she let herself cry and remember.

She was hiding in a closet in the house her family lived in before they moved to Horseshoe Road. She was hearing the sounds of her parents quarreling and in an attempt to escape from the hated sounds, she had pulled the clothes off the hangers and burrowed under the pile, leaving only her head uncovered.

Then the scene changed. It was years later and they had moved to the house in Old Westbury. The quarrels had escalated. She remembered watching television in her bedroom on a night not long ago when Daddy's voice had blasted its way into her psyche. "Why do you always piss me off?" he was saying to her mother. "I don't want anything to do with you. The money just goes out the door. When will it stop? We are always helping others. You buy too many things—food, clothes . . . It's either 'Title I' or 'Title V' or the children or the school. Everything is so important to you, everything but me."

There was a pause in which her mother's soft voice couldn't be understood over the sound of Cindy's television; then her father started screaming again. "No, I'm not going to calm down. I want you to answer me— when is it ever going to stop? How many times do I have to tell you that no one is ever going to be as generous to you as you are to everyone else. These people shove it up your ass and you take it and say 'Can I have some more?' "

"Howard, please."

"Get away from me. I'm sick of your activities and your precious doctorate. I want you out of my life. I've had it up to here!"

Suddenly a loud noise rang out downstairs. Cindy pulled herself back into the present, not wanting to dwell further on her poor mother begging him to stay, pleading with him while her father mocked her. His stomping around that night had terrified Cindy—she worried he might be packing to leave. *No one could have been kinder to him than Mommy. She did everything for him. Do all couples who are married a long time argue like they did?* wondered Cindy. *Was it just a fight or did it mean something more ominous?*

Finally, Cindy found a dress that would have to do. She wanted it to be better, perfect. Tears stung her eyes. She wished she had something more suitable—something that would really represent her mother.

A short time later, Cindy returned downstairs and forced herself to talk to her relatives. People she hadn't seen in ages were arriving, many carrying food. Paula and a cousin were busy arranging the platters on the dining room table—fried chicken, cakes, salad. She wondered how people had found out so quickly.

"Darling," one neighbor gushed, "they say that most accidents are in the home. I'm so sorry about your dear mother."

"Thank you," Cindy said, automatically taking the bowl of fruit salad from the woman's hands and placing it very carefully on the table. Cindy kept telling herself everything must be just right. "Thank you," she repeated.

Through the front window, Cindy saw her father get out of an unfamiliar car. He was with two detectives—

one of them was that Detective Sharkey who had been in Cindy's room earlier. When her dad spotted Paula coming down the drive towards him, he hurried to the girl's side. He hugged her, said something in her ear, then ushered her down the long sloped driveway. Watching, Cindy felt puzzled. He hadn't even talked to *her* yet. She saw the two enter Paula's car and drive away. Paula was like their father in many ways, bright and assertive. Cindy could understand their closeness, but she couldn't help feeling left out. Especially now.

When Paula and their father returned to the house, he still didn't make any move to speak with Cindy. There were plenty of other people in the house to talk to, however, and plenty for her to do. She knew that in the Jewish religion they were supposed to have the funeral very soon after the death—within twenty-four hours if possible. Someone said her mother's would be delayed for some reason.

As Cindy moved through the living room, speaking to the guests who kept arriving, bringing them coffee or tea, making small talk which she couldn't remember later, she was suddenly aware of her mother's touch everywhere. As if for the first time, Cindy noticed the beauty of the cathedral ceilings, the polished mahogany mantel displaying the valuable beer steins Mommy had collected, the blue and white delft tile, the grand piano.

And she began remembering others things from the past—like how, when Daddy would go off on trips, he'd bring presents home to her, Paula and Mommy. And he'd whisper to Cindy that she was the easiest to buy for with her petite, slender body. She sighed. *Daddy couldn't have killed Mommy.* She had to get that thought out of her head.

Her thoughts were interrupted by the doorbell's ringing for possibly the twentieth time. She paused by the balcony. Although the top of the front door was blocked from her view, she could see her father opening the door.

"What are you doing here?" His voice was measured, very controlled. *Who could he possibly be talking to like that?* Cindy thought.

"I'm here to see Cindy," was the answer.

Recognizing the voice of her boyfriend, Mark, she started down to greet him, but stopped midway when she heard her father say, "Leave now and if you ever try to see her again . . . you'll be sorry! I'll . . ." She couldn't hear her father's next words, but she could see him angrily slamming the door.

Howard Band then turned and started up the stairs. "Oh, you're here. Here. These are for you." There was no emotion in his voice. He handed her a crystal vase full of red roses and returned to his friends in the living room.

She believed the cops and detectives were still in the house—at least they had been a little while before—and she wondered if they'd heard her father with Mark. Why hadn't he invited her boyfriend in?

The encounter left her angry, confused and so weak she had to sit down at the head of the stairs with the vase of roses beside her. Her father never liked Mark and she had to sneak out to see him. Of course, she had other boy "friends." But she and Mark were steadies. Fran had introduced them. They'd really hit it off. *What if Daddy caught us when we went out?* she suddenly thought. Cindy's breath felt tight, as if someone were sitting on her chest.

Well, she wouldn't think about that now. She couldn't. It was enough to get through this day minute by minute. Cindy went to look for a place to put her beautiful roses.

* * *

As Detective Jack Sharkey stepped into the kitchen from the basement, he noticed Howard Band starting up the stairs carrying some flowers in a vase. Sharkey had no idea of what had just transpired, however. By the time he reached the living room, the episode was over and Band was chatting with friends by the fireplace.

"Mr. Band," Sharkey said, keeping his voice low and calm on purpose. "You understand we need to do an autopsy on your wife, sir."

"Oh, no. No autopsy, detective. Our religion," Howard stopped and cleared his throat. "I'm sure you're aware the Jewish religion doesn't permit such a desecration."

"I'm sorry, sir. Despite that, this is a legal matter, now. I'm afraid we'll have to insist, sir."

"What is it, Daddy?" A feminine voice interrupted them.

The two men both turned to see Paula approach them from behind.

"Paula, the police want to perform an autopsy on your mother."

"No, detective. We can't permit it." Paula's voice was firm.

Saying they'd speak later, Sharkey walked away. When he spotted his sergeant, he motioned him over. Together, they walked out on the patio.

"We have to have an autopsy, Tom. Without the husband's consent, I guess we'll need to get the papers and present them. I understand his feelings, but the autopsy is a must."

The sergeant patted his face with a handkerchief. The August sun was hot. "Yeah, I think you're right."

"Incidentally, Tom, headquarters cleared that car we both noticed along the road. Just car trouble, it seems. But, of course, if the autopsy shows this isn't an accident, someone might have seen the husband drive away and figured no one was home. He might have gone in to burglarize and been surprised by Mrs. Band."

"And ties her up, then gets scared she can ID him and decides he has to kill her and throws her down the stairs. Right?"

"Well, if that's so, then let's hope our guys beating the bushes out there behind the house find some evidence. But first things first. Come on, Tom, we've got to take official statements from the girls. Artie French talked to Cindy, the younger one. She's pretty shook up. But I want to take her somewhere quiet. After that, we'll take a statement from the other daughter. Even though she wasn't here, she may have some insight we haven't heard before."

Moments later, Detective Sharkey saw Cindy and said, "We've got to take your statement, Cindy. We need to take your sister's, too. Do you want to go first or second?"

He watched her consider. "Second, please, if you don't mind, sir."

He nodded, touched her shoulder lightly in encouragement and walked off to find the older Band girl. He found the eighteen-year-old talking to some neighbors and asked her to come out on the patio for her interview. Paula followed him there and sat down. He never used a tape recorder and seldom wrote the interviews down until later because he liked to keep the questioning as natural as possible. Today, however, he pulled out a small notebook.

In taking Paula Band's statement, Detective Jack Sharkey felt the young woman was somewhat resistant. Nevertheless, she was extremely intelligent and she answered his questions perfectly. Her attitude, on the other hand, indicated she thought the police should be looking elsewhere for whatever caused her mother's death. However, he received most of the answers to the questions he asked and then excused her.

Afterward, he took a deep breath, then walked through the crowded house seeking Cindy. He found her in the living room looking dazed and apprehensive. He signaled to her and she followed him onto the patio. "We'll do this as quickly as possible, Cindy," he told her, the expression in his eyes relaying his sympathy.

Cindy took a seat on a marble bench. She decided she could trust this big, strong-looking man. She liked his down-to-earth voice, his *I'm-here-to-help-you* attitude. Heaven knows she needed someone she could trust. "Yes sir," she said quietly, "I know you will."

"Cindy, first of all, I need your full name and year of birth, okay?"

"Cindy Ruth Band, November 6, 1963."

"Really? Well, we have something in common. November 6 is my birthday, too."

She smiled despite her nervousness. Perhaps it was an omen of some sort that they were both Scorpios born on the same date; perhaps it meant she really *could* trust this detective." She smiled more broadly and he smiled back.

"Cindy, I can only imagine how hard this is on you. I want you to repeat some of what you told Detective French up in your room about last night's events. Then I'll ask you a few more questions, okay? We have to have an official statement from you, because we don't know yet the reason for your mother's death. I know you want to find out what really happened to your mother, don't you?"

She nodded, fighting tears. She managed to tell him again about the party, about her friends and about how she came home later than she was supposed to.

"Is that so?" he said, tapping his pen against his chin as if he were weaving her statement into some sort of solution.

His next questions puzzled her, as she couldn't think of any reason for them or how in the world they'd help solve the case.

"Did your mother usually wear slippers when she was in her nightgown?"

For some reason this was a tough question for her to consider. "Usually yes," she finally answered. "But why?"

"What did she have on when you last saw her, Cindy?"

"She was wearing a white terry cloth wrap-around robe. It had sort of a halter-top look. It was Roman-like with a long straight skirt bottom. She still had her taupe-colored bathing suit on underneath. And, oh yes, she was wearing white sandals on her feet."

"Do you know what nightgown she would have worn last night?"

"No. Was it the one my sister and I got her for Mother's Day? It was a matching set. A nightgown and jacket, light orange and white with purple paisley swirls?" She hoped he'd say no. "Yes" would be too painful.

The lawman shook his head. "Her nightgown was blue."

"My mom always dressed properly, Detective Sharkey. And she always wore her ring. It was her mother's wedding ring. The other thing she always wore was a gold watch that my dad got her for her birthday. And she wore glasses and contacts, though she didn't have glasses on when I left." Cindy could see he was listening intently.

"How did she seem when you last saw her, Cindy?"

For a moment, remembering, she couldn't answer. The tears wouldn't stay down. "Mommy was so nice and gentle; she was calm, easygoing and pleasant as always when I last saw her. She came to my door and knocked. Carol and I were just talking. She said 'Hi' to

Carol and she said she had some new clothes for me. I didn't really give her any of my attention. I was in a hurry to get to the party." Her voice cracked. She took a deep, trembling breath, then went on. "I thanked her. She left and went back into her room."

"Was your dad there when you left?"

"Yes, my dad was in their bedroom and very quiet. The television was on. I don't know—it just seemed uncomfortably quiet and I knew that he was not going to be nice to my mom." She covered her face with her hands. This was so hard. *What happened to Mommy? What is going to happen to me?* she thought. Her life was dissolving in the space of hours.

Detective Sharkey offered her a handkerchief and waited for a few moments before continuing. "Take your time, kid," he said in a soft voice. "Just a few more questions when you're ready."

She couldn't imagine how her answers could possibly help him. At last she pulled herself together and finished answering his questions.

Extracting his card from his wallet, Sharkey handed it to her. "If there's anything at all I can do for you, Cindy, or if you think of something that you believe I need to know, call me. Any time, okay?"

As Sharkey watched Cindy walk away, he knew in his heart that the future wouldn't be easy on her. She had definitely loved her mother—was probably a lot like her—and the woman's death was hitting her with the force of a stun gun.

As Sharkey stood there, one of the men signaled that Florence Band's body had been taken to the morgue. Next, Sharkey would secure the writ to have her autopsied, eliminating the argument Howard Band had evoked.

* * *

Unfortunately, when Sharkey was handed the autopsy results he found they provided few answers. The medical examiner, Dr. Leslie Lukash, listed the cause of Florence Band's death as officially "undetermined with an associated condition, contusions and abrasions of the skin."

To the press, Lukash declined to describe the marks around Florence Band's wrists and ankles, which Sharkey had seen and made note of, other than to say they were "non-lethal." The medical examiner assured the press that "only about five or six cases a year of the approximately 1200 cases annually in Nassau County" remain undetermined. "Our determination of death is based on anatomical findings of the body and chemical, thermal and electrical studies. In these undetermined cases, no apparent findings are discovered to establish the reason for the person dying."

The autopsy report did not satisfy Sharkey. Nor did it satisfy other people connected with the case. The victim's close friend, Ellen Robertson, who had raced to the house on Horseshoe Road when Dr. Sultan called her after pronouncing Florence Band dead, said, "Here is this forty-two-year-old woman in good health who died. People simply don't die for no reason."

Florence Band's brother, told reporters, "I am angered at medical science for not being able to determine the cause of death. Somebody dies for a reason; they are saying she didn't die from the fall."

Sharkey's lieutenant, Detective Lt. James Short, commander of the Nassau County homicide squad, told the press, "The case is an open case and we are investigating as thoroughly and aggressively as we can until we find out what caused her death. We are not going to be satisfied and our investigation will continue as it would with any other undetermined or suspicious death."

Chapter 6
Funeral Rites

Cindy's questions about her father would not let her rest. She told herself, *I have to try and believe in him; he's still my father.* But she conversed with him only when she had to and those brief exchanges were only possible because of the shell she'd formed around her real self. Mostly she'd avoided him, but today she could not. It was the day of her mother's funeral.

"Come on, Cindy," Howard Band ordered as he opened the front door to leave for the funeral rites. "Get in the car. And remember, after the service you will ride in the first car with Paula and me." Newspaper and television people with cameras were standing in the front yard. He ignored them. Others could not. Florence Band's suspicious death was making headlines.

As Cindy stood there looking first at her father, then the limousine waiting by the curb, he added exasperatedly, "Well, come on. Get in. We'll be late for your mother's funeral."

She shook her head and stepped back, ignoring the expression on his face. *I can't go with him,* she thought. *I don't want to. I won't.* "Daddy," she said, "my friend

Eddie asked if I could ride with him and his mom and dad. I'd like to do that."

Her father was angry. She could tell by the flinty look in his eyes and the way his hands clenched into fists. She felt certain, however, he wouldn't make a scene in front of the media, so she slipped off to wait for her friend. As she walked away, she saw her sister Paula climb in the car with their father.

By the time Eddie and his parents picked her up in their Mercedes and drove to the funeral home, all the close relatives were already seated in the family waiting room, a private lounge adjoining the chapel.

Cindy stood at the door looking in for a while. She dreaded joining them. It made everything too real.

Al Saffer, her grandfather was there. How she loved him! His head was down. He never lifted it even once. He was very, very sad. Her mother's brother and his wife were also there, as were her father's sister and brother-in-law and, of course, Paula and her father. All the relatives were trying to console each other.

"Do you have your eulogy written?" Cindy asked Paula as she sat down on the couch beside her. "I wrote mine just before I came here." She longed for her big sister to turn to her. She wished they could comfort each other.

But wrapped in her own grief, Paula merely nodded. "Yes, I did, too."

At that point, undertakers entered the room to usher the grieving relatives into the chapel. Through a strange sort of haze, Cindy was aware that every row was full except for those in front reserved for the family. The faces were a blur. *The entire community must surely be crammed into the pews,* she thought. *People cared about Mom, they really did.*

In the front of the chapel was the plain wooden coffin that held her mother. It was closed. There were no flowers. Tradition said it was better to help the poor. Suddenly, just as Rabbi Robbins went up to the podium, Cindy was struck by an overwhelming conviction that her mother wasn't in the coffin at all, that this whole thing was some kind of bad dream. But the prayers commenced and the rabbi began to tell the vast audience what a wonderful woman Florence Saffer Band had been. How she was the highest sort of woman. One who'd made a fine home for her husband and children and one who'd honored God. Cindy, whose heart was breaking as tears rolled down her cheeks, knew these things were true.

When the rabbi called for eulogies, he invited Paula to speak first. Cindy heard her sister praise their mother. It was a good eulogy. Then it was her turn. When she climbed onto the podium, sick with grief and wondering if she could even speak, some hidden part of her took over and she began.

"Mommy," she called out, her voice rising in an arc that filled the entire hall, "Can you hear me? I love you and I miss you and I know you're watching over me. I'm thankful for being your daughter. You're the best thing in my life. I know that you're going to be proud of me some day. I'll work so hard to do right. I'll make you proud of me, I promise." A hundred pairs of eyes were on her. She could see, as she returned to her seat, that everyone in the chapel was crying.

The rabbi intoned the traditional prayers, then brought the service to a close with an invitation to go to the cemetery for the burial and later to the Band's home for refreshments.

Just before they left the chapel, Cindy saw her grandfather weeping silently, his shoulders shaking, as the undertakers removed the casket. Suddenly, the room became pin-drop quiet. Then her grandfather shattered the still of the chapel with a loud, long wail, a scream that sounded like it was being ripped from his heart. "Flo-o-o-rence." His son guided him towards the exit, his arms around the older man's shoulders, but the agonized cry lingered in Cindy's mind and she felt herself trembling.

When Cindy went outside where well-wishers were extending their sympathy to the family, she spotted the hearse about fifty feet away. As the men loaded the casket into its open rear door, Cindy started running towards it. "Mommy, no!" *I'm in some kind of nightmare,* she thought. *Why can't I wake up? They can't take Mommy away!*

At that moment, Eddie and his parents embraced Cindy and led her to their car. The long procession caravanned to the burial grounds. In the back seat of the car, Cindy, still trembling, felt weak.

"Cindy, lie down, put your head on my lap, okay," Eddie told her.

She had never before felt so helpless. Questions ricocheted through her mind. *What really happened to Mommy? Was it an accident? Was it . . . murder?* She gasped; even just thinking it, the word murder lunged at her.

At the cemetery, Cindy managed to walk to the gravesite. As she looked around, she guessed there were probably a hundred and fifty people gathered around that hideous hole in the ground. Her breath grew ragged; her legs felt unstable.

After saying prayers, the rabbi passed the shovel to Howard Band, who poured some clods of dirt onto the coffin suspended at the edge of the grave. Paula repeated the rite, then offered the shovel to Cindy.

Maybe she was losing her mind, but there was something she *had* to do first. She walked toward the edge of the casket and knelt down. "May I touch it?" she asked the rabbi in a whisper. He nodded. *If I can just touch it,* she thought, *I'd know whether Mommy is really in there or not.*

Cindy bent down. She pushed on the raw wood of the coffin, not wanting the crowd around her to realize she was doing so. It moved only slightly; there *was* weight in the box. She felt overwhelmed. *Mommy is in there. It's real,* she thought. *Florence Band, my beautiful, beloved mother, is in that coffin. Oh, how can I possibly survive thinking Daddy might have done this to Mommy?* The faces of the assembled mourners began to revolve around her, dissolving into blackness. Cindy fainted.

What happened next, she didn't know. Later, she assumed someone had carried her across the cemetery. When she woke up, she was lying under a tree some distance from the gravesite. Surrounding her was a crushing mob of people. All she could see were sympathetic eyes looking down at her. She took a deep breath and struggled to sit up.

"It's over, honey," a neighbor told her.

Cindy got up and started back to the grave. One of her relatives stopped her.

"No, child, it's over," he said. "It's okay, it's okay."

Moments later she was sitting in Eddie's car.

During the trip back to the house she was only half-aware of where she was or how she was. At home, people took her arm and led her inside where a buffet had been prepared by a catering company to feed those who had attended the funeral. Everyone wanted her to eat.

"Please have something. It's really delicious," a cousin said, coaxing her toward a table with mounds of food. She knew he had to be right, it must be delicious, but she couldn't eat.

"No," she said, "I just can't."

Vaguely, she wondered why her boyfriend hadn't

shown up. He'd sent flowers. Why hadn't he come to the funeral?

The phone rang while everyone was eating. She answered it. Mark was on the line.

"Why haven't you been by?" she asked him, after thanking him for the vase of roses.

"Your dad warned me I'd better not come around again . . . or else."

"What are you talking about?" Nothing made sense to her any more.

"Don't worry about it. How about coming out and meeting me, Cindy?"

She'd have liked nothing better. She needed comforting with all her heart. She felt like a little girl whose caretakers were too busy for her. "I can't, Mark. Not yet. You know—the mourning period. I couldn't do anything to hurt my mother."

"But your mom is . . . Okay, I understand. But maybe we can get together next week, okay?"

"Okay." She wondered what it would be like next week and the one after that. Maybe by then she would know what happened to her mother. Maybe . . . She began to tremble again.

Chapter 7

Grave Suspicions

Detective Jack Sharkey was completely immersed in the Band case. Although he'd made a vow early on in his marriage that he would be an active father and husband, he had been putting in long hours, working until late at night following down leads. He was aware that this had to be difficult for his wife, Jeanette—the kids being so young—yet she never complained. *I'm one lucky man,* he reminded himself whenever there was time to think about it.

Right now, the most important thing was contacting everyone that Florence Band and her husband had known—neighbors, associates, relatives, everyone. The Bands knew one heck of a lot of people. It seemed to be taking forever to find and interview everyone. But, of course, they had to do it. The most innocuous person, the simplest of clues—he didn't want to overlook anything in order to best determine if this was an accident or a homicide.

Mentally, Sharkey reviewed the people to whom he had already spoken. He had met the Band's neighbor, Dr. Leon Sultan, at the house on the night of Florence

Band's death. He had spoken with him since then, but tonight, hoping to pick up something new, he stopped by Sultan's house again. The home, large and elegant, was on the other side of the street from the Band mansion, several hundred yards down Horseshoe Road.

After some small talk, Sharkey turned to the physician and asked, "Can you remember anything more to add to your statement?" When the man answered "No," the detective told him, "I just want to clarify a few points." He looked at the doctor, trying to gauge where the man's sympathies lay. "You specialize in orthopedic surgery, isn't that right, Doctor?" the detective began.

"Yes, it is."

"How did you happen to go over to the Band house the night of August twenty-fourth, or more accurately the morning of August twenty-fifth?" Sharkey continued. "Would you please just go over that again in detail for me, sir?"

The doctor nodded, his expression grave. "It was shortly after midnight on the twenty-fifth of August, when I heard some noise in front of my house, in the way of shouting, knocking or banging on the door and possibly the doorbell ringing." He paused, remembering. "I opened my window and it was a moonlit night. I asked, 'Who's there?' Mr. Band was outside, saying, 'It's Howard. Howard Band.' He said, 'It's Florence. She's hurt.' "

"What happened next, sir?"

"I immediately put on my pants, shirt. I mumbled some words to my wife, said I'd be right back."

When the doctor stopped, the detective prodded. "Where did you meet Howard Band after he called to you?"

"Right in front of my house, the front steps, on the front patio. We both got into his car and he drove around and down my circular driveway and up into his driveway just outside the back of his garage. The quick trip took a mere ten seconds," Dr. Sultan said quietly.

"And about what time was it when Mr. Band came to your house?"

"About five or seven minutes after twelve."

"Were the lights on in the Band home?" Sharkey probed.

Sultan scratched his chin pensively. "I believe they were."

"When you went into the kitchen area, was the basement door open or closed?"

"It was closed. I asked Howard where Florence was and he pointed to that particular door. I opened the door and saw the basement light on. At the foot of the stairway was Florence. I told Howard to sit down in one of the kitchen chairs at the dinette table and I went down to the basement." He shook his head. "Obviously, the memory of what he saw at the bottom of the stairs was painful."

"Was anyone else in the kitchen at that time, Doctor Sultan?"

Sultan shook his head. "No one else was there. I could see right away that Florence was not moving or breathing. She had no pulse. Her face was devoid of color and there were purplish discolorations on the right side of her neck and the clavicle area, the collarbone. I stayed in the basement perhaps twenty or thirty seconds and then came back up."

The doctor took a deep breath then slowly let it out. "I approached Howard," he told Sharkey. "He was at the top of the stairs in the kitchen. I said to him, 'It's too late, Howard. She's gone. I'm so sorry.' "

And then, Sultan said, he told Howard Band to call the police.

As Sharkey thanked him and got up to leave, he

turned and said, "Please call me, Dr. Sultan, if you think of anything more."

"You know, there is one more thing." The doctor hesitated, stroking his chin as he considered. "It was a little over a year ago, actually, I remember the date— December fourteenth. Howard called me over. Florence's head was bloody. Howard said she'd been asleep and hit her head on the night table. I went to the house and saw she was hurt. I took her to Mercy Hospital. I thought, of course, it was an accident, so we didn't call the police. Do you think . . . ? No, she must have had a nightmare, some disturbed sleep."

Sharkey's heart beat a little faster, but outwardly he remained calm and professional. He asked a few more questions about the "accident" that December night, then left. The detective thought about this new morsel of information as he drove back to his office. He'd already looked at the nightstand in the master bedroom. He was sure there was no way she could have hit her head on the edge of it and broken the skin, because the edge of the table was rounded and considerably higher than the bed.

Had Band been trying to kill his wife that night and failed? Sharkey asked himself. *And if so, had he figured that if he called his physician neighbor, the same pattern would unfold as before? The police would not be called, because Sultan was a doctor. Howard would be off the hook.* "Now, Jack," he muttered out loud to himself, "don't jump to conclusions. This has to be done very, very carefully." Sharkey knew he needed a lot more information than he had to prove whether or not Howard Band had killed his wife. Nevertheless, the thought had now become an active suspicion.

Chapter 8

Such Good Friends

"Cindy and Paula, we're all going to a friend's house tonight for dinner. Her name is Liz." Howard Band, dressed in gray Gucci pants and a navy blue La-Coste shirt, approached his daughters as they stood in the foyer, talking quietly.

Cindy looked at her dad. It was the first fairly pleasant statement he'd made to her since the funeral a few weeks before. She was torn between hope and annoyance. Since her mother's death she'd avoided him as much as possible. *But who,* she wondered, *was such a good friend that they should visit her while they were still in mourning?*

She was surprised when her sister, who always seemed on such good terms with their father, turned to him with a frown on her face. "Dad, look, I don't want to go anywhere, okay?"

"Where are we going?" Cindy asked.

"Now Paula . . ." her father began.

"No, I am not going!"

Cindy nodded. "Right! And I'm not going either."

"Oh yes you are!" She could see he was getting

angry. His lip curled and he was getting loud. At this point, still feeling numb over the loss of her mother, she did not care.

"If you're saying 'Oh yes you are' to *me,* Dad, forget it. I am absolutely *not* going." Paula stalked off.

"And neither am I." Cindy headed after her sister, but her father grabbed his younger daughter by the arm. "Ouch, Daddy! That hurts."

"You *are* going and that's final."

"Well, why does Paula . . ."

"Not one word." His face was reddening, his jaw clenched.

For a moment they locked eyes, then Cindy lowered her lids. *Okay, I'll go. I'll take food to this stupid dinner party just like Mommy would have done,* she thought. Suddenly Cindy felt compelled to make something special. She didn't have a lot of time but maybe she'd make a French apple pie and thus make her mother proud. "All right, Dad, all right." The words came out in a rush, forced through her teeth. "At least tell me who Liz is."

"That's better." Howard Band showed a small smile. "Her name is Elizabeth, but they call her Liz. She's been a friend and business acquaintance for a long time. You've seen her once or twice."

Cindy shook her head. "I don't think so."

"Incidentally, she's got kids around your and Paula's age, too, so you'll have a good time."

Good time! Why, Cindy thought climbing the stairs, *would I want to have a good time with Mommy barely in the ground? What is wrong with Daddy?*

Once in her bedroom, Cindy could hear her sister moving around in the adjoining room. She went into the bathroom, which separated the two rooms, and tapped on the door. "Paula?"

"It's unlocked."

"What's going on? Who is this Liz?" Cindy entered

Paula's domain, a spacious room carpeted in plush navy with a grid of white lines and white-painted furniture. "Why are we going there for dinner? It doesn't seem right." She sat down on the leather chair by her sister's desk, a custom-made white Formica and chrome creation which she'd always admired.

Cindy had always admired Paula, too. She wished they hadn't grown apart. After all, Paula was just one year and eleven months older than she. As kids, they'd had so much in common. They'd both been active in school—things like Brownies, Girl Scouts, bakeoffs and music. And because they'd both been accelerated in school, they got to go to specialized camps for gifted children every summer. She'd attended art classes; Paula had gone for music. Cindy sighed. Now they hardly spoke. She missed her sister's company.

"Paula," Cindy said again, trying to arouse her sister's attention.

Paula was sitting on the edge of her wide bed reading. She read a lot. Behind Paula, the bed's headboard consisted of inlaid shelves filled with books. "Cindy, it's *you* going to Liz's house, not me."

Cindy didn't feel like arguing so she ignored her sister's dig. "Yeah. Well, who is she—this Elizabeth person?"

"Liz. She goes by Liz." Paula blew her nose. She laid the book down on the bed open to the page she'd been reading.

"Okay, then. 'Liz.' But who *is* she?"

"Oh Cindy, for cripes sake. You mean you really don't know?"

"Know what? Come *on*!" She and Paula never used to snap at each other.

"I think she's Dad's girlfriend. Don't be so dumb."

Cindy was glad she was sitting down. The news hit her in the stomach. She shuddered. How much more didn't she know about her father. "Oh geez! How long's that been going on? Did Mom know?"

"Of course, she knew. Our mother wasn't stupid."

"But Paula . . . What did Mommy say? On top of everything else she had to take—Dad's bad temper and all—you mean he cheated on her with a real girlfriend? I knew he'd get mad at Mom and go out lots of nights. I figured he was stepping out sometimes, 'cause he'd splash on cologne, but I never thought it meant anything. Oh, this makes me want to barf!"

"I don't know how Mommy took it. They fought a lot. I was away at school, but I knew that much. How could you *not* know?"

Suddenly, the now-familiar dark mental fog rolled back over her. All Cindy could do was sense—and feel—the extent of her mother's pain. *Mommy loved him,* she thought, *but Daddy had some woman on the side. He was two-timing her!* She longed to hug her mother, tell her how sorry she was about everything.

"Please, Paula, fill me in. I can't stand it, but I've still absolutely got to know. I don't know—maybe I did suspect and just didn't want to admit it. For a long time, he's been coming home after work and napping. And, of course, talking on that stupid phone up in his room, then having a bath and taking off for the evening. No telling what time he was coming home." She paused for a minute in thought, then went on. "And now I remember that often the phone would ring, but if Mom or I answered it, the person would hang up."

"See? You should have guessed, Cindy."

"Maybe I was in denial or something. A girlfriend! Geez, poor, poor Mom."

Paula looked at her sister appraisingly. "You've seen Liz, Cindy. Remember last year, after we took that cruise when we got off the boat there was this ditzy babe, about a size six, wearing skin tight pants, high heeled boots and a long mink coat? She had big boobs, a clingy blouse and blonde hair that was absolutely perfect—hanging just below her shoulders . . . She came to meet us."

"Okay, Paula, I get the picture, okay?" Cindy snapped. She thought of her lovely mother—refined, never gaudy, soft lipstick, expensive, tasteful clothes. She always made life so wonderful for all three of them. *Oh, how could you, Daddy!*

"Well, don't get snippy. You asked! Anyhow, she met us as we docked. And we saw Daddy kiss her. Really Cindy, how in the world could you forget that? Don't you remember?"

The scene came back to Cindy in a flash. She had wondered who that brazen woman kissing her father was. The woman had said she was their travel agent and had come to welcome them home. It hurt Cindy to even think of this woman. It seemed disloyal to her mother. She sighed. So that's where they'd be going tonight. To her poor mother's rival. Cindy's stomach was churning. She turned and went back to her room. Lately, she just seemed to go from one nightmare to another.

Later that evening, Howard Band drove too fast and talked too loud. In the car on the way to the dinner party, he spoke of work, the neighbors, food—everything except her mother. Cindy felt tired before she ever got out of the car in front of Liz Diamond's house. A maid answered the door and ushered them inside.

The woman who came up to greet them and gave her father a peck on the cheek had streaked her hair a bit, but up-close Cindy could see she was indeed the same woman from the travel agency who'd met them at the pier when they returned from their vacation the year before. And suddenly, with sinking heart, Cindy realized something else. This was the same woman who had rung their doorbell and said she had car trouble when they were in the pool with their friends the day her mother died. That day, Daddy had called her "some strange woman." Cindy felt a coldness inside which extended down to her toes.

"This is my daughter Cindy, Liz. Isn't she pretty?" Her father's words made her face redden.

"Hello, dear. I'm so glad to meet you. Your daddy's told me so much about you." The blue eyes were gazing at her intently, sizing her up.

Cindy couldn't answer. She nodded, walking past the woman to place her apple pie on a table already ladened with luscious looking food. In fact, it was so crowded, she decided there was no room for her dessert and took it to the kitchen. When Liz followed, Cindy handed the large dish to her without a word.

There was a beautiful, long dining table—oval, covered with a linen tablecloth on which sat two silver candelabra. Three kids were there, somewhere around her age, waiting to sit down and eat. She looked at them. They looked at her. She didn't speak.

"Cindy," Liz said, "I want you to meet my son, Donny. Donny's twenty-three, honey. He's my 'take-charge' boy. Donny, this is Howard's baby, Cindy. You'll be seeing a lot of each other now."

Cindy saw a tall, lean, good-looking, million-dollar guy, dressed in Gucci shoes and looking absolutely superb. He surveyed her with interest and said all the right things. Yet Cindy was completely unaffected by his charm.

To her surprise, she heard Donny say, "Hi, Howie." As they talked together, she could sense that Donny knew her father very well and she wondered how.

Liz introduced Cindy to her other teenage children, Shelley, who smiled briefly at her, and Bart, the youngest, who nodded noncommittally.

When dinner was announced and they finally sat

down, Cindy took only small portions of the food. The meal went on endlessly. The conversation with Liz was over her head. She couldn't think, she didn't want to speak. When the interminable evening was finally over, Cindy was relieved to go home.

To Cindy's horror, Liz began coming over to their house every day. It upset Cindy, who was more and more unsure of what her father had or had not done. Now he was flaunting his girlfriend in her face.

One evening her father and Liz went into the bedroom and locked the door—*Mommy's bedroom,* Cindy thought angrily. She could hear the two of them arguing. In her fuzzy state of mind since her mother's death, she did not try to analyze the conversation. Ordinarily, one couldn't understand what people were saying through the heavy door, but her father was shouting. He sounded furious.

"Who *cares* how it will look? Okay, when DO we get married then? Look what I've done for you and this is how you treat me!"

". . . done for you . . ." What did that mean? Cindy asked herself.

The words, however, were filtered through the protective haze that still surrounded Cindy. They scarcely registered in her brain five minutes after she heard them. She felt she was in another world—a confused place where she didn't know how to act or what to believe.

But, of course, nothing was the same as before—even talking to her boyfriend. He came by the house and her Dad, so preoccupied with Liz, finally let Cindy go out with him. Mark was very understanding. He took her for a long drive, saying little. Finally, they stopped along the water, got out and walked onto a large rock. His words to her were soft and comforting and that was what she needed. The warmth and comfort he gave her helped her to function.

A week or so later, Mark, Fran and Cindy went to a tennis match. Mark drove them to Flushing, New York for the U.S. Tennis Open. They sat in great box seats where the action was directly in front of them. Cindy, of course, was dressed in black. She appreciated her friends; they said not a word about the tragedy that surrounded her. She longed to be "like everyone else," something they seemed to know and that's the way they treated her.

Afterwards, she could scarcely remember the matches. She knew it was very hot and she knew she'd been very quiet. It was impossible for her to concentrate, though, with some difficulty, she did notice the happy spectators. She could not help feeling that she didn't have the right to enjoy herself or laugh. She sat there as long as she could. Finally she told Mark, "I need to go home."

Mark looked thoughtfully at her for a moment and nodded. "Sure. Let's go now."

In the days that followed, wherever they went, Cindy was unable to sit still or concentrate for more than a few minutes. She suspected she was still in shock, but she needed companionship desperately. It saved her from the endless questions about her father, which now filled her mind whenever she was home. She did not even have her sister to talk things over with, for Paula had returned to college.

Cindy realized that, thankfully, school would be starting soon. She was anxious to return. She knew it might be hard to concentrate because of her mother's death. Still, she had skipped a grade, as had Paula, so she did not worry about her marks. She told herself it would probably just come naturally.

Though many of her schoolmates called she didn't

seem able to converse with them as she once had. She felt "different" now. She almost felt as if she were a different person. A person whom she didn't know and didn't want to know.

As the days wore on, Liz continued coming to the house on Horseshoe Road every day. It seemed impossible to believe. Cindy wished the woman would just go away and leave them alone. But she didn't.

The day before school started, as she was talking to her in the kitchen, Cindy tried to take a long look at Liz from an objective point of view. Cindy saw that she was a striking woman, her deep blue eyes accented by the matching camel hair sweater and velvet slacks she was wearing and the diamonds that seemed to sparkle everywhere a person looked. Cindy could sense between her father and Liz a certain excitement about their romance. *He must love her,* Cindy thought, *he must have loved her even when my mother was alive. And Mommy just happened to be in the way.*

The thought made her weep inside. *Poor, poor, good Mommy.* She tried not to think that this was anything but the romance of a lonely man and an available woman. *They couldn't have harmed my mother! They couldn't have!* She tried to perceive Liz as her Dad must have seen her—a woman whose husband had died, a woman lonely and on her own. She tried to feel sympathy for Liz. She had to. Otherwise she couldn't survive and Cindy was determined, for her mother's sake, to survive and someday do things that would make her mother proud. She'd find a way to do something that would be beneficial to people. Florence Band had always, always helped others and Cindy wanted to do the same.

Chapter 9
School Woes

Cindy scarcely had time to assimilate the fact that her father was in love with Liz Diamond, when she had to face the prospect of going back to high school. Summer was turning into autumn. Leaves seemed to turn red and yellow overnight. The mourning period for Florence Band was not yet over when school began that clear, summer-like September day and Cindy was still dressed in black. She realized it would be difficult to study after what had happened, but she did not feel that a couple of B's instead of the A's she usually got would hurt her record. Her father had always insisted on top grades.

This was her senior year—supposedly a magical time. Despite the shock over her mother's death, Cindy couldn't help looking forward to being back at Jericho High School with her friends once again. She felt sure they'd help her through this terrible time of her life.

In Cindy's opinion, there was no school better than Jericho. The kids in her neighborhood all rode a small private school bus to the handsome red brick building about seven miles away. Great teachers, fantastic students. She just loved the school.

That first morning, as she stepped through the entrance of the school building, a crowd of sun-tanned students, their smiles tempered with sympathy, immediately surrounded her. It warmed Cindy's heart to realize they had been standing near the door waiting to see her before heading for their homerooms.

"Oh, Cindy!" "We heard you were coming back today." "Hi, girl." "How you doing?" they called. One girl who'd been away all summer screamed, "Omigod, Cindy, I *just* heard, honey. I'm so sorry!" The girls took turns hugging her neck; the boys, looking equally as concerned, hung back. Instead of embracing, they stood around dropping inane remarks to cover their emotions.

When the bell rang and the young people hurried towards their homerooms, Cindy was shocked to be confronted by a woman holding a notepad and pencil and a man carrying a large camera. They had pushed through the group of students surrounding her.

"Cindy Band," called the woman, clearly a reporter. She held a microphone up to Cindy's face. "Can you give us a statement about your mother's death, please."

Cindy stared, not knowing what to say. She had tried to forget the media frenzy and the endless speculation in the newspapers that would not go away. She was aware that reporters still lurked around her home, trying to talk to whomever entered or left. But to enter her school! She couldn't believe they'd do that.

"I . . . I can't. I have to get to class, I . . ."

"Only a short statement, Cindy, that's all. How do you feel about your mother's death?"

Tears filling her eyes, Cindy clamped her jaw together and shook her head. She couldn't answer.

The reporter went on. "People are saying it could be

murder, you know. There'll be all sorts of people wanting to write your story, Cindy. You're very in demand these days. Sooner or later, you'll need to . . ."

A flash went off in Cindy's face as the photographer clicked his camera, then clicked again. She saw spots. "No!" she cried out and began to run, her shoes clipping along the concrete floor of the hallway.

Behind her, the photographer caught another shot as Cindy stumbled. Then he hurried in front of her, his camera flashing again and again.

Why are they doing this to me? Cindy thought as she grabbed the doorknob of her classroom. Some students were staring at her from down the hall as she repeated, "No!" opened the door and fell into the first empty seat. A low murmur went through the room. She felt the caring—and curiosity—of her fellow students. The homeroom teacher called the class to order, sending Cindy such a look of kindness, she felt a soothing, momentary warmth.

Despite the upsetting incident with the press, the day went well. For long moments, Cindy forgot her troubles. She was so happy to be in school with her friends. Despite her stress, school was still going to be easy for her. Cindy knew she was lucky; she didn't need heavy studying to get good grades.

At noon, she and a couple of friends walked over to the nearby cider mill and, although the weather was still warm, they ordered steaming hot cider with their lunch. *Mmmm, I feel better already,* she thought.

That week and the next, she enjoyed the sanctuary of Jericho High, the joy of her companions, the relief from the tension at the house. She got an A on each of the first two tests she took. But then, the following week, she was sitting in her third period class—American History—when the teacher came to her desk and motioned her to follow. Placing the paper she was working on under her books, she followed Miss Cheney into the hall. They both noted the loud chatter from the classroom, which began the moment Miss Cheney closed the door. Cindy heard her name mentioned over and over. She looked up at Miss Cheney to see if she had heard it, too.

"Cindy," her teacher said, placing her hand on her shoulder for a moment, "First I want to tell you I am so sorry about your mother. I . . . I never got the opportunity to say so last week. She was a very lovely lady."

As always when anyone spoke of her mother, Cindy had to stifle tears.

"Right now, the dean wants to see you, dear. I believe a family friend is waiting for you there."

As she walked down the hall towards the school office, she wondered who was there with the dean. *Family friend? Her uncle, perhaps? Or Dr. Sultan from across the street? Her father often turned to Dr. Sultan when something was up.*

Cindy suddenly recalled that her father had been called to the school yesterday for a conference. She'd assumed it was because she was a senior and there were plans that needed to be made or perhaps the dean had merely wanted to extend his sympathy. Her dad had not said anything about the meeting when he returned home and she hadn't asked. The only thing he told her was that while he was in the high school, "some idiot" had flattened his new car's two back tires. She had no idea who would have done such a thing or why.

After the school secretary motioned her into the dean's office, Cindy saw—of all people—Liz Diamond seated at the horseshoe-shaped desk talking to the dean and the assistant dean. Both men wore serious expressions on their faces. A tight, unfamiliar feeling welled up in her chest. *What earthly right does Liz have to be here? This is ridiculous,* she thought. *Obscene!*

The woman was dressed in tight white pants. Sparkling stones dangled from her ears and caught the sun's light streaming in from two large windows. *Mommy would have never dressed like that,* Cindy thought.

"Cindy," the dean said, his brown eyes glistening with sympathy, "we have been discussing what's best for you. Mrs. Diamond here is very kindly offering to help in your tragedy. We owe her our thanks, don't you think so?"

Outrage threatened to choke her, but Cindy forced herself to swallow the feeling as her father's girlfriend turned bright blue eyes upon her. Trying to imagine herself anywhere but there with Liz, she stared at the two men, then nodded.

"Sit down, Cindy," the dean continued, his face reddening slightly. "Now here is the situation. We are confronted with a terrible problem. My dear, it truly hurts us to say this, but we are going to have to ask you to leave school. I am so very sorry."

"What!" She couldn't be hearing correctly. She looked at the assistant dean, but that gentleman, too, was nodding his head. Cindy took a seat quickly in a straight-backed chair.

"Now, now. You're a very intelligent girl," the dean continued. "You only lack one credit to graduate. Only one small English credit. You truly don't need this year here. Just take a course somewhere."

"But . . . but . . ." *Not go to school? I'll die without my friends. School and friends are all I have left in my life.* Deep, dull pains suddenly began to rake her stomach.

"Think about the good of the school. You can understand, I know, that the media, that all this attention . . .

well, it's disrupting the entire school, Cindy. You surely don't want to be facing all this unwanted attention, do you?"

"I . . . I'm okay. I can handle it. I . . ."

"Oh, my dear, I'm so sorry. It's not your fault that the reporters are causing such a commotion. No. But the whole situation—well, it's not good. And it's especially not good for the school. In this case, as much as the administration wants to make your life better and as normal as possible, we don't feel equipped to do so. Therefore we must ask you to leave. Mrs. Diamond understands. Your father understands. They'll help you. Just go take a course somewhere where nobody knows you . . . And of course you can come back in June and graduate with your class. You don't have to go today, dear. Finish this first marking period if you like."

The dean's voice, kind as always, was nonetheless saying the unthinkable. It droned on. Liz answered. The assistant dean said a few words, too. Cindy felt dazed.

What am I going to do? she asked herself. *No friends, no school, no mother—nothing. If this is what the rest of my life is going to be, I might as well be dead!*

At last the meeting was over. Cindy thought she recognized sympathy and concern in the two men's eyes. She felt Liz's hand on her arm, propelling her up from her chair and out of the office away from the two school administrators. As Liz led her down the hall, the woman kept chattering about all the "fun we're going to have—your dad, my kids, you and me."

Cindy's nose was filled with Liz's perfume—a spicy, sensual aroma, strong but not unpleasant. But she *couldn't* like this woman. *Couldn't, wouldn't.* Despite Liz's friendly demeanor and constant chatter, Cindy couldn't help wondering if her mother would still be alive if Liz hadn't been in the picture.

Then her thoughts turned to her father. They raced back and forth, up and down, yes or no. *Had he done something to Mommy?* she asked herself. *Am I blaming him wrongly?* She was so confused her head ached.

Struggling to hold back tears, Cindy returned to history class to finish the day, unable even to smile at the classmates who wanted to know what happened. Finally, when the bell rang, she hurried from the room and started to her locker.

"Cindy."

She heard a voice and turned. It was her English teacher, Elizabeth Murphy. "Cindy, I'm so sorry. I just heard about you leaving. Look, I know you only need one credit and that's in English. If you'll stay after school for the next few weeks while you're still here, I'll tutor you every day."

Cindy felt the love projected towards her and appreciated it deeply. She wanted to hug this kind lady. "Ms. Murphy," she said tearfully, "thank you so very much."

From that day on, true to her word, Elizabeth Murphy stayed after school and tutored Cindy each day. It was just one of many kindnesses she experienced with her teachers and friends in that most difficult time of her life.

But the media didn't give up. Men and women alike called and accosted Cindy offering to write her story. *But I will never talk to anyone about it. Never, never, never,* she told herself.

After a few weeks, Cindy steeled herself to leave. Liz came to pick her up on Wednesday, November 12, the last day she attended Jericho High. Her friends hugged her. There were tears. There were also books to take home and a gift or two. As Cindy climbed into

Liz's car, she gave a last wave to her friends and the life she was leaving forever. She knew nothing would ever be the same. The drive home was long and silent. *How can I escape this pain?* she asked herself repeatedly. It was another question for which she found no answer.

The days inched by. One evening, lying on her bed in her room, Cindy could hear Liz speaking to her father at the foot of the stairs. "It's hard on Cindy not being in school, Howard. All her friends are there and she's home. That's not right. You've got to do something!"

"I suppose we could call Sarah."

"Sarah? The shrink cousin?"

"Yeah. Florence's cousin. I bet she and her husband would take her for a while."

"Oh, that would be wonderful. It would be fine for Cindy, too. Call them, Howard, right now. Something has to be done."

That night, Sarah Cohen and Steven drove to the Band house from their home in Greenwich, an affluent community in Connecticut.

When her father called Cindy down to the living room, Cousin Sarah held out her arms. Cindy ran to her and received a warm hug. "Steven and I want you to come and live with us for a while, honey," she said, smoothing Cindy's auburn hair back from her face.

Sarah's hand on Cindy's head felt so soothing. Her mother used to do that. But nobody since . . . "All right," she said. *I hate to leave my friends,* she thought, *but everything is so different now, anyway. I might just as well go.*

After packing her bags and phoning Mark and a couple of her girlfriends, Cindy climbed into the back seat of her cousins' car, ready to leave this place she'd always loved so much. She forced herself to look straight ahead.

The drive was so smooth and quiet she almost fell asleep. But once at the Cohen's beautiful, serene home, her cousins took Cindy into the kitchen and offered hot cocoa. Their children were both in bed, having been tucked in earlier by the babysitter.

"You'll see the girls in the morning," Sarah said and gave her a reassuring smile.

"Cindy," said Steven. "We're both so glad to have you here. There are already some messages waiting for you, although I don't know if you'll want to return them." He shook his head.

"Who?" Cindy didn't think Mark and her girlfriends had had time yet to let the gang know where she was.

"Reporters are trying to reach you."

"Oooh, give me a break! Well, I don't want to talk to *them*. No way!"

"We thought that's how you'd feel." Sarah patted her back. "Cindy, let's sit and talk," she said, pointing to the kitchen table. Steven grabbed the whistling kettle from the stovetop while Cindy and Sarah sat down. "Look, Cindy, we know you've been through a very, very bad time and we know you can't get over it just like that."

Steven brought over some mugs filled with creamy hot chocolate and sat across from Cindy, giving her a warm smile.

"We will do everything we can to help you, honey. And," Sarah added, "if you can't sleep, just call us and we'll get up and talk, okay?"

Steven nodded. "Any time, Cindy. I don't care if it's three in the morning, you call us!"

They're being so kind, Cindy thought, biting her lip. *I'll try not to bother them.* "Thank you," she said. Sarah showed her to her room and after she changed into pajamas, both she and Steven tucked her in. It was soothing to be treated like a little child again.

"Goodnight," they called as they left the room.

Cindy fell asleep a few minutes later, exhausted.

The next day, Sarah took Cindy to her new school—Greenwich High School—and enrolled her in the senior class. To Cindy's relief, nothing was said about her mother's death and no one seemed to have read the articles that had been filling the newspapers. Maybe kids in Connecticut didn't really care about murder cases in New York. Well that was fine with Cindy. *She* had no intention of bringing it up, that was for sure. The kids were friendly and she responded to them. She knew her mother would have wanted it that way.

On the following Saturday, Cindy asked Sarah and Steven if she could go find a part-time job. They seemed somewhat surprised but didn't object. Two days later, Sarah drove Cindy to the local shopping mall. Cindy wanted to stay super busy so she wouldn't think so much about what had happened. Since she needed only one credit to graduate, she'd be taking two classes in school, physical education and English. She'd have lots of extra time, she supposed, and a job would help to fill it.

Cindy told her cousin that she preferred to look for a job at a retail clothes shop of some sort. "Because after graduation," she said, "I want to enroll at the Fashion Institute of Technology in Manhattan. I'll major in fashion buying and merchandising. And I'll minor in advertising and display and exhibit and design. Mommy and I've been talking about it for the longest time. It's all planned. And it's all prepaid, too."

After applying at a number of stores, Cindy found a

neat shop that sold little kid's clothes. The owner hired her and she began work the following Monday evening.

But that night, feeling tired and a little stressed from training at the shop, she had a horrible nightmare.

She was at a party, a beautiful party in a big hotel. Lots of people were around her enjoying themselves. There was music. She was happy. Then the elevator came down. There were mirrors around the elevator. She watched to see who was going to come out of the elevator.

She saw the elevator door open. To her surprise, her mother stood there in the middle of the elevator. She was alive and beautiful, dressed in a splendid white dress, like a bridal gown, all lacy and lovely. Cindy felt so happy. But then her mother stepped out onto the floor and walked away without saying a word. Moments later, she returned, dressed all in black. Still not speaking, she climbed back into the elevator, the door shut, and the elevator rose. "No, Mommy, no. Don't go!" Cindy cried out.

Terror such as she'd never known washed over her in waves. She wanted to scream, but knew if she did, she wouldn't be able to stop. Finally, willing herself to open her eyes, she saw only darkness at first. Then, as her eyes adjusted, she saw through the bedroom window the faint glow of a waning harvest moon and knew she had been dreaming.

She was drenched in sweat, her heart pounding. She climbed out of bed and headed for her cousins' room. She felt embarrassed, but she was too afraid to be alone. She needed them.

Sarah and Steven got up and fixed Cindy peanut butter and crackers in the kitchen. The three of them talked for what seemed like hours.

The weeks went by. Though she was getting through the days, the nightmares did not stop.

Chapter 10

Dark Hunches

So far, Detective Jack Sharkey had made little progress on the Band case. He was aware that the two Band girls had left the area. Paula had gone back to college. Cindy was at her cousins' house. *Better for her,* he thought. There was still too much talk around Jericho High and Old Westbury about the "accident." Of course, it was no accident—he was pretty sure of that now. There was just too much evidence to the contrary. He and Martin Bracken, the assistant district attorney, had been comparing notes.

In spite of a strong hunch about Florence Band's death being murder, Sharkey was stymied as to how to get the proof necessary to convince a jury. He hadn't been back to the house on Horseshoe Road for almost a month. He didn't want to be accused of harassing a bereaved husband. If only he could find someone who *really* knew something, who perhaps knew the husband more than just superficially, he could work that angle.

Sharkey looked up to see two Nassau County detectives standing in front of his desk. Like himself, both were dressed in coats and ties. Al Martino, beads of sweat on his brow, fanned himself with a file folder. Although it was November, Long Island was in the midst of Indian summer. The men looked pleased with themselves as they told Sharkey they finally. might be on to something.

Detective Gary Schriffen handed Sharkey a report. As Sharkey reached for the paper, he indicated that the men should sit down in the two other chairs in his small office. Notes from the Band case were spread out on his desktop where he'd been puzzling over them, trying to figure out where to go next in this twisted mass of innuendoes and gossip.

"So you have a lead, do you?" he asked the two men.

The entire homicide team had been tracking down all the Band family acquaintances, whether they seemed pertinent or not. Among the many people they'd been interviewing, the two detectives had met that morning with a woman who lived in Manhasset Hills, but seemed to be spending an inordinate amount of time at the Band home. She was a looker, they told Sharkey. Really striking.

"Liz Diamond, huh?" Sharkey mused, one hand behind his head, the other holding the detectives' report. "Oh, yeah, I recall the name. Travel agent over in New Hyde Park, right?"

"Yeah, Jack," Martino said. Schriffen nodded. They sat down while Sharkey finished reading their report.

The Diamond woman was their travel agent and, evidently, a friend of the Band family. Or, perhaps solely a friend of Howard Band. In fact, there were those who felt that Mr. Band was a womanizer.

Sharkey had already delved into the fact that the Bands had done considerable traveling. Usually it was a family thing—all four of them on a cruise or a trip to Mexico, whatever. A lot of that stuff in the past. So it was perfectly natural that they should know a travel agent. Of course, there were a number of occasions when the husband had tripped off to Holland either by himself or with his father-in-law, but Mr. Band had made those journeys for the business in which he worked.

The company belonged to the victim's father, Al Saffer. The older man was a real nice guy. He was just devastated over his only daughter's death. Sharkey had made it a point to probe into the business. Very legit and all. In fact, Saffer's company had been the first in the floral business to bring a couple of innovative products over from Holland, which had paid off nicely. It certainly brought the company *and* Howard Band big bucks.

Apparently Band had a lot of charm when he wanted to. As a salesman, he'd done great for the company—and himself.

After Sharkey finished reading the report he nodded to the men. "So you interviewed this Elizabeth Diamond at her travel agency, is that right?"

"Oh, no," Detective Martino said with a chuckle. "She insisted we meet her elsewhere. We ended up at a diner drinking strong coffee. Guess she didn't want her associates to think the police were questioning her."

"Is that right? And it's your opinion that she is a little closer to Band than just booking his cruises? An affair, you think?"

"Well, we couldn't say that for sure," said Schriffen. "It's just that she hedged around a little, you know."

"If the husband was in a relationship with this woman—well that's a motive for murder as old as time. Got her home address here? Yeah, I see it. Okay, I'll go check it out this evening. Thanks, men. Good job!"

After the two detectives left, Sharkey wrote a few notes on a legal pad he pulled out of a desk drawer, then rummaged through the papers on his desk looking for notes he'd made at the time of Florence Band's death. Probably wouldn't be anything to this Diamond deal, but he'd go see what his own vibes told him. *Sorry, Jeanette, honey,* he thought ruefully. *Another late night, but I have to find out about this woman and her connection to Howard Band.*

It wasn't quite dark yet when Detective Sharkey pulled up in front of Briarcliff Circle in Manhasset Hills that evening. He saw a brown house with a gabled roof on a quiet, tree-lined street. It was an affluent neighborhood, he noted. A teenaged boy burst out of the front door, called goodbye to someone inside, then took off down the walk taking long strides.

At the lawman's knock, a maid opened the door and said "Good evening," with just the slightest trace of a Spanish accent. When he told her who he was, she excused herself to notify her employer. Moments later, an attractive blonde came to the door.

"Are you Elizabeth Diamond?" Sharkey asked. He put on his most engaging smile. Martino and Schriffen were right—she was a looker. "I'm Detective Jack Sharkey of the Nassau County Police Department. I'm investigating the accident in which Florence Band died. I believe you were the Band's travel agent?"

The woman said something about having already answered questions for the other gentlemen earlier in the day. For one brief moment he thought he saw a flicker of fear cross her face. Then she composed herself and asked him if he wanted to step inside. He did. At her suggestion, he took a seat on the living room couch by the window. She sat opposite him, crossed her legs and smiled confidently. She was obviously a woman aware of her feminine powers.

He had to admit this woman was attractive in an earthy, vixenish sort of way. Something about her perfectly manicured hands, her vivid blue eyes and the way her well-shaped legs filled out the tight slacks she was wearing. Definitely a female, he noted, a very collected, unrattled female. But there was something else. Sharkey noted her eyes had a sort of glazed look, as if she wasn't clearly focusing. He wondered if she was on something. A tranquilizer, perhaps? It was just a hunch.

But in spite of her placid exterior, as he interviewed the woman Sharkey soon realized—just as had Martino and Schriffen—that there was indeed more than a casual relationship between her and the husband of the victim. "How did you first meet Howard Band, Ms. Diamond?" Sharkey asked.

She twisted slightly in her chair, then turned back to face him. "I was at work one day and decided to take a break and go into the pet store. It's only a few feet away . . ."

He assumed she meant that the pet store was across from the travel agency in the same mall.

She looked at him and smiled, ". . . and Mr. Band happened to be in the pet store at the time. We got to talking about—we just happened to speak about dogs with the owner, and then he said something and I said something. That's how we met. And when he learned I was a travel agent, I began handling his travel arrangements."

"When was that?"

"A few years ago . . . three or four."

"Did you ever go out with Mr. Band? Socially, I mean." The other detectives had ferreted out that the two had been places together. Sharkey felt this woman was smart enough to know that Al and Gary would have already reported that fact.

She hesitated, then said, "Yes, but it wasn't really a

social thing. I was his travel agent and we became friends."

"Was this before the death of his wife?"

"Uh . . . yes."

"Where did the two of you go?"

"Once in a while we went out for lunches, different restaurants. Sometimes we went out for dinners." She paused a moment. "Or we went to a show."

Sharkey kept his expression bland, his voice a monotone. "Just when was it that you learned of Florence Band's death? Was it on August twenty-fifth?" For a minute the detective thought she wasn't going to answer. Technically, of course, she didn't have to; she wasn't under arrest nor did he have a subpoena for her. But he hoped she'd continue.

Liz Diamond excused herself and headed towards the kitchen. Sharkey heard water running. When she came back she smiled at him, her eyes appearing slightly glassy. He wondered if she'd taken a pill. Steeling herself, maybe?

Finally, she answered his question. "Yes. I was awakened from a deep sleep by the telephone ringing and I didn't have a clock on my table. It was dark in the room and I just couldn't see the time. So I would be guessing to tell you an exact time."

The caller, she said, was Howard Band. He was in tears.

"What did he say, Ms. Diamond?"

"He said something happened. Something happened to his wife. I said, 'What do you mean? What happened?' He said, 'She had an accident.' I said, 'How is she? Is she all right?' He said, 'No.' And then he told me that she was dead."

"What else did he say?" Sharkey asked.

"I asked, 'What happened?' and he said that she fell. She fell down the stairs."

As Sharkey carefully jotted down Ms. Diamond's words, he already knew what his next step would be: He'd subpoena the telephone records of the Diamond residence for the time period around August 25. It was a long distance call from Manhasset Hills to Old Westbury. The number of times and the time of day Band and Diamond had talked might give some indication of the extent of their involvement.

Although he'd interviewed Al Saffer, the victim's father, and her brother, several times since August 25, Jack Sharkey reached out to them again after he left Liz Diamond.

The old man, czar of a floral empire, still appeared utterly crushed. His daughter, so much like her late mother, was the light of his life. Her violent death was the most devastating event he had endured—even worse than the death of his first wife, Sarah, whom he had adored.

It was hard for Mr. Saffer to speak about it. Even his voice sounded broken and hoarse, Sharkey noted, as he spoke with him at his house. Al's second wife, Shirley, made the detective feel welcome by serving tca and cookies.

"You have to find out what happened from my son-in-law. He was there," Saffer said. "It couldn't have been an accident. It just couldn't."

After murmuring promises and saying goodbye, the detective drove to Pleasantville in Westchester County, about an hour away, to talk to Florence's brother, David, a married man in his thirties. David also felt his sister's death wasn't an accident. He talked at length—seemed glad to talk, in fact—emphasizing points the detective had already unearthed.

But he brought up one thing that was unknown to

Sharkey: "Did you check into the loan Liz Diamond made to Howard? That woman has got to know more than she's told you. She's probably afraid if she talks to you, she'll never get her money back."

"Is that so?" *A loan. This is news,* the detective thought. He decided to investigate this new matter in more depth before he approached Liz Diamond again.

A few days passed before Sharkey returned to the travel agent's house. As soon as he walked in the door, Liz Diamond began talking rapidly about the weather, her kids, her maid and the cost of groceries—everything, he decided, except what she knew he wanted to hear. He could see his visits were making her nervous and he decided to capitalize on her jitters.

He'd come to expect Liz's usual trip to the kitchen for Valium or whatever it was she was taking. She didn't disappoint him this time. When he mentioned the word "investigation," she excused herself. When she came back, she began to pace. Well, he could wait her out. But today, like a patient postponing a dental appointment, she went on and on, finding excuse after ridiculous excuse to avoid answering his questions.

"Ms. Diamond," he finally broke in, "what about this money?"

"What money, Detective Sharkey?"

"The seventy thousand dollars you loaned Mr. Band."

Her face flushed for a moment. She sat down on the edge of a chair. "That was a business arrangement only."

"To help him invest in the Al Saffer Floral business."

"Well, uh—yes."

"Ms. Diamond, I've made some inquiries. I can get these things in writing. I believe you don't want to cooperate with the police investigation, because you're afraid you'll lose your money."

"Well . . ."

"Seventy grand—that's a lot of cash. But, Ms. Diamond, here's something to think about—Al Saffer has told me he will make good on the seventy thousand if you talk to us about what really happened the night Florence Band died."

Liz Diamond didn't answer. She just listened.

Chapter 11

An Ill-Omened Offer

"But Sarah, you're the psychologist," Steven Cohen was saying with concern. "Can't you help Cindy? She is still having nightmares, poor kid. She isn't getting much sleep."

Sarah nodded thoughtfully. "Maybe I ought to take Cindy to see my partner. Therapists don't do well treating their own family members. They can't be objective enough. And Cindy might prefer to talk to a stranger." She sighed. "I feel for her. She is still practically a child."

"I think it's a good idea taking her to see Richard. Let's do it soon."

A couple of days later, Sarah Cohen drove Cindy to her office and introduced Cindy to her partner, Richard Jannsen. Sarah left Dr. Jannsen and Cindy alone to talk. The psychologist seemed like a comfortable, gentle man, with thick brown hair and a mustache. He talked with her softly for some time, asking about school, her friends and what she thought of Sarah and Steven's twin daughters. That made her laugh. Little

Amanda and Carolyn were very cute and often said the funniest things.

After a while, he got down to the reason for her visit. "Cindy, your cousin says you've been having dreams, bad dreams. Do you want to tell me about them?"

She swallowed, then began to speak. "Yes. I can't sleep. I have nightmares . . . frightening ones. I'm horrified when I awaken from them," she told him. She explained about the dream, every night the same, over and over, in which she pleaded with her mother. *Mommy, don't go!* Then she told him about her mother's death and how she had to leave school.

When she finished, she saw concern etched into the doctor's face. "Cindy," he said, "I'm going to try to help you." He stood up and walked over to the window and stood gazing out for a moment. Then he turned back to Cindy and sat down in the chair next to her.

Cindy," he continued in a low, calm voice. "I'm going to hypnotize you. We'll do this for a while in order to help you handle the trauma you've suffered." He smiled warmly at her. "Okay?"

Cindy nodded. At this point, she would try anything.

Dr. Jannsen nodded back to her. "Now, I want you to lean back in your chair and watch my face as I count. Are you okay? Are you comfortable, Cindy?"

"Yes."

"Think of a calm, peaceful place. Somewhere safe and beautiful. Can you do that?"

"Yes," she answered, trying hard to please, attempting to find that "safe" place he wanted her to imagine. "All right. I'm on a country road. I see a place with lots of apple trees. An orchard. It's so beautiful. There's a wonderful fragrance in the air and the apples are shiny and red. It's nice. Is that what you mean?"

"Exactly. Keep thinking of that good place with the sweet scent. Relax, now. Ten, nine, eight . . ." he counted backwards.

Cindy felt the strain and tension leave her muscles. She trusted this man and in a short period of time slipped just to the verge of sleep. Dr. Jannsen was still talking, telling her over and over that things would be better. Much later, she became completely awake. She smiled.

That evening, Cindy slept through the night. It was the first time since she'd arrived at her cousins' house that she didn't have the bad dream.

A few nights later, though, the dream returned. This time she was able to turn over and go back to sleep by herself. Cindy went to see Dr. Jannsen twice a week after that. He was always empathetic and always comforting.

While they were driving home from one of her visits with Dr. Jannsen, Sarah asked, "How is school, Cindy?"

"It's fine. Of course, I'm only taking two classes so it's no big deal."

"Right."

"And the kids are either super scholastic or jocks. Most everybody in school is Christian. They seem to have high morals; they're really polite and they're 'old money wealthy'. I love the houses they live in—all these big, old colonial homes." Her arm swept towards the window. They were driving through the elegant community as she spoke.

"And you know what, Sarah? Nobody here seems to know I'm one of the daughters in the Band case or, if they know, they're too polite to say anything. Isn't that great?"

"Yes, that is good. Have you mentioned it to any of your new friends?"

"Just a few, but they don't talk about it. It surprises me. It pleases me. Because everybody knew about it at Jericho High—even all the teachers. I hear that the accounts ran in the Long Island papers, on television and probably other media all over the world, because they said it went out on Associated Press and United Press International. That made me feel so, I don't know— different. I hated it."

Her cousin was quiet for a moment, giving Cindy a moment to reflect on how "different" she felt.

"I'm glad Mark drives over to see me from time to time," she went on. "You don't mind when he drops by, do you?"

"Of course not."

"He's wonderful," she said, noticing Sarah smile. "But somehow I don't feel like the old carefree, have-fun Cindy I used to be. I don't know . . . this is just so difficult."

It was a weird feeling, as if she were acting in some Greek tragedy the drama department was putting on at school. Nothing seemed real to her anymore. And although she had made many new friends at Greenwich High School, she had the sensation of being in limbo, of waiting, waiting—she didn't know for what.

"I know, honey. It is hard, especially for you," said Sarah. "It's tough on the whole family and for me to lose my cousin. But she was *your mother.* Of course it's hard." She pulled into the driveway and let Cindy out before putting the car into the garage.

Shortly after they entered the house, the telephone rang and Cindy answered it.

"Cookie baby," Howard Band's voice over the telephone crooned like that of the father she'd known as a child, "I miss you. How about coming on home?"

She hadn't expected him to say those words. For a few brief seconds, it made her beam. As a child, she'd always been so happy when he did something nice for her or praised her. Of course, the good feeling couldn't last; her mother's death, in all its gruesome agony, hammered into her mind a succession of such bruising scenes, the pleasure of his words evaporated like drops of water on a hot stove.

She saw Sarah watching her from where she was sitting on the couch. She was frowning. She probably suspected the caller was Cindy's dad.

"How are you? Are you doing all right, Daddy?" Cindy didn't know what else to say.

"Fine, fine. But I'm serious about this. Listen little girl, you belong here. Come on home. The holidays are coming up. The house isn't the same without you."

"Daddy, I really can't. I have to stay here or else I can't graduate. But I'll be finished by February."

They talked awhile. She wondered where his girlfriend was. She really hadn't expected him to call and ask her to come home like that. Finally, he said goodbye and hung up.

From the living room couch Sarah cleared her throat and gave Cindy a long look.

"That was Daddy," she said in a low voice. "He wants me to come home." Cindy had the feeling her cousin didn't approve. Sarah and Steven had been so good to her, but they couldn't know how mixed-up she was feeling. She wanted desperately to do the right thing. But what *was* the "right thing?"

Chapter 12

Searching for More Leads

Detective Jack Sharkey felt at times as if his wrists were shackled. Newspapers were still covering the Band story and turning to him for information that he wasn't free to give. He read the official autopsy report again, looking for something he had missed.

We, Leslie Lukash, M.D., Chief Medical Examiner, Gil Figueroa, M.D., Deputy Medical Examiner, Minoru Araki, M.D., Deputy Chief Medical Examiner, hereby certify that we have performed an autopsy on the body of Florence Band at 9:10 A.M. and said autopsy revealed as follows: Cause of death: Pending investigation. Final diagnosis: Undetermined cause. Associate condition: Multiple contusions and abrasions of the skin.

Sharkey sighed. The medical examiner, Dr. Leslie Lukash, had listed the cause of Florence Band's death as officially "undetermined with an associated condition, contusions and abrasions of the skin." To the press, Lukash had declined to describe those marks other than to say that they were "nonlethal."

Lukash had assured the press that "only about five or six cases a year of the approximately 1200 cases annually in Nassau County" remain undetermined. "Our determination of death is based on anatomical findings of the body and chemical, thermal or electrical studies. In these undetermined cases, no apparent findings are discovered to establish the reason for the person dying."

When the reporters hounded Howard Band, he complained because homicide detectives were still investigating his wife's death. He told one newspaper reporter: "I don't understand that. I thought it was over. I've had enough with this."

Band referred the press people to his attorney, who told them, "It's a sad commentary on forensic medicine that they can't come up with a cause of death. I'm shocked and so is Mr. Band."

The person Detective Sharkey thought could best provide the information he wanted, after Band's daughter, Cindy, with whom he kept in touch and was growing to like, was Liz Diamond. Sharkey continued his many calls to her. She had quit her position at the travel agency and could usually be found either at Howard Band's mansion or at her own house on Briarcliff Circle. The detective went only to the Briarcliff Circle home in Manhasset Hills. Sometimes her kids were there, sometimes not. Often when he'd drop in, they were napping or watching television. It didn't appear that any of the children had jobs, although he knew that Bart attended college.

As always, the young Guatemalan housekeeper, Marina, let him into the house. He waited in the living room for Liz Diamond. When she appeared, she was coiffed perfectly as always and well dressed, even though she no longer went to the office.

"Detective," she greeted him. There was always a touch of worry in her glance, he thought. That's all right. Perhaps she would worry herself into telling him what really happened. He felt positive she knew.

"How are you, Ms. Diamond? Did I interrupt anything?"

"Oh no. That's fine. What can I do for you?" She indicated he should sit down on the couch. She took a seat in a soft chair nearby. "Haven't you exhausted all your questions by now?" She smiled.

"Perhaps I just stopped in to see how you are getting along."

"No, I know you're after something but I can't imagine what. I believe I've answered every question you could possibly have."

"Let's go back to that night, Ms. Diamond. Your phone tolls indicate . . ."

"You got my phone records? Is that proper, Detective Sharkey?"

"This may be a murder case, you must remember. Your phone tolls show that you called someone August twenty-fifth at 3:30 A.M. in New York City."

"Oh no I didn't. Who would I have called?" She stood up, went to the window and looked out, moved some magazines around on the end table, then sat back down.

"It's here on this page. See?" He pulled a paper from his briefcase and showed it to her.

"Oh, that was just . . . Say, Detective Sharkey, I was just going to have a hot dog for lunch. May I fix you one?" She started towards the kitchen.

He held up a hand to detain her. "Why no, thank you very much, Ms. Diamond. It sounds fine, but I have to get back as soon as we finish discussing why you called this person on August twenty-fifth." *No hot dogs,* he thought. *No need to get that chummy.* What's more, anyone could see Ms. Diamond was very uncomfortable about the phone call.

"Well, I . . ." She sat back down in the chair, but couldn't seem to sit still. She kept fooling with an invisible piece of lint on her freshly ironed slacks.

Sharkey already knew exactly whom she'd called and why, because he'd already gotten the person's statement. He persisted. "You called this number, a Mr. Samuel Levy, at close to four o'clock in the morning. You were trying to reach your girlfriend, but when Mr. Levy answered the phone instead, you became confused and told him, 'your wife is dead.' Perhaps you thought you were talking to Howard Band, but Mr. Levy is willing to testify as to what you told him. I assume you had taken a little too much . . . uh, medication."

She looked at him for several seconds with her intense blue eyes. She was chewing on her bottom lip. "I may have done that. I was tired and upset about Howard's wife having fallen. But really, Detective Sharkey, are you sure you don't want something to eat? I'd be glad to make you a bite," she said, flashing that electric smile. She quickly jumped up and headed into the kitchen leaving Sharkey alone to ponder her strange behavior.

Chapter 13

Shadowed Homecoming

After the difficult holiday period, in mid-January when the weather was dark and gloomy, high school was almost over for Cindy. She'd complete her exams and secure her two credits, only one of which she really needed, within a couple of weeks, so there'd be no trouble getting into design school. Still, at the eleventh hour she wasn't sure what to do about going home. Her cousins didn't seem to want her to leave and she was sure they were only thinking of her welfare. But her father had been calling pretty frequently these days and he was a hard person to ignore when he turned on his charm. No wonder he'd always had women flocking around him.

Cindy asked herself over and over, *Why does Daddy want me to come home so badly? Is it really because he misses and loves me that much? Or could it be because Daddy is such a control freak? On the other hand, he might think I'm telling Sarah stuff about him and Mommy. Or maybe Daddy doesn't trust me away from him. Or maybe he thinks I've told something about him to the police.*

* * *

Her father called her constantly, day after day.

"Butchie-girl, how are you? We've been talking about you. We want you home. Here it is the new year already and you're still away. You don't belong over there. Come home and I'll buy you a car. And jewelry. Any kind you want. C'mon, your home is here!"

"A car!" She couldn't believe it! A car! She'd be free to go see her friends. She could have a life other than work, study, eat and sleep. "Thank you very much, Daddy. But I'm still going to school, you know, and . . ."

"As smart as you are, you don't even need that one little credit."

"But Daddy, give me a break, I want to go to college and without graduating I can't, and . . ."

"Well, I want you home. Go ahead and finish, then come home, you understand?" In the background, she could hear a woman's voice. *Probably Liz.* The thought irritated her.

When Cindy hung up, she saw both Sarah and Steven looking at her. She heard Steven mutter something *sotto voce.* She was so mixed up. She supposed they both hated her father. She did, too, not only because of Liz, but for what he did do and might have done to her mother. But he was still her dad and, in his way, she felt sure he loved her. She had to believe that even though he'd cheated on her mother, he wouldn't harm anyone and certainly wasn't capable of murder.

Once a long time ago, he'd told Cindy he'd never harm her. "You're my own flesh and blood," he'd said. "I would never, ever hurt you." She remembered it as if it were yesterday. And when he went away on trips— which he did quite frequently—he'd bring gifts for Paula, her mother and her. From Holland he brought Delftware—exquisite pieces, which her mother loved. He often brought clothes for Cindy. "I like buying for you, little girl," he'd told her. "You're a perfect size, you're so easy to buy for. Everything I get for you looks good."

"Cindy," her cousin's voice shattered her reverie.

"Yes, Sarah?" She walked back to the table and sat down with them.

"Look, honey, I assume that was your dad and he's telling you to come home."

"Mmm." She nodded.

"I just want to tell you something. Think very carefully about what you really want."

"I will," Cindy promised.

Her father called again one evening a few days before school was finished. "Cindy, little girl, I've bought your car. You'll love it. It's a Honda and you know they're good cars. I chose a color I thought you'd like, too. Just say the word that you're coming home and I'll have them deliver it right to our driveway. Like I keep telling you, it just isn't the same around here without you."

His voice sounded so sincere. He really wanted her home. Why else would he have bought the car? "Okay, Daddy, I'll be there next week. I'll get Mark to bring me home."

It was a chilly day in February when Mark drove her home from her cousins' house. True to Howard Band's promise, there was a new Honda Prelude waiting for her at the top of the sloping driveway beside the house.

"Oohh!" She gasped with delight as they pulled in from the main road. "Daddy got my new car! Look at it, Mark. I can't wait! What would you call that color? Sort of a pearlescent cranberry?" She jumped out of

Mark's car and ran up to the Honda, excited and ready to take off immediately. However, just as she'd expected, the keys were not in it. Mark helped Cindy into the house with her suitcases and kissed her goodbye. He didn't stay. She knew he didn't want to court any more trouble by speaking with her father.

Cindy entered the house with mixed feelings. She tried to stifle the horror and merely accept what was to be, reminding herself that, in her mother's memory, she must survive.

"Thanks, Daddy, for the car!" she told him when he came into the living room to greet her. He held out the keys, smiling happily. She immediately slipped them into her jeans pocket, the smile on her face equaling her father's. Daddy's gesture reminded her of earlier times when he used to sing her to sleep at night with songs like *Hushabye* or *Over the Rainbow*. Music meant a lot to him and he had a beautiful voice. She was very small when he used to do that and he looked so tall and powerful to her. Those were happy days. But the memories were bittersweet, because her mother was dead and she could not shake the thought that her father could be to blame.

Nudging her suitcases towards the staircase, Cindy looked around the house. Suddenly, the house seemed unfamiliar to her, as though it were someone else's home now. Obviously, Liz was mistress here and was making her presence felt. Little keepsakes, books, a pillow here and there had changed the very ambiance of the house. Even the smell of the place was different. Liz's perfume seemed to cling to the furniture and permeate the rugs. Nothing was the same.

Her father had his hand on her elbow and seemed bursting with news. "Guess what, Cindy? Liz and I are going to be married. Isn't that great?" he said, the proud grin making his often fierce face seem almost handsome. Before Cindy could answer, the new maid, Nevalda, came to take the bags upstairs into Cindy's childhood bedroom, leaving Cindy free to follow her father into the family room where he sat down at a small desk. She took a seat on the leather couch. "And we want you to be our witness at the wedding, Cindy my child. We've set the date for June, a little more than four months from now."

She wasn't surprised. She knew now he had loved this woman before her mother died, even if he never admitted it. Yet he was still her father and Cindy knew she should be glad for him, but she couldn't force any feelings of happiness. Something deep inside her felt like a volcano ready to erupt. Cindy resented this marriage. In an instant, the questions she had about her mother's death began rumbling through her brain once again. Her stomach began to hurt. "Congratulations!" Cindy's voice sounded small as she said the word. How was she going to bear living here until she was of age, knowing her mother, her most precious friend, had died here?

Wanting desperately to escape the house, Cindy pulled the car keys from her pocket and ran out the front door to take a drive in her new car. Her father followed right behind her. "By the way," he called to her from the doorway as she seated herself behind the steering wheel, "it's a stick shift. You've never used one, have you?" He walked over to the Honda and climbed in on the passenger side. "I'll ride with you and tell you what to do for a few blocks, then you're on your own." Though she wanted to be alone, Cindy didn't argue. She knew her father was not making a request.

For a moment or two, the stick shift seemed difficult, but Cindy was always very quick to absorb new things. A short while later, she was driving like a pro. Back in the driveway, her father climbed out of the car and gave her a little wave.

Cindy pulled out of the driveway and onto Horseshoe Road. Driving the new car was wonderful. She felt so free, free of the craziness inside the house. Because she was a minor and was forced to remain with her father until she came of age, this car would be her salvation, she was sure. It would keep her from going stark raving mad.

One night, Cindy heard her father's loud, angry voice in the den. When she walked in the room, he was just hanging up the telephone. He turned to her and said, "I'm glad you're home, little girl. You should have come back to your old dad a long time ago." He was growing angry, she could see. His voice was rising and he was waving his arms around.

"Daddy, are you thirsty? I'll get you a soda," she said and ran to the kitchen, glad to be out of reach of the brewing storm.

"Did I tell you," he said after she put a cold Coke in his hand and placed a bowl of hard pretzels on the lamp table by the couch where he was now reclining, "I'm going to sell this house. Why? Because I see what's coming. Old Al Saffer is trying to force me out of the business. So we're moving to Florida. How'd you like that, Butchie-girl? There's a college down there where you can enroll and I'll start my own business."

Cindy, shocked, didn't answer. It sounded as if her father had made up his mind. That meant the move was as good as done. *When,* she wondered. She really wanted to start college in New York City at design school. She and her mother had discussed it many times. In fact, Florence Band had pre-paid the tuition last year and classes for the spring semester would start later this month.

Hearing the front door open, Cindy looked up to see Liz Diamond coming towards them, her usually impeccable blonde hair tousled from the strong February wind. "Well, hi, Cindy and Howard. I see you two are getting reacquainted. That's nice."

Cindy's stomach lurched but she repeated her congratulations on their coming marriage. She wanted to more than survive this life; she wanted to do something good in this life to make her mother proud. That's what she'd pledged at the funeral. So she *had to* accept this marriage. She had to make the best of it, somehow.

"Thank you, dear," Liz answered as she kicked off her high-heeled boots and sat down on the couch beside Howard. But Cindy saw something in Liz's face that she hadn't expected to see. Was it fear or distaste? Intuition told her that this woman no longer felt the same about her father. *What has changed,* Cindy thought, *since I've been gone? Has Daddy begun to verbally abuse Liz . . . or worse?*

A few days later, Cindy heard her dad and Liz fighting. Nasty, screaming voices which almost made her feel ill. As she listened, Cindy realized her dad was being just as unreasonable with his new wife-to-be as he'd been with her mother. Howard Band was a walking time bomb some days. You never knew when he was going to explode. She wondered if Liz ever feared that one day she might have an accident just like her mother had? Or did Liz know more about that than she admitted?

On Saturday, as Cindy was upstairs in her bedroom, she heard her father call. "Cindyyyy!"

"Yes?"

"Come in here."

"Where's Liz?" Cindy called out. Although Nevalda had unpacked Cindy's clothes and hung them in the closet, she wanted to rearrange them herself and she really didn't want to stop before she'd finished the job.

"I said get in here. Liz is over at her house on Briarcliff Circle with her no-good kids," he called, twisting the words "no-good kids" to sound like something obscene.

Oh, Geez, he's in an awful mood, Cindy thought. *I'd better go see what he wants.* She hurried down the hall to her father's room. He was lying on the bed smoking a cigarette and watching television. From time to time, he flicked a few ashes into a beautiful Delft ashtray he'd brought from Holland, careful not to let a speck escape onto the bedspread. As usual, the phone was close by. "Here, Cinnamon, sit down beside me on the bed."

Dad called her little pet names when he was feeling sentimental about his daughter, so she assumed his reason for calling her this time was not to chastise her. However, Cindy didn't want to be close to him. In a way, she guessed she still loved him, remembering the nice things he used to do for her, but thoughts of her mother's death—no matter how hard she tried to push them down—would never go away. So she stood at the bedside for a moment making no move to sit, until he reached out his hand for her to take. Cindy pulled back. She didn't want to hold his hand. Then in a decisive voice he urged, "Come on, sit down right here and hold my hand."

He forced a smile, apparently trying to be nice. Then he stared at her until finally, she sat down solely to keep him from getting angry again. "All right, Daddy. What do you need?"

"Do you know that I love you very much? You're my baby. Cinnamon, you just don't realize. I miss

Mommy, too." For a moment, there seemed to be a catch in his voice, but the tone immediately changed to disgust as he added, "Liz is nothing like her!" He reached up and patted Cindy's hair. His voice became soft and paternal, "You're so pretty. You'll always be Daddy's little girl. Sit down with me on the bed and we'll watch television. I like this program and you will, too."

She shook her head. He was such a control freak. "No, Daddy, I have some things I need to do to straighten my closet. I'd better get back." She hurried out of the room before he could say anything more.

"Why don't you let the maid do it, whatever it is?" he shouted after her as she walked down the hall, "What do we pay a maid for if you're going to do her work? Stupid maids keep quitting anyway. One right after another!"

Cindy kept walking, pretending not to hear. Back in the safety of her own bedroom, she returned to her closet to straighten the clothes but instead sank down to the floor, the weariness of dealing with her father's mood swings and temper tantrums wearing on her. *I have to get out of this crazy house!*

Cindy soon discovered that Liz had quit the travel agency before Cindy had returned to Old Westbury from her cousins' house. By now, the blonde woman was at their house practically every hour, except for the times she went to Briarcliff Circle to see her three grown kids.

Howard Band's relationship with Liz, Cindy had also discovered, was growing more volatile yet more encompassing. Her father was obsessed with Liz. He wanted her by his side all the time. Unlike the distance he'd always put between himself and his first wife, he chased after this woman constantly, sometimes calling her as often as twenty times a day. Also, when he and Liz went to bed, he always locked the door, something he hadn't done when her mother was alive.

Despite the appearance of all-consuming love, Cindy was shocked as the weeks wore on to find that Howard's relationship with Liz—somehow easier to bear when she thought of it as a passionate, never-dying romance—had deteriorated into a dog and cat fight.

Her father, she was surprised to see, had taken on household duties in a way he never had with her mother. Since the maid usually left in the late afternoon, he almost always cooked dinner, which frequently was steak. One night, however, he prepared what looked like a delicious stuffed and roasted chicken and placed everything out on the table at their usual dinnertime. Cindy was sitting at the table with him waiting for Liz to come home so they could eat. She could see her father become increasingly annoyed the later it got. He was picking nervously at his fingers, an annoying habit he'd acquired recently. His face was contorted and crimson.

Oh, geez, she thought, *he's going to fly into another rage!* Watching him plunged Cindy back into the past. *Had he been enraged like this that last night with Mommy?* Cindy couldn't stop thinking about it.

When Liz finally arrived, she slung her coat on the sofa and rushed to the table to take her place. She was talking fast, possibly to cover her tardiness. Howard interrupted to ask where she'd been.

"Oh, I stopped off at home to see if the kids were okay. I hurried, Howard, but got caught in traffic. I'm sorry. You should have gone ahead and eaten. I'm really not hungry, dear."

Howard let his breath out with a puff. "Not hungry,

huh? Been over to that miserable Briarcliff Circle again!"

"Well, really, I mean it. I'm not hungry. You two go ahead. Please."

"You don't want this chicken? Are you quite sure you don't want it?" His face was almost purple with rage. Cindy saw it. She wanted to speak up but didn't dare for fear of being punished. "Okay," he began in a conversational tone, "if you don't eat it, you're going to wear it. Try me!" He picked up the chicken in its glass Pyrex pan, complete with stuffing and juices, and dumped the whole thing into Liz's lap. He then stalked out of the house, cold as it was, grumbling under his breath.

Total silence filled the room. Liz seemed frozen, her eyes wide with disbelief. Then she, too, jumped up. Cindy gasped, aware that Liz's beautiful velvet slacks were ruined. In silence, the woman went to the kitchen, then returned to clean up the mess.

The scene had made Cindy lose her appetite.

"He didn't used to be this way," Liz finally said to Cindy. Her voice sounded thick and hoarse. There were tear marks on her cheeks as she swiped at spilled food.

But Liz doesn't know how Daddy used to be! When Mommy was alive, Cindy thought, *she made dinner every single night, sometimes simple roasts and steaks, but sometimes she'd cooked delicacies like lobster thermidor or stuffed Rock Cornish hens.*

As Cindy helped Liz clean up the food from the table and floor, she remembered one evening a couple of years before when she, too, wasn't hungry for dinner. Instead of helping herself to the rich entrée that sat on the dining room table, Cindy had gone to the kitchen and brought back a bowl of cereal for herself. She sat on Daddy's right; her sister Paula was at his left. Their mother went on talking, realizing instinctively that Howard was growing irritated and trying to forestall the outburst of anger. Howard stared, his breath becoming heavier. Finally, he pushed back from the table and stood up.

"I'm not sitting at this table with that kid just having cereal after you made a beautiful meal," he exploded. His voice cut. He stormed upstairs. A little later, the front door slammed.

Tonight, recalling her past humiliation at her father's angry behavior, Cindy knew what Liz must be feeling right now. Against her will, Cindy felt sympathy towards her. The distraught woman was suffering from Howard Band's bad temper. Just as Cindy tried to say a few words of sympathy to Liz, her father stormed in through the front door, gave them both dirty looks and went up to his room.

A short time later, he bellowed down the stairs, "Liz, get up here! Now!"

Liz gave Cindy an almost apologetic look, took a pill from the pocket of her slacks, poured a glass of water and swallowed the pill, then went upstairs.

Cindy wondered what the woman was taking. Whatever it was, Cindy didn't blame her in the slightest. Sometimes things got so bad, a person had to escape one way or another.

Whether it had been their joint sharing of sympathy that night or not, shortly after this Cindy noticed that her father's girlfriend was going out of her way to be nice to Cindy. The next Saturday, Liz took Cindy to the cemetery where Florence Band was buried. It was an icy, frigid day and Liz was wearing one of her lavish assortment of furs—this one a beautiful silvery mink full-length coat, which not only made her look alluring but also protected her from the wind.

As they picked their way across the frozen ground between the tombstones, an immense sadness filled Cindy. When they reached the gravesite, she stepped forward to the grave alone.

She looked down at the grave, tears filling her eyes. *My mother,* she thought, *was a saint, a wonderful woman, always a lady. How am I going to make it in this changed, topsy-turvy world in which I find myself? Oh Mommy, I miss you so much!*

She stood by the grave and faced the headstone, almost able to feel her mother's presence. An immense pressure beneath her ribs threatened to rob her of her breath.

As if she sensed the girl's thoughts, Liz came up behind her and put her hand on Cindy's shoulder. "Cindy, what happened wasn't meant to hurt you, you must believe me." Her voice was strained, full of emotion. "I know I can never take your mother's place, but I'll do everything I can to be like a mother to you."

Cindy knew the woman was being sincere, but she couldn't answer her. She still wondered if Liz somehow was involved in her mother's death. Could her father's girlfriend have helped kill her mother? Cindy stared at Liz for a long moment thinking over what the woman had just said. What did Liz's words mean? Had something slipped out? Was it an admission of guilt or just an expression of sorrow? Cindy moved away thinking, *You couldn't even begin to touch what my mother meant to me.*

As they stood there, Liz's words made Cindy aware that she had to talk to someone, perhaps even the police. She couldn't let her mother's death be swept aside. No, she had to do something so the truth would be found out.

Cindy squared her shoulders. "I'm ready to leave now," she said softly. Cindy threw a kiss towards the grave and tried to ignore the ache in her heart.

But the ambiguity of Liz's words about her mother would not let Cindy rest. When she arrived home, she knew what she had to do. In her bedroom, Cindy picked up the telephone and dialed Detective Sharkey's office number. When he picked up, she managed to say, "I have to speak to you . . . alone."

Chapter 14

Lethal Vision

A few evenings later, Detective Sharkey came to the house and was greeted by the maid who was staying late that evening. Cindy, her father and Liz were sitting at the table following dinner, which again Howard Band had cooked. He usually cooked steak and tonight was no exception. The dinner was delicious; Howard had ruined it for all of them, however, by yelling at Liz because she was late again. She'd been to see her kids. He acted as if he couldn't stand for her to be with her own children. When the lawman entered, Howard finally shut up.

Cindy was very glad to see the detective. He'd been so nice to her last summer after her mother died and so it was he who she'd telephoned and in whom she'd confided her thoughts about her father and Liz, thoughts which continually plagued her.

"Hello Mr. Band, Ms. Diamond. I hear congratulations are in order!"

Cindy saw her Dad and Liz exchange glances as if they wondered how the detective had found out so quickly about the engagement.

"Cindy," Sharkey said, smiling down at her and ignoring Liz and Howard, "when I heard you'd gotten home from your cousin's house, I wanted to come by and see how you were doing. I'm still working on your mother's case, you know. Do you think we could go somewhere and talk?"

"Sure, of course," Cindy answered, jumping up from the table. She ignored her father's glaring eyes and walked over to the detective standing at the edge of the dining room. She held out her hand and shook Sharkey's, squeezing it a little to let him know she understood why he was there. She also wanted to signal her gratitude for his not letting her father or Liz know she had called him.

Cindy put on a jacket she had retrieved from the foyer closet. Sharkey led the way outside and they talked as they walked around the property. The detective asked how she'd been and how she was getting along now that she was back with her father and his soon-to-be new wife. She could hear genuine concern in his voice. As soon as they were far enough away from the house, Cindy said, "Mr. Sharkey, I called you because I've been thinking about my mother's death . . . and my father . . ." She stopped abruptly, unsure of what she should say.

Sharkey broke in, "Cindy, how do you feel towards your father? Do you think he killed your mother?"

She drew in her breath and then the words rushed out. "Well, Detective Sharkey, I don't want to think that about my dad, but he has a temper, you know, and he hurt my mother one night awhile back and Liz, I now know, has been his girlfriend for a long time. And . . . and I do want the person who killed my mother to be punished, even if it is my father!" Suddenly, it was all she could do to keep from crying.

Cindy looked up at the detective and leaned closer. "Have you spoken to our neighbors?"

"Yes," he answered. "Several times. A lot of the neighbors and friends to whom we have spoken seem to think your father may have been involved in her . . . her accidental fall."

Tears filled Cindy's eyes. It was one thing to have such thoughts, another to hear them spoken out loud. But she almost felt relieved. "I've been thinking that, too," she said, the realization slowly taking hold that almost from the beginning, though she hadn't wanted to, Cindy had feared the worst about her father. "I don't want to think that, but I do," she said and began to tell him all she had seen and heard and what she felt.

"Now Cindy," Sharkey said softly after she was finished, "I know you loved your mother. With your help, we can get justice for your mother. I want you to meet the assistant district attorney. He and I want to bring this case before a Grand Jury. I know this is hard for you, but will you help?"

She took a deep breath and let it out in a shaky exhalation. "I will. I want to help. I'm afraid things are going to get worse and worse for me around here. In fact, I'd better get back in the house right this minute before my father gets mad." Spontaneously, Cindy reached out and put her hand on Sharkey's arm. "Detective, I really want to thank you so much for trying to solve this case for my mother."

He smiled. "You're very welcome, Cindy."

Back at the front of the house, he opened the door for her and told her good night as she slipped inside.

When she returned to the dining room and sat down at the table, her father continued talking to Liz, ignoring Cindy for several minutes. Finally, turning to face her, he said in a cold voice, "You know what you're doing, Cindy Ruth Band? You think that man's your friend, don't you? He's not your friend, you know. He's trying to put your daddy in jail."

Cindy sighed and stared hard at her father for a moment. Then, without replying, she got up and went to her room. Her father's voice calling after her to come back followed her up the stairs.

Chapter 15

Preparing for Anguish

Detective Jack Sharkey, carrying a leather briefcase, opened the huge wooden doors of the Nassau County Court House in Mineola, New York. The building was an imposing cinderblock structure, stuccoed to look like gray granite. Entering, he passed the six jury rooms on the first floor and took the stairs to the second. A short way down the hall he came to a door marked *Martin Bracken, Assistant District Attorney*. When the ADA bellowed, "Come in," Sharkey entered. The two men shook hands and sat down. The detective opened his satchel and pulled out a bulky file marked "Band."

"Okay, Jack," Bracken began, "so what do we have? Let's hear it step by step." The ADA was a man of medium height, broad-shouldered, attractive and slightly balding at the front of his dark brown hair. He was blessed with an excess of energy, which invigorated everyone in his presence. He never sat still. From time to time, his arms flailed or he jumped up to emphasize a point.

Sharkey cleared his throat and removed a paper

from the folder. "Well Marty, we're pretty positive Band is guilty. What we have, though, is mostly circumstantial. Do you think the jury will buy it?"

"That's what we'll find out, Jack." Bracken smiled. "Okay, tell me what you have."

"First of all," Sharkey began, "we have Florence Band's body. Her position at the bottom of the basement steps is the first clue; it's not the way a person would land if she had fallen down the stairs. And her nightgown was neat and tidy, not mussed or half pulled up over her head as one might expect. My sergeant, Tom Mangan, is the one who noted that there was undisturbed dust on top of the five-gallon drum located right next to Mrs. Band's hand. Logically, she would have reached out as she fell and grabbed for the drum or, at the least, her falling body would have disturbed the dust as she landed right next to it. And there was a suitcase situated so that one might think she had tripped or fallen over it, which had undisturbed cobwebs running from its top over to the top of that drum.

"I talked to their friends, the Robertsons, who were with the Bands earlier that day. They said she had slippers on when she was at the pool party. When we found Mrs. Band, she was barefoot. Strangely enough, there was no dirt or dust on her feet, even though the stairs were dusty. Nor did she have any of the spilled spaghetti sauce on her feet or clothes. Forensics checked the nightgown thoroughly. All of these things suggest that she did not fall and was placed at the bottom of the steps after the death had occurred.

"Another significant thing—there were ligature marks on Mrs. Band's wrists and ankles, strongly indicating somebody had tied her up. We looked for signs of a break-in, but there was no evidence of forced entry. The police did a very thorough perimeter check of the grounds and there were no signs of intruders and no pry marks on the front or back doors or any of the ground floor windows. Believe me, we had officers scouring the entire estate.

"We know from interviewing Paula Band that she was upstate at Lake George, New York, waiting for her parents to drive up the next morning. Also, I interviewed Neil Ferrick and he will testify that Cindy Band was at a party over in Jericho and didn't leave till he did. He drove her home.

"So that leaves Howard Band as the only person in the house with his wife that night. Of course, the defendant's lawyer could argue that the ligature marks were made during some bizarre sexual activities between them before Mrs. Band went to the basement. But during the autopsy, we learned that when those marks were made on her wrists and ankles, she was already dead—they didn't bleed internally. And that wouldn't be consistent with bondage. We also learned at the autopsy that the victim was not killed by a spinal cord injury from falling down the stairs. She died from traumatic homicidal asphyxiation."

Bracken nodded and was about to speak.

"There's more, Marty," Sharkey said, holding up his hand. "One of their friends, Frank Robertson, said Howard Band told him that he wanted out of the marriage. He told his friend he was no longer in love with his wife. Band said the same thing to Mrs. Band's brother, David Saffer.

"Another indication: Howard Band has changed his story several times. For instance, he told Tom and me that he had helped his wife wash dishes and clean up. We know that wasn't true because Ellen Robertson said they only used paper plates and it was she who helped the victim clean up the kitchen. There were, she told us, no dishes to wash."

"Okay, Jack," Bracken said, leaning forward in his chair. "There's a lot here to work with."

"I think so, Marty. But you never know how a jury will take it. You work and interview, investigate and probe and sometimes what seems so obvious to us is just ignored by the jury or enough doubt is implanted in the jurors' heads by a good defense attorney."

"We'll soon see," said the assistant district attorney. He rose to shake Sharkey's hand. "Good work, Jack."

After Sharkey left Bracken's office, he immediately called Cindy, who he expected to be the state's star witness. He knew having to live with her father while preparing to testify in court was becoming increasingly difficult for her. He wanted to be sure the girl was alright, as well as let her know what was happening.

The phone was ringing as Cindy opened the French double doors from the patio. She ran to answer it.

"Cindy? It's Detective Sharkey. Can you talk?" the familiar voice asked.

"Yes," Cindy said, dropping her voice to almost a whisper. "I just stepped in the door after spending the night at Liz's house. It's bedlam here. Actually, it's bedlam there, too, but in a different way. Hey, how are you? How are things going?"

"Well, Cindy, we'll be getting those subpoenas out soon, as we've finally got this thing all set up for the grand jury. So now I'll need to discuss some more things with you. I'll probably be by tonight to see you for a minute or two. If you can talk then, fine; if not, we'll do it another time. Also, Marty Bracken is the Assistant District Attorney, and you and I will want to go over some of the material with him, too. Are you ready? Will you be alright?"

She felt a twinge in her stomach. This was untraveled ground. Cindy had known, of course, that impaneling a grand jury would be the next step, but the idea of getting on the witness stand and talking about her mother's death and her suspicions in front of her father made her turn pale.

"I'm afraid, Mr. Sharkey."

"That's understandable, Cindy, but remember you said you wanted justice done, right? I'm afraid this is the only way to get it."

"I know. But Daddy's going to be so angry. I'm not sure what he'll do."

"Look, I know living in the house with him must be a nightmare, suspecting what you do. Sometimes it makes me sick, knowing what you're going through. But you're still a minor and he will remain your guardian until we can prove in a court of law that he's guilty. Believe me, we're trying to get it over with as soon as we can."

"Okay. I understand. I'll be ready," Cindy said, sounding more confident than she felt.

She sighed as she hung up the phone. She remembered that Liz's son Donny was going to come by tonight. She, Donny, her father and Liz were all going out to eat. She wasn't looking forward to it. She wondered if Jack Sharkey would come by before or after they went for dinner.

That evening, Donny Diamond arrived about seven. Nevalda, who was staying late to do some extra chores, opened the door for him, then retired to the kitchen. Cindy, dressed and ready, met him in the living room.

He kissed her cheek. "Beautiful as always," he told her. "Where's the parents? Reservations are for eight, have they forgotten?"

Howard and Liz were taking them to *El Parral,* an upscale Spanish restaurant in Syosset.

Liz Diamond and Howard Band, after putting on

their sartorial finishing touches, came downstairs. Donny whistled at his mother who wore form-fitting black velvet pants and a soft cashmere sweater of slate blue, which was crocheted with a dainty design along its edges. With it, she wore diamond stud earrings and a bracelet of pink, white and yellow gold in diagonal stripes. She also wore her favorite high-heeled, leather boots. They walked into the living room and sat on the couch while Liz changed purses to complete her ensemble.

Before she could finish, they heard a knock. "I'll get it, Nevalda," Liz called out, rising and walking to the front door. She was back in a moment.

"It's Detective Sharkey with another detective and they want to see Cindy," she said.

Donny jumped up, rushing past Liz to get to the front door, his Bally shoes clicking as he walked on the parquet floor. His raised voice filtered in from the foyer. "No!" he was saying.

"Get out of the way, Mr. Diamond," Sharkey said firmly. "We have a subpoena for Cindy to testify before the grand jury." The two lawmen brushed past him and entered the living room.

An angry Donny rushed in and stood between them and Cindy. "Look, you're not talking to Cindy without me present! Come on, Cindy, come here." Donny motioned to her.

Instead, Cindy rose and walked towards the men. "Donny, no, I'm fine. I'll see the detectives."

Detective Sharkey met her eyes. "This is for you." He put the subpoena in her hands and gave her a quick smile. With a nod to the others in the room, the two detectives turned and left.

Cindy went back to the couch and sat down, almost afraid to look at her father and see his reaction. Instead of being angry, however, he was slumped over in his chair, both palms against the side of his head.

"Oooh," he moaned.

"Howard, what's wrong?" Liz asked, touching his shoulder. "Are you okay?"

He looked up and said, "It's this stress! I'm telling you, the stress is just so great my head is exploding."

Silence filled the room. Cindy felt a chill. *Was Dad having a stroke or was he just trying to get her sympathy?*

Donny broke the impasse. "Come on, let's go. Cindy, you're driving with me. We'll meet you there, Mom, Howie."

Cindy nestled back into the leather seat as Donny raced his Corvette towards the restaurant. With relief, she saw Donny flip on the car radio. She wouldn't have to talk. When the sleek sports car braked to a halt in the parking lot, she was almost sad that the ride had ended. Now she would have to be in her father's company again.

Leaning against the side of the car as they waited for their parents, Donny bent towards her and hissed, "Okay, so you got a subpoena. You ought to have slammed it back at them. What the hell's the matter with you?"

Cindy didn't answer. She was watching Liz and Howard drive up at that moment and pull into a nearby parking space. Her father looked ashen. She couldn't interpret her own feelings concerning the episode; she didn't even make an attempt. *What if he'd had a heart attack or a stroke? What if he'd died right there in the living room? What would she have felt? Sadness? Relief? Elation? Freedom? Fear?*

"Howard had a migraine," Liz said, patting his arm. "But he's okay now, aren't you, dear?"

"Good for you, Howie. I knew you were going to be all right once you left the house," Donny said, leading the group across the street.

The four of them went inside the restaurant. To begin their Spanish feast, Howard ordered each of them *mariscos,* a huge bowl of tempting bouillabaisse loaded with lobster and shrimp. It was delicious, but Cindy had no appetite. She sat playing with her spoon, waiting for her father to scream at her. But Howard Band didn't even look at her. Silence prevailed at the table. For the rest of the evening, Cindy tried to wrap herself in a protective cocoon, to pretend she was someone and someplace else. She tried not to think of what lay ahead in the days to come.

A few nights later, Cindy and Liz were together in the den. Each of them had a glass of herbal iced tea from which they took occasional sips. Liz was helping Cindy fill out a form to turn in on Monday when she was to begin the college of her choice—the Fashion Institute of Technology.

"I've wanted to go there forever," Cindy told Liz. "I want to be a fashion buyer."

"Well, you've got good taste in clothes, Cindy. That will be a distinct asset. Okay, we're down to question number eleven. 'Are you acquainted with any members of the faculty?' You aren't, are you?" Liz paused, absentmindedly chewing on the end of the pen she was using on the questionnaire.

"Yes, actually," Cindy answered. "We had a barbecue here one time and Mommy invited the dean of FIT. He was very nice. She introduced me, we talked and he said to let him know when I was ready to enroll, that he'd help any way he could."

"Okay," Liz said, marking "Dean" in the space for question eleven. "What's his name?"

A male voice from upstairs interrupted. "Liz, come to bed."

"All right, Howard. In a minute."

Before they could do much more, Howard called a second time, a little louder this time.

"I said I'll be there in a minute," Liz replied. She rolled her eyes.

A scarce five minutes passed before he yelled at the top of his voice. "Get up here now, Liz. NOW! Do you hear me?"

"I'm sorry, Cindy." Liz grabbed a pill from the pocket of her blouse, swallowed it with a gulp of tea, then walked upstairs.

Cindy tried to focus on filling out the form, but before she could finish she heard the sounds of Liz and her father quarreling. *Living at this house is like sitting on Mt. Etna.* She may as well go to bed, she decided.

Once undressed and in her bed, Cindy tried to sleep but the angry invective coming from the master bedroom continued. Suddenly her door swung open and a frightened Liz rushed in, slamming and locking the door behind her.

Moments later, her father pounded on the door. "Open this thing or I'll kick it in! Do you hear me?"

Cindy jumped out of bed and pulled on her bathrobe. Her hand was on the lock to open it when Liz screamed, "No, don't, Cindy. Please don't!"

"Open this door or you'll be very sorry!" Howard Band shouted.

Liz bit her lip and stared at Cindy. "Don't let him in!"

Cindy felt herself trembling, thinking, *What should I do?*

"I said open up. OPEN IT!"

She was terrified of what her father would do. "Liz, we've got to open it. It'll be better. If we don't, he—he *will* break it down. I'm sorry." She turned the lock.

Her father almost fell into the room. "You don't belong in here, Liz," he said, his voice quieter now. "Get out of here now." Then he turned to Cindy. "And as for you, you think that man Sharkey is looking out for you. Well, if he puts me in jail, just think about what will happen to you then."

Cindy couldn't stop shaking as her father pushed Liz through the doorway and slammed the door shut, leaving Cindy alone in her bedroom.

At her desk, Cindy forced herself to finish the questionnaire on her own. It was three in the morning, but she couldn't sleep.

The next morning she drove into Manhattan and parked at FIT. She was ready to begin college. The Fashion Institute of Technology was a state university located in the heart of the garment and floral districts in New York City. The nearly forty-year-old campus had recently added six new buildings. It was the place to study for prospective fashion designers and people in the fashion field. The institute's alumni included Calvin Klein, among others. She'd wanted to go there since she had been a freshman in high school.

Cindy remembered how she and her mother had checked out FIT on one of their fun shopping tours—those delightful trips when she and her mother were like two girlfriends. That's when they decided this was the school for her.

As Cindy strode into the building, she began to feel more and more apprehensive. A year ago this would have been so easy and wonderful. But today—well, she wasn't the same person she'd been a year ago. The events of the past six months had made her fearful and jumpy. She told herself she'd be able to get away from everything here, to begin a new life. She was sure she didn't know anyone at FIT so no one would be aware of the circumstances of her mother's death. Yet as she surveyed from afar the clumps of kids laughing and talking together in the hallways, she didn't even know how to act. Not long ago, she'd been happy and popular. Now she didn't understand how to "join in."

She forced herself to go to her appointment, where her advisor mapped out a schedule. Much of what she'd be doing the first year, the advisor said, was to take the same required courses offered at any college. That way, she'd get them out of the way before settling in with the actual design regime.

As she rode down in the elevator after leaving her afternoon class, her gaze caught that of another girl who looked familiar.

Recognition showed on the other girl's face. "Cindy?" she asked tentatively. The two hugged. "How are you? It's been what—eight years, maybe? Your family and mine were such good friends."

"Laurie!" Cindy said, excited at seeing a familiar face. "When Daddy and Mommy used to come to Brooklyn to see your parents, Paula and I would play with you and Melissa. It's so good to see you."

"So what have you been doing, Cindy?"

Cindy searched her old playmate's face but saw no signs that she knew of the tragedy. Cindy's stomach tightened. Quietly, she said, "My mother's dead."

After hearing Laurie's shocked gasp, she knew she had to explain further. When they got off the elevator, she told the girl the story as briefly as she could, noting the sympathy that drew down the corners of her childhood pal's mouth.

"You poor girl," Laurie told her, "come on over to the cafeteria with me and I'll introduce you around, okay?"

Cindy shook her head. "I need to get home," she said and with a small wave walked away.

Although Laurie made several overtures to her, Cindy felt too much like an outsider and didn't accept the invitations. She, who had been so outgoing and popular, was now subdued and silent. All she could think of was testifying about her mother's death before the grand jury. That and her suspicions of her father's part in the death.

One day shortly after beginning at FIT, Cindy left the school after classes let out and drove directly to Mineola on Long Island. She was slated to meet with an assistant district attorney. Detective Sharkey was waiting for her in the lobby of the courthouse and escorted her to the ADA's office.

"Marty, this is our best source of information and, hopefully, star witness, Cindy Band," the detective said. "Cindy, this is Marty Bracken, the Assistant District Attorney who's going to see that justice is done. Please take a seat and get comfortable."

She reached across the desk to shake the man's hand, then sat down as Jack Sharkey had requested.

"Ah, yes, Cindy." Bracken smiled at her. "You remember, I'm sure, that Detective Sharkey took your statement on August twenty-fifth, right after your mother's death. I'm going to go over it with you right now. The person who is going to record everything you say today is on his way to my office as we speak. Just remember, Cindy, the statements you made to Detective Sharkey last summer must correspond to what you say in front of the grand jury, okay? I have those statements here. You may refresh your memory with them."

"Okay . . . okay." Cindy felt very small and vulnerable. She watched as a man came into the office and set up his transcription machine with which he would type her answers to the ADA's questions.

"Don't worry, Cindy. Remember, we're your friends," Detective Sharkey encouraged her, while Bracken spoke with the stenographer. "If Mr. Bracken sounds tough to you, it's only because he wants to prepare you for the opposing attorney. We don't want them to surprise you, if possible. You'll be okay."

"Okay, Mr. Sharkey, thanks," she whispered in return.

Summoning her courage, Cindy confessed her suspicions about her mother's death. Once she did, Bracken asked her every possible question about her revelations. When the session was over, two hours later, she felt drained.

Jack Sharkey walked Cindy out to her Honda and opened the driver's side door so she could get in. "Nice car," he told her. He leaned toward her. "Cindy, I'm so proud of you. You did fine!"

"Thanks, Mr. Sharkey," Cindy said, sliding into the driver's seat. *But what will my father do when he realizes I'm helping the police?* she agonized.

Chapter 16
Witness for the Prosecution

For the next few weeks, while they waited for all the witnesses to be deposed, Cindy and Jack Sharkey spent time together almost every day after Cindy's classes ended, either on the phone or at the house on Horseshoe Road. He had her go over and over the answers she would give so that they'd sound natural when she had to testify before the grand jury. That way, he told her, she wouldn't become tongue-tied and freeze up. On the days he came to the house, each time the lawman left, her father invariably exploded at Cindy. The very sight of Jack Sharkey set him on fire emotionally.

"That man is a bloody bastard!" he ranted one day.

Cindy winced.

"I told you he's trying to put me in jail. Are you helping him? Answer me, Cindy Ruth Band!"

Cindy did what she could to avoid an argument, mainly by not answering. But her sister Paula, who had came home from college for a long weekend, walked in as Howard Band stalked out of the kitchen. Paula did not hesitate to show which side she was taking.

She confronted Cindy. "How can you do this? I just don't understand you," Paula said, glaring at Cindy with accusing eyes.

"Do what?" Cindy knew what she meant.

"Try to put Daddy in prison. He's your father. He's taking care of you. How can you! Do you actually *know* what you're doing or are you just too stupid to see?"

"To see what, Paula? I believe he killed our mother. And you know it, yet you . . ."

"I don't know it at all. Not at all! What will happen to us if Daddy's taken away because of your whim."

"My whim? There's plenty of proof."

"According to whom? Your new cop friend? What's his name—Sharkey?"

Cindy turned away and walked out of the kitchen. She felt as if her insides were churning. *Was she doing the wrong thing? Could Daddy possibly be innocent?* Then, for a moment, the face of her mother appeared in her memory and Cindy knew that she couldn't give up now. The grand jury proceedings would be coming up in less than a week.

At this point, Jack Sharkey lived the case night and day. He knew his wife Jeanette must be getting irritated at his constant preoccupation with Florence Band's death, but she never let on. As she kissed him goodbye before he left for work one morning, she tenderly touched his cheek. It was as if to say, *I understand.* It gave him the feeling of bright sunshine on a cold day. It was a wonderful encouragement and, as always, he felt blessed.

Sharkey drove over to the Mineola School on Jackson Avenue where Florence Band had spent much of her time. Perhaps he could learn something there he had missed. One more brief session with her principal wouldn't hurt, he told himself.

The principal, Sheldon Dumain, had praised the victim to him before. He reiterated his praise now. "She was one of the most dedicated and knowledgeable persons I ever knew," he said. "I feel a sense of loss both as a human being and as an educator." He had recommended Florence Band years before to be the Director of Title I, a federally funded program, for the tri-district of Mineola, Herricks and East Williston. She had become director and district coordinator of the program, which supplemented students' work in reading, mathematics and English as a second language.

Although he didn't learn anything new, the principal's words gave Sharkey an even greater urgency to bring Florence Band's killer to justice.

To his surprise, as Sharkey left the school office and strode back down the hall, he almost ran into Paula Band. Her mouth opened in an "O" as if she had not expected to bump into him, either.

He spoke in a careful tone. "Good morning, Paula. How is the world treating you?"

"What are *you* doing here, detective?" Paula asked huffily. "I didn't expect you to snoop in Mother's business, too."

Sharkey noted her antagonism. "I'm still trying to find evidence about your mother's death and this was where your mother spent much of her time."

"Well, I certainly know that! I don't think you have any right to be here. All you're doing is trying to find stuff against my father and I resent that."

"Cindy says that . . ."

Paula broke in angrily, "I don't want to hear what my sister has to say. And I would certainly get a warrant if I were you!"

Rather than further arouse the older Band girl, Sharkey

said goodbye, turned around and left. He'd save his questions for another time. Perhaps talk to Ellen Robertson, Florence Band's friend, once more. He knew Florence had confided in her, sometimes by phoning in the middle of the night, just to talk.

As he made the trip down the highway to the Robertson home in East Norwich, Sharkey remembered having gone to the Robertson's house with Artie French shortly after Florence Band's death to interview Ellen Robertson. When they had arrived, they found Seth, the Robinson's little boy, celebrating his birthday. However, the pain of mourning was so evident in the house that it overrode the happiness of his day and caused everyone to look downcast. Sharkey and Artie had sat down on the floor to play with the child. Seth's eyes lit up with delight as they showed him their handcuffs and badges while Ellen watched. She told them later that his visit had made her son's day and she was very touched. Ellen Robertson always cooperated fully with the police. She was sure Florence's death was no accident.

Now, after Sharkey rang the doorbell and was invited in, Ellen told him that Howard Band had taken to calling her at night to say he "didn't do it." Finally, her husband had taken the phone from her a few days before Sharkey's visit and told Band to stop calling.

"She was my best friend. I'd begged her to leave him," Ellen Robertson told Detective Sharkey. "But she always told me she knew he'd find her if she left."

"Unfortunately, she never even got the chance to leave. He made sure of that," Sharkey said bitterly.

Chapter 17

Grand Jury Questions

When the Grand Jury Presentation of the County of Nassau of the State of New York against Howard Band convened on March 24, the earth was still frozen and Cindy felt the same.

Assistant District Attorney Bracken ran through his witnesses with an enviable smoothness. He had subpoenaed far more people than he expected to use in the actual trial, but the one person he was sure he was going to call was Howard Band's younger daughter.

A frightened but determined Cindy waited in the hall outside the grand jury room for her turn to speak. To her surprise, Liz, who had also been subpoenaed, waited with her part of the time. She was a striking figure in her silver fox coat and high-heeled boots.

"Have you noticed a drinking fountain on this floor?" Liz asked her.

"It's over there," Cindy said huskily, pointing to the end of the corridor. She watched as Liz went to get a drink. *Probably popping a pill or two,* Cindy thought, *to make answering the questions a little easier.* When

Liz returned and took her seat, she was wearing a wide smile. Cindy sighed.

Several days into the testimony, Cindy was finally called. Taking a deep breath, she shakily followed a bailiff into the courtroom. Before testifying, she looked over at Detective Sharkey, who gave her a brief smile and nod. To Cindy, the policeman was a kind and good man who she could trust. She wondered many times where she would be if he had not been there as a friend for her when she was so distraught.

"Do you swear to tell the whole truth and nothing but the truth?" The bailiff swore Cindy in and she took a seat in the witness box. She counted twenty-three jury members occupying the first few rows. She felt all their eyes upon her.

Despite her fear of her father, Cindy was about to give testimony that she knew would help the prosecution show that there was cause to believe her father had murdered her mother. She wondered what the jurors thought of a daughter who would do that.

"Miss Band." ADA Bracken's voice was firm as he questioned her, "please tell the ladies and gentlemen of the jury what was taking place at Nine Horseshoe Road when you pulled in the driveway in the early morning hours of August twenty-fifth?"

Although her mouth felt dry, she had gone over her testimony a number of times with Detective Sharkey. She spoke in a clear voice. She didn't stammer. "When we got home from the party that night, we saw a number of police cars sitting in our driveway. I thought, *Oh, the cops must be having coffee with my folks.* Neil . . ."

"Is that Neil Ferrick—the young man who brought you home?"

"Yes, Neil Ferrick. Neil pointed out that it was after midnight. I still wasn't alarmed. I thought maybe the burglar alarm had gone off by mistake. Dad had been doing wiring on it in the afternoon. There were five police cars. I got out of Neil's car. Even though there was crime scene tape there, I still thought it was the alarm, so I said to Neil, 'Goodnight. Thanks for the ride.' "

As Cindy went on describing the night of her mother's death, tears filled her eyes and rolled down her cheeks. In a soft but firm voice, she told the jury about her father's and mother's argument that afternoon and the many which had preceded it. Finally, glancing over at her father then back at Bracken, she stated that, in her opinion, her mother's death was not an accident.

Eventually it was over. The prosecutor thanked her, and Cindy climbed down from the witness box.

Although she didn't get to sit there and hear the other witnesses, she watched people go in and out of the grand jury room and knew they were testifying for the prosecution, just as she had.

What she didn't know was that the nearer Marty Bracken came to the end of the hearing, the more he feared that his case was not strong enough and it probably wasn't going to make it. When it was time to ask for the jury's decision, the prosecutor made an unexpected plea to the jury, saying, "I am going to withdraw the vote."

When Cindy saw Sharkey walk out with a crestfallen look, she ran over to him. "What's wrong?"

"Marty thinks we would lose if it comes down to a decision, so he made the announcement to withdraw the vote. That means that no decision will be made."

Cindy was so disappointed she couldn't speak. *All this for nothing,* she thought. *What will my father do to me now?*

Sharkey watched her with concern in his eyes. "Still, this keeps the case open," he said. "It may take a while to get an indictment, but in a case like this, it's a good decision." Somberly, Sharkey patted her shoulder. "We'll have to get more evidence, Cindy. I'll need your help."

"I know," she said calmly, her voice low. But inside she was thinking, *No, no! My God, how can I go on living with a murderer?* She realized she would have to retreat into her own world. She would have to do whatever it took—act, pretend, talk herself into it—in order to endure.

"I know it's rough, kid, but don't you worry. I am not giving up. I refuse to quit on this case until Florence Saffer Band gets the justice she deserves. I promise you, Cindy, that your mother's death won't go unpunished."

She felt like crying, but she held her emotions in check. "Thank you," she said quietly.

She was glad her father hadn't testified. Sharkey had told her that defendants are never called as witnesses in a grand jury presentation, thank goodness. Nonetheless, Cindy knew her father would be more than angry about her part in the proceedings. Now she had to go home. How she dreaded it! *Today is April 16,* she thought. *How, oh how, am I going to get through the next few days and months? How am I going to get through this until Sharkey has the proof he needs to get the indictment?* And then an even more ominous thought arose in her mind. *If Daddy killed Mommy and now knows that I am going to testify against him, what will he do to me?*

Chapter 18

Walking a Tightrope

From that day on, Cindy was always on guard, listening, watching. She was mistaken, though, in what she thought would be her father's first response after her grand jury testimony. He somehow curbed his anger, although his eyes were flinty and hard as he pleaded with her that he could not, would not have done such a thing. How could she think he was a murderer?

Cindy's head ached all the time. What if her testimony had convinced the jury of his guilt and he hadn't actually done it? Could she be wrong? Could he be innocent? Yet, in her heart of hearts, she could not stifle the vibration of the awful truth contradicting her doubts.

And this respite from his temper was only momentary. As time went on and Sharkey's investigation intensified, things got worse in the house. She saw her father becoming increasingly nervous, picking at his hands, flying into rages at the smallest impetus. Cindy was becoming more afraid of him every day.

* * *

In June, soon after college let out for the summer, two important milestones took place. First, Cindy graduated from Jericho High School with her former classmates as promised. She'd looked forward to the ceremony, but when she went to pick up her diploma, hardly anyone from her family was there. Nothing was the same. Nothing ever would be again, she realized.

Then, her father married Liz Diamond. The ceremony took place at an office in Temple Beth Emanuel in New Hyde Park as planned. Cindy was the only one to attend the rites. Paula said she couldn't miss the summer classes she was taking and Liz's three kids did not want to attend.

Liz looked attractive as usual. She wore a two-piece suit with gold and diamond accessories. Howard Band, who had changed his style of dressing since his wife's death, wore black pants and a very expensive black and white silk shirt. This choice of colors was the bulk of his recently purchased apparel, Cindy observed.

A rabbi officiated. Her father's secretary and Cindy served as witnesses. The rabbi performed the ceremony quickly. It is customary in the Jewish faith to wait at least a year before remarrying after a spouse's death. Her father and Liz hadn't waited that long. Cindy wondered if the rabbi felt uneasy.

As the three of them got in the car to go home, Cindy felt as though she were living in a surreal world. *This can't be true,* she thought. *It just isn't happening. Any minute Mommy will walk up to the car and tell me this has all been a dream. Less than one year ago, everything was normal—fairly normal, that is. Now my whole life is twisted into something unrecognizable. And Daddy and Liz are married!*

On their wedding night, Cindy observed that the couple seemed lovey-dovey.

Then the fighting resumed.

Why did Daddy marry Liz if their love affair has turned cold? As Cindy mused about this, another ominous thought shook her. *Was it, perhaps, because a wife can't be forced to testify against a husband?* Cindy shuddered.

She went out with her friend Mark a few nights later. They drove around the beautiful countryside and the ride calmed her. As always, Mark was kind and comforting. It helped push her own turmoil from her mind—at least for a few short hours.

Late one Thursday night, after her father and new stepmother had gone out for the evening, an exhausted Cindy fell into a troubled sleep, only to be awakened by a burst of light and the sound of loud, quarreling voices coming from downstairs. Creeping to her bedroom door, she soon realized the voices were her father's and Donny Diamond's. They were both yelling at Liz. Cindy couldn't decipher their words; she could only sense that the argument was escalating. She tried getting back into bed and putting the pillows over her ears to obliterate the noise, but it didn't work. The screaming went on and on. Cindy didn't know what they were fighting about and she didn't want to know. Finally, silence came and she fell back to sleep.

But the next morning, Cindy knew she needed to get out of the house on Horseshoe Road as quickly as she could.

That evening, as if she'd read Cindy's mind, Liz asked the girl to go with her to the Diamond home on Briarcliff Circle. Not wanting to stay home, Cindy agreed. She got along okay with all of the Diamond kids. But she soon learned that they did not like Howard any better now than they had last fall before their respective parents were married. Donny, Bart and Shelley had no intention of ever living in the big house on Horseshoe Road with him and told her so.

"No way," Shelley said once. The tall, beautiful-as-a-model twenty-two-year-old wore an angry look and stared defiantly at her mother.

From that night on, Cindy often stayed over at the Diamond home.

Still, because of Sharkey and their mission to achieve justice, she felt compelled to return to Horseshoe Road in the daytime. Almost every day, she communicated the goings-on at the house to Sharkey.

One morning when she was at home, her father called to her from the kitchen. He was sitting at the table reading the newspaper dressed in a Ralph Lauren polo shirt and slacks. He motioned to a chair. "Sit down."

She sat, not wanting to anger him.

"You know, Cindy, your grandfather's trying to get rid of me."

"What!"

"That's right. I've helped him build up his floral business until we both became multi-millionaires and now to show me how much he appreciates my help, he's trying to kick me out of the company. It's one big headache." He put his hand on his forehead. "And you and your cop friends don't help! Every day that Sharkey detective is telephoning or coming here to see you."

Cindy said nothing.

Her father changed the subject. "Why do you stay over with Liz's kids so often?"

The question surprised her. They were his stepchildren, after all. "Well, I—"

" 'I can't' are the only words they know," he burst

out. "They sleep all day and go out all night. They don't work and they leech off Liz. Donny should be out of the house and on his own. I don't know if you know it, but their grandmother has a lot of money. She's a depression baby and, as a result, has saved all her life. Did you know that?"

"Well, no, Daddy, I . . ."

"You know who Carl was, don't you?"

"Liz's husband who died." Somehow, the next sentence tumbled out of her mouth before she knew it. "What did he die of, Daddy?"

Her father stared at her strangely for a moment then narrowed his eyes as if she had said something indecent. "He died of a heart attack. Why do you ask?"

Cindy felt unnerved for a minute. "I just wondered."

He gave her a second penetrating look, then went on. "He made it big in the garment industry. Well, Carl had a huge life insurance policy, plus Liz got part of the business, although the partner has kicked her out. They did okay financially, the Diamonds. They still have a live-in maid, Marina."

"Yes, I know, but—"

Howard wasn't going to quit. "Liz's daughter Shelly is going out with the biggest piece of crap and *he* stays there at the house, too, on and off. Bart, her youngest, is a snotty teen. He hangs up on me as if the phone were on fire whenever I call for Liz. She has no control over them. She gives them money; the grandmother buys Donny a brand new Corvette every two years and Shelley and Bart get a brand new whatever-they-want car whenever they ask. Liz buys all the groceries and pays all the bills."

"They *are* her children."

Her words obviously irritated him. He raised his voice. "They are a bunch of spoiled brats. Listen to me,

I don't want you staying with them and I mean it. They should go to work, get their own cars and, until then, walk. Those kids are in complete lala land." He threw down the paper and stalked out of the kitchen.

On one of Cindy's rare evenings at home, a warm night in early July, her father called her into his room.

"Liz's out again," he said.

Liz is probably at the house on Briarcliff Circle. That means Daddy will be in a temper until she comes home, Cindy thought. She sighed and was careful not to mention it.

Howard Band was preparing to go out. Cindy noted how nattily her father was dressed. He was dressing more upscale since her mother had died. His clothes were expensive and trendy. Sometimes, she'd learned, Liz bought them for him—gorgeous Calvin Klein sweaters, Armani jackets. Liz had all kinds of connections in the garment business because of her late husband. Tonight, Daddy was splashing his neck with a sensuous-smelling cologne, something he always used to do when he went out without her mother. *What is going on here?*

"Did you want something, Daddy?"

He dropped a sudden kiss on her cheek. Although he rarely did more than snarl at her now, his moods seemed to be becoming more Jekyll and Hyde-like these days.

"Listen, cookie-girl," he said, "if Liz calls for me, just say that I had to run an errand that came up suddenly, so then she won't know that I'm out all evening."

Cindy sighed watching her father go out the door. Inside she felt numb and sick.

That night, lying in her bed in the empty house,

Cindy remembered how it had been in the last few years before her mother's death. There had been cheating then, too, she knew now.

She recalled often hearing her mother and father quarrel. In fact, in the final weeks of her mother's life, most evenings had progressed in an identical fashion. Suddenly one evening in particular flooded back into Cindy's mind.

Her father had asked her mother at the dinner table how her day had been. She talked about it, delighted that he seemed interested. She shared her ups and downs with him—she always did when he asked. She started talking about one of her associates, a Dr. Alfred. Her father butted in, "Dr. Alfred is a piece of shit." Then he began screaming at her mother. Finally, after yelling at her for several minutes, his tone became downright brutal. "You get up early to make a homemade cake for a meeting with these people and they don't deserve it." Even though her mother kept quiet, her father screamed on and on. He ranted until he was hoarse, then finished eating and went upstairs. Her head aching from the yelling, Cindy quietly excused herself from the table and went up to her room. She could faintly hear her father talking on the telephone in his bedroom, an activity he'd been doing almost every night. Shortly thereafter, she heard him pass her door and go downstairs. Cindy tiptoed from her room and went halfway down the stairs where she stopped and listened. "I have to go out on business," her father said in a raspy voice.

Then she heard her mother beg, "Stay home tonight, can't you please?" But he yelled back at her. Finally, her voice broke as she said, "Howard, I love you!"

He mimicked her in a nasty voice, then screamed, "I want a divorce."

Cindy put her hand to her mouth, shocked to hear her father's angry demand. Then she heard her mother choking and crying and finally retching with empty dry heaves. Her mother's nature was so gentle that her father's constant abuse often made her break down that way. Tears rolled down Cindy's cheek as the sound of her father's feet descending the basement steps floated up to her. She quietly raced back to her bedroom when she heard her father coming up from the basement and heading toward the main staircase. With her door open a crack, Cindy glimpsed suitcases in her father's hands as he stormed past her bedroom. She could tell from the sounds of drawers opening and banging shut that he was packing his clothes. Her mother came up the stairs and went into the master bedroom. She cried and begged him not to leave. "Please, stop it, Howard. I love you. Don't go. Please think about what you're doing!"

"Get away from me," he roared.

Unable to stand the bickering any longer, Cindy burst into their bedroom. "What's going on?"

Her mother, sobbing, said, "Daddy is leaving."

"Don't go, Daddy," Cindy begged, feeling so sorry for her mother.

Abruptly, he stopped packing and smiled. "All right, Cinny-baby, for you I'll stay home."

When her father had gone downstairs to the kitchen for a snack later that night, Cindy asked her mother why she put up with being treated so badly. "Divorce him, Mommy!" she had said.

"It will be all right some day, honey. Things will get better. They really will."

Of course, they never would. Now, lying in bed remembering, Cindy began to ache for her lost mother. *Dear, wonderful Mommy. What horrible agony! And then to have it end as it did.* Cindy wept. Her mother had deserved better.

And now, she deserved justice. "I have to hold on," Cindy murmured, "to give her that."

Chapter 19

Hellish Summer

Detective Sharkey's visits were the brightest points in Cindy's days that somber summer. She felt as if he truly understood how horrible her situation was living with her father and that he was doing his best to make her life a little better. They had become good friends and Cindy, at his request, now called him Jack.

Often they'd go outside on the patio to talk. If it were too hot, she'd take him to the air-conditioned recreation room. The maid was in and out, doing her work, paying little attention to the lawman and the auburn-haired girl who were so engrossed in their conversations.

"You know, Cindy," Detective Sharkey said one afternoon as they sat on the couch in the recreation room, drinking sodas taken from the fridge in the corner. "I'm sorry that I have to ask you to go over this tragedy so many times, but if we're to prove the truth about what happened, we can't let one fact slip by. Last night it occurred to me that I've never asked you if you had talked to your father about what happened the night of your mother's death. Did he ever tell you what happened? Did you ever ask him?"

Cindy sighed. "Yes, I finally asked him after the funeral, 'Daddy, what happened?' And he said, 'I was upstairs with Mommy in bed and I mentioned that I had a tummy-ache. I looked in the medicine cabinet for some Pepto-Bismol. None. She said she would go to the pharmacy. I said I would go. I got there and it was closed, so I went to Swensen's and they didn't have any, so I came back home. I fell asleep watching television. I awoke a little while later and didn't see Mommy, so I called her name and no one answered. I went downstairs and called her name. No one answered. I went to the kitchen, noticed the basement door open and saw Mommy at the bottom. I ran down the stairs and shook her. Then I drove to Dr. Sultan's house.' " Cindy looked at Jack Sharkey. He nodded his head.

"Yes. Your dad has basically stuck to that story, but he's also changed it in several small ways at times. How do you feel about what he said, Cindy?"

Cindy felt hot emotions rising within her chest and she looked away. She told herself she shouldn't still cry so much, but she couldn't seem to help it. For a few moments, tears choked her. When she could speak, she told Sharkey, remembering how terrible it was. "You know, it took weeks before I could even enter her room. Everything was just as she left it—tons of clothes and shoes, purses in each closet and dresser. I couldn't stay long and I couldn't touch anything. Oh, Jack, I wanted so badly to smell the scent of my mother, to breathe in the traces of her perfume, but I couldn't bring myself to do it. I tried on several more occasions, but it was a long time before I could actually touch anything of hers. And then suddenly, a new woman was in my mom's room, in her bed and everything! My Dad was with Liz all the time. Can you believe it—he was trying to get her to marry him as soon as possible because a wife can't testify against a husband—at least that's what I think."

"You told me Liz seemed to keep putting him off. Did your Dad and Liz quarrel because of her not wanting to get married right away?"

"Yes. I used to hear Dad arguing with Liz about it sometimes and also about her children when he didn't know I could hear them. It was like I was—like I still am—in a bad dream all the time. It just keeps going on."

"Can you remember anything at all that he actually said that sounded suspicious to you, Cindy? Anything?"

"Yes, more than once I'm sure I heard him calling out, 'I did it for you and this is how you treat me!' "

After the lawman had left the house that afternoon and Cindy had gone upstairs to her room, her father called her into his bedroom. She could tell by the mean look on his face that he was angry.

"Damn it, Cindy. The grand jury dismissed this thing. Why is that Sharkey still hanging around? I can't believe you keep trying to help the police put me in jail. I saw you outside with that detective. Is that really what you want to see—your father in jail?"

Cindy knew she was playing with fire, but she stared into his eyes and answered calmly, "I want to see whoever killed my mother put in jail, Daddy."

On August 25, the anniversary of her mother's death, Cindy was able to get through the day because she was involved in registration for the fall term at the Fashion Institute of Technology. She signed up for *Advertising*

& *Promotion*. It was her second attempt at this course. *What is going wrong with my brain?* she thought as she filled in the forms. *Will I ever be able to concentrate again?* She hadn't done well in general in the spring courses, because she'd had to miss so many classes to prepare for the grand jury hearing. Late that afternoon, Detective Sharkey came by, a gesture Cindy really appreciated. He told Cindy how sorry he was for her loss. No one at home mentioned the fact that a year had passed.

The twelve months of mourning were finished and Cindy knew it would no longer be a dishonor to her mother to wear whatever colors Cindy wished. She pushed her black clothes to the back of the closet and wore a smart beige pantsuit when she returned to school. Several students and a teacher commented on how fashionable and pretty Cindy looked.

Cindy had much more homework that night, the first of her second term, but each time she began in earnest to work on a problem or write a paper, the intense arguments between her father and Liz blasted the thoughts out of her mind. Once during one of their quarrels, she heard her father say "Look what I did for you and now you're giving me trouble!" Cindy cringed.

Around eight, Liz left the house—probably headed for Briarcliff Circle—and Howard Band turned his temper on Cindy.

"Cindy, get in here," he barked at her from his bedroom.

She'd been talking to Mark on the telephone but hung up abruptly. Mark always understood. Not anxious to defy her father, she went to him. "Yes, Daddy?" she asked pleasantly. Maybe he merely wanted to ask her about school. That would be very nice, since he knew how much she'd looked forward to returning to FIT.

"I have something very important to say. You'll be

turning eighteen in a couple of months and I know what you're going to want. You're going to try and claim your inheritance, aren't you?"

She smiled. Her mother had taken out a small insurance policy at school and Cindy was due to receive six thousand dollars from it when she turned of age. "Well, Daddy, I would like that, yes."

"I don't want you to take it."

She was shocked. "Why? It's mine, isn't it?"

"Now Cindy, I'm just trying to think of you. You'll just dribble it away and waste it. You're too young. We'll invest it. Leave it alone and . . ."

"Daddy!" She was disappointed. She had no intention of "dribbling it away." It would just be nice to have a nest egg she could call her own, especially now that she was in college. Maybe it would make her feel better, make her feel more secure. Plus, it was something from her mother.

He wouldn't tell her sister to wait, Cindy thought. *Oh no! Paula will get her share, all right.* To her father, Paula was the "perfect one," the one he always held up to Cindy to emulate. There was a breathtaking 24-karat gold bracelet worth about ten thousand dollars that he had bought her mother on a trip to Europe. The piece was beautiful, with an elegant raised design. Cindy loved it. When Paula had gotten all of their mother's jewelry out of the vault the day after she had died, Cindy wore the lovely bracelet for a little while. It made her feel so close to her mother. But Paula made her sister put it back. "It's too expensive for you to wear," she insisted. Now her father had given Paula the bracelet and most of the rest of the jewelry, besides.

Howard Band's voice had become a shrill growl, "Quit arguing. Who do you think you are? You never listen to me. All you do is talk to those damn cops! Well, the grand jury didn't work out for them, did it?"

He laughed. "Maybe now that nosey, overbearing detective will stop trying to get you to spy on me."

"Daddy, I've got to go. I just started back to school today and I've got lots of homework." She turned to leave, but he yelled at her.

"Liar! That's what you are, Cindy Band. Don't you dare turn your back when I'm talking to you."

She turned around to face him. "Dad, I have homework to do."

"You've 'got homework'? That's a lie! You haven't got 'homework' when you talk to your friends on the telephone, have you? You didn't have 'homework' when you spoke with Liz before she left." The grimace on his face made her want to run. "That Liz. She's always over at Briarcliff Circle." His voice grew louder. "Briarcliff Circle, Briar . . . cliff, Bri-i-iarcliff C-i-i-rcle!" He contorted the address a little more each time he said the words. He was frightening her.

How in the world am I going to continue to live here? Here it is, the very first night of my second term and I can't even get my homework done, she thought. *I'd be better off somewhere else, anywhere else than here.*

As she stood there waiting for her father to finish yelling, he reached under the bed and pulled out a pistol. He stroked it, sending cold chills up and down her back. She couldn't keep her mouth from flying open. Of course, she'd known he'd had guns and rifles all her life. He even used to shoot target practice with the Old Westbury police and, when she was little, he hunted deer. But what . . . ?

"Hand me that rag on the chair, Cindy," he said in a calmer voice. "I started to clean my guns before Liz left, but that woman got me so upset that I stopped and put them back under the bed. Isn't this one a beauty?

Always keep your firing tools spotless, Cindy. You never know when you might need one of them. Okay, I know you want to leave. Go on, if you have to study, go do it. Who cares about Howard Band anyway?"

Her stomach and head churning, Cindy went back to her room and opened her textbook. She found herself reading the first page over and over without making sense of anything. Her insides were doing flip-flops. The thought of her father with those guns kept flashing in front of her eyes. In her mind, she tried to count how many firearms he actually owned. He always had kept one under the bed "for burglars," along with a pistol in his car, four rifles in the basement, and—if her memory was correct—at least five other handguns. She shuddered.

That night, after she finally fell asleep, something awakened her in the darkness. Someone was in the room. She lay very quiet for a moment, her heart pounding, waiting. A few minutes passed in silence, but she could tell that whoever or whatever was in the room hadn't left. Was it her imagination? Had someone let the dogs out of the kitchen? At last, gathering courage, she sat up in bed and turned on the lamp on the little side table.

"Daddy! What are you doing here?" she asked when the soft rays of the light showed who was standing beside her bed.

"Oh, nothing. Just checking, cookie-girl. Go back to sleep."

He left. She turned off the lamp. But the eerie feeling didn't go away as she lay there, eyes wide open.

Chapter 20

Deadly Repetition

Although she lived with fear and apprehension, nothing in Cindy's life prepared her for what would happen one night in early October.

She'd gone out early with an old friend. Her father was too obsessed with Liz these days to object as he once did. As always, he'd given her a curfew, this time 11:00 P.M. Coming home late wasn't her fault. Her date just wouldn't leave the party without a scene, which she refused to make. But, as the guy so loudly pointed out, it seemed ridiculous for a parent to be telling a college student to come in at that early hour, anyway. Her date had embarrassed her by pointing it out; her father embarrassed her by trying to enforce his childish rules. However, her date also knew what a difficult man her dad could be, so he soon relented. They were only fifteen minutes late. Nonetheless, Cindy was in an apprehensive mood when she walked through the unlocked door.

And her apprehensions were well-founded. Her father, his hands tightened into fists, his face livid, stood waiting for her in his pajamas at the head of the stairs. Her first thought was that he and Liz had been quarreling and he was on his way downstairs to cool off.

"What are you doing coming in at this hour, Miss Band? This is my house. I make the rules. D'you know you really piss me off?" He rushed down the stairs and barred Cindy's way up to her bedroom.

She tried to speak carefully and softly. "Sorry, Dad. I wanted to come home early, but my date insisted on staying."

"Then you shouldn't go out with the bastard. Now, you listen to me and listen good. You are late and I think I'm going to ground you."

Not again! This is too much. "Daddy, this is stupid. Give me a break. I'm almost eighteen now and I'm not even that late." She turned her head away from him.

"Dammit, look at me when I talk to you!" He was pacing back and forth, working himself up. She had to get away. She tried to slip past him and go up the staircase.

He grabbed her and pulled her back. "Don't you walk away when I'm talking to you!" His grip was like iron. She tried to pull away, but he wouldn't let her. They wrestled and she fell to the floor, staring up into his face as she lay there. A large, pulsing vein popped up on his temple; his face was crimson and his expression pure evil. She tried to crawl away, but he kicked her and slammed her back onto the floor. Grabbing her by the hair, he smacked her head against the hard wooden floor.

Cindy screamed for help. "Liz, please help me. Get him away from me."

"What's going on down there?" Liz called as she rushed down the steps. Cindy felt relief, but it was short lived.

At the bottom of the steps, her stepmother screamed, "Cindy, what have you done?" She began wailing and waving her arms about.

Cindy couldn't believe what happened next. Liz reached over and hit her. *They've both gone crazy.* Her father now had Cindy pinned down on the floor with his full weight on her chest. He let go of her hair and put his huge hands around her neck, squeezing. He was strangling her. She couldn't get her breath.

"You're trying to kill me," she choked out the words, "just like you killed Mommy!" Cindy gasped for air, feeling herself losing consciousness.

"Don't you ever say that to me again, you little bitch," he snarled.

Liz was still screaming and running back and forth in the foyer, but she wouldn't help Cindy in any way. Every time the girl managed to push herself a little bit away from her father, he slammed her back onto the floor. His hands found her neck again. All she could think of was that eventually he'd cut off all her oxygen. She couldn't breathe. She was dying. *Like Mommy.*

The last thing Cindy remembered before passing out was her father's grimacing face, distorted with hate, his hands closing like a vise around her throat.

When Cindy regained consciousness, she was amazed to see paramedics and police from the Old Westbury station lifting her onto a gurney. She tried to ask where she was and what was happening, but instead she began to retch. Her neck ached; her throat felt raw and inflamed. But the memory of what her father had done to her and what his intentions had been, hurt much more.

Seeking protection and safety, she retreated into a world of her own making, a world she had created for herself since her mother's death. In this place, anything and everything was acceptable, no matter how insane it might be. Since she didn't know how to physically escape from this upside down, *Alice in Wonderland* world, she retreated down the rabbit hole and hid there. Thoughts passed in and out of her mind. *Did Mommy feel this way sometimes? Did she cope with the pain of what was happening to her by pretending everything was okay, by pretending she was acting in a movie rather than suffering in real life?*

Paramedics surrounded her, she could see, but it was the police who were carrying her gurney to the ambulance. One of the officers—she didn't recognize who because her eyes wouldn't focus and everything looked fuzzy—told her as they loaded her into the rescue wagon, "Miss Band, you must never go back there. Never. Someone must have heard you screaming and called 911. When we saw the address, we pulled out all the stops to get here in record time. We're taking you to the hospital."

"Call Detective Sharkey," she managed to whisper as they loaded her into the vehicle. *Whoever called 911 saved her life. Was it Nevalda? Was she staying overnight in the house as she sometimes did? Or was it Liz?*

At Mercy Hospital, Cindy was placed in a small glass-enclosed room in intensive care until the doctors could ascertain how badly she had been injured. She was relieved to see that her room abutted the hallway in such a way that allowed her to see who was coming from either direction.

At first, she only wanted to rest. She was aware that Detective Sharkey came by, but she was too dazed and tired to say much.

The next morning, she tried to sit up, but fierce pains exploded in her head. A nurse told her she was on "twenty-four-hour observation," because they suspected a concussion. As she carefully laid her head back on the pillow, she thought she saw her father coming down the hall and heading for her cubicle. He was neatly dressed in a blue sport coat worn over a white knit shirt. She blinked once or twice as a cold shiver ran up her spine. Then her long-time coping mechanism kicked in. She told herself, *This can't be happening. I must be hallucinating.*

But it *was* real and her father was drawing closer, closer. And then, before Howard Band could push open the door to her room, five police officers sprang from different directions and barred his way, their guns drawn. She couldn't hear their conversations through the glass, but she knew they must have said "Put your hands in the air," because her father lifted his arms in a hurry. One officer reached over and opened her father's coat. In the harsh, fluorescent light of the hospital corridor, she saw a gleaming silver pistol in a holster. The officers quickly disarmed Band and escorted him down the hall out of Cindy's sight.

Daddy, Daddy . . . she thought, as tears seeped out of her closed eyes. *Why is he carrying a gun? Is he planning to finish what he started the night before? Is he really going to kill me, too?*

She knew the police officers would stay out there, protecting her. Nonetheless, she couldn't stop sobbing and trembling.

On the day she was released from the hospital, she was taken to Juvenile Court. She looked around as she entered the courtroom and saw her father and Liz. The judge, a woman, asked Cindy a few questions and then called her father to the bench.

"You are not to go near your daughter, Cindy Band, for a period of three weeks. This," the judge said, handing him a writ, "is a restraining order. Do you understand me?"

Howard muttered, "Yes," and took the paper.

Where am I going to go? Where am I going to live? she asked herself. For lack of an alternative, Cindy went to Liz's house on Briarcliff Circle and stayed there for the three-week period. Her father honored the restraining order.

She was too upset and embarrassed to tell Cousins Sarah and Steven about her father's attempt to kill her. She was ashamed. After all, they had wanted her to stay with them in Greenwich and she hadn't listened. Why, oh why had she gone back to her father's house? She had been mentally and emotionally wrestling with the question of whether or not her father was guilty. Her hope had been that her suspicions were wrong. When he insisted she live at Horseshoe Road, she thought maybe this meant he hadn't done anything wrong. She had only wanted to know the truth and her father was the only one who had the answer.

This can't be the way other people live, she thought. *Something has to change. Soon, the restraining order will expire and my father will be back in my life. I can't go on this way!*

Chapter 21

Romantic Interlude

During the weeks Cindy spent at Liz's house, her schoolwork at the prestigious design school suffered. She put in the hours, but her heart wasn't in it. Much of the time in class, she found herself being drawn back to the past, thinking of her mother and staring out the window. She had taken *Advertising and Promotion,* an interesting course, but she couldn't keep her mind on it. She hated her inability to concentrate. She'd always gotten excellent grades in high school and now nothing seemed to stay with her.

Sometimes she could scarcely wait until lunchtime to get out of the building. One brisk fall day, Cindy ambled over to the floral district, where her grandfather's offices were located. She noted the familiar landmarks such as "Holiday Plants," and "Hawaiian Cut Flowers." It was like stepping back in time.

She recalled that one of the offices of her grandfather's company, as well as an entire building that he had purchased to house the burgeoning Saffer empire, was on West 28th, the very street she saw in front of her.

Florence Saffer receives wishes of good luck from her father, Al, shortly before she is to marry Howard Bund.

The bride and groom at their wedding reception.

The picture of innocence at age eleven, Cindy Band remains blissfully unaware of what was to come.

Florence Band arrives home from her work with a local school system, less than a year before her untimely death.

The garage and a portion of the Band home on Horseshoe Road in Old Westbury hint at its size.

On the night of Florence Band's death, the kitchen stands eerily vacant. The slightly ajar cellar door hides a horrific scene at the bottom of the stairs.

The grim scene that greeted Cindy Band the night of her mother's death.

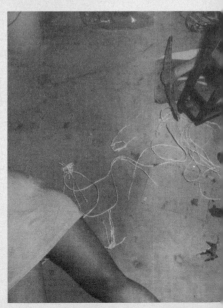

Next to Florence Band's body lie numerous pieces of thin rope that were used to bind her arms and legs.

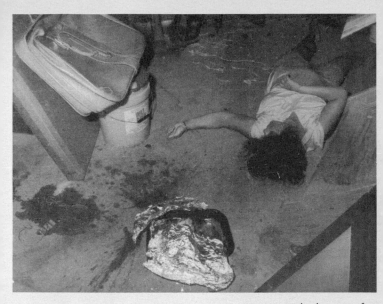

At the bottom of the stairs, police find splattered food from containers that Florence Band was supposedly carrying when she "fell."

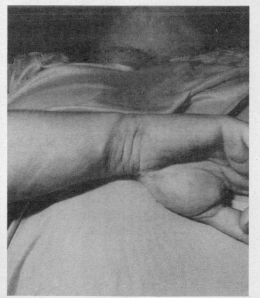

Florence Band's right wrist shows ligature marks inconsistent with the claim that she died from an accidental fall down the stairs.

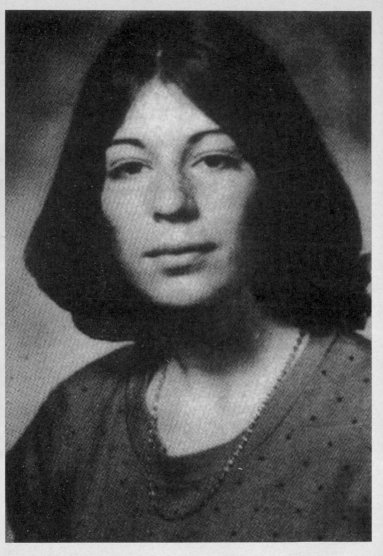

At the time of her high school graduation, Cindy Band still grieves for her mother and is faced with growing doubts and suspicions about her father.

After finishing high school, Cindy moves into the Rainberry Lake home in Florida with her increasingly violent father and her step-mother.

Determined to help Cindy and seek justice for the family, Detective Jack Sharkey doggedly pursues the Florence Band murder case.

With her mother's murder solved, Cindy was free to move on with her own life. Here she stands inside La Vielle Maison, the famed Florida restaurant where she served as events manager.

She took deep breaths. The streets were sweet-smelling and colorful, lined with flower shops and warehouses. This was the realm of her father and grandfather. This was where they had become successful in the floral industry. This area, in Chelsea, bordered the part of the city known as Hell's Kitchen.

Tilting her chin upward, Cindy caught the scent of myriad blossoms and, for a moment, remembered back to her childhood walking along these streets on those days when her father had taken her to work with him. She remembered how early they had climbed out of bed—3:00 A.M., usually—and how much fun it had been to be with him and see her grandfather, who always told wonderful stories and doted on her.

I must remember to tell Sharkey about that sometime, she thought, *as well as report what's going on and how Daddy treated me when I was little, although I can't imagine how that could help the investigation.*

As she walked, she let her mind relax and remember.

So many times, she thought, *people told me how ingenious Grandpa was to bring back innovative inventions from Holland: things like the now-common plant pot with holes in the bottom for drainage and the little sensor-meter which indicates moisture level so you know whether or not a plant is too dry. Daddy was—or rather had been—the sole distributor for a huge ten-thousand-dollar machine that sorted roses by ultra violet rays. And then, of course, Daddy sold all those inventions and made them so popular that the money just rolled in.*

When the money "rolled in," Daddy decided to have a new mansion custom built in "the best community on Long Island." That was also when he met Liz and everything started to change.

As Cindy strode along, her hair blowing in the cool, brisk breeze, people on the street recognized her as Al Saffer's granddaughter and Howard Band's daughter. They called to her in a way that showed fondness and respect. Perhaps they were paying her homage because of her grandfather. Everyone down here loved Al Saffer, she knew.

One elderly man came out of his shop and shook her hand. "Miss Band, I'm Sol Field. Your daddy used to bring you down here, all dressed up so pretty. Your face hasn't changed a bit. I've known your granddaddy for years and years. He has so many pictures of you in his office. How is he?"

"He's doing fine," she said smiling, not sure if the kindly man knew what had happened to their family.

But he added, "I heard the stories. I read them. I'm so sorry about your mother, Miss Band." After asking her to wait a moment, he rushed inside the shop and came back with a bouquet of large, perfect roses, which he handed her with a smile.

Murmuring her thanks, she buried her nose in the bouquet, savoring the wonderful raspberry aroma of the flowers and reveling in the scent.

"Give Al—uh, give your granddaddy my best, child. Come back and see us."

The encounter cheered her and she kept walking. Others along the street spoke to her, too. Some were workers, some owners. So many knew her name: "How are you, Miss Cindy. It's so good to see you again!" "I hope you're well, Miss Band. We are so sorry about what happened. If there's anything we can do . . ." She was surprised and pleased by their words of consolation for her loss and the deep respect they showed her because she was the granddaughter of Al Saffer.

Farther down the street, she came to the Saffer Company office. She didn't go in. She knew her father was no longer welcome there. Her grandfather had already headed south for the season. He was spending a lot of time in south Florida these days. She continued walking down the street.

"Hello, Miss." Hearing the masculine voice, she turned to stare at the young man who had addressed her. She wasn't sure if she knew him or not. She didn't think so, for surely she would have remembered someone as good-looking as he was. He was dressed in neat, clean working clothes—jeans and a turtleneck sweater. Tall, sandy-haired and slender, he was probably in his early twenties. His skin, she noticed, was clear and beautiful. But his eyes were the most striking feature of his face. They were the saddest yet most appealing brown eyes she had ever seen. She wasn't in the habit of talking to strange young men on the streets of Manhattan, but he possessed a fascinating charm that radiated from his head to his toes.

She smiled, curious that he'd spoken to her. "Do I know you?"

"I hear these others call you 'Cindy.' That's your name, Miss?" He had a strong accent but she couldn't place it. It certainly wasn't Spanish, Italian, French or Portuguese, because she was familiar with those. "Cindy your name?" he repeated.

"Yes, I'm Cindy." She waited, not sure what he wanted.

"I saw you coming down street. So beautiful. So very beautiful. And so friendly. All those men come out and greet you, give you flowers. I had to meet you too, Miss Cindy."

He told her his name—a long, unintelligible name of numerous syllables. She knew she would never remember it. Then he added with a smile that lit up his sad eyes: "You call me Nick, like my friends here." His hand indicated the flower warehouse behind him. He told her he was from Yugoslavia.

"You work in there?" she asked. The company was a large one, well-known in floral circles.

"Yes. This all belong to my uncle. I help with plants, make deliveries. I help uncle." His flushed expression told her he found her attractive. "You come in and meet him, please."

She wasn't sure why she went. *Things are so jumbled already that they can't get any worse, can they?* At any rate, she followed him inside and into his uncle's office. No one was at the desk. Nick looked crestfallen.

"I'm so sorry. I not mean to lie."

She laughed. He seemed so worried. "It's okay, Nick."

"I tell you what. You come with me. I live close by. I make us sandwiches for lunch. You hungry?"

Her stomach grumbled. "I guess I must be." She laughed again.

"Please come home with me. I fix it."

She looked at her watch. She didn't have another class for two hours. *Why not?* she thought. As she walked beside him to his apartment two blocks away, however, she asked herself if she was crazy. This was New York City. She didn't know this guy. But he seemed very sweet and kept talking to her in the shyest, most respectful way. Besides, she was in an area of the city she'd known from childhood. She knew the people here; she had no feeling of fear.

"I'm over here with uncle," he told her as they walked along the sidewalk. "I like America. But soon I must return to Yugoslavia. Be in army. We all be in army for two years. When they call, I must go."

"Oh, when do you have to go?"

"I do not know, Cindy. They let me know when it's time." He stopped abruptly.

"Here is my building. Come upstairs, please." He held the door open for her.

The ground floor of the building contained another floral store. Tall potted plants occupied most of the floor space. They walked through the store and at the back of the huge room were metal stairs. Nick indicated they should climb up. When they reached the second floor, there were wooden steps to climb.

"Wow, you get your exercise, don't you, Nick?" she said as she reached the third floor. Beyond were more steps covered in carpet.

"Yes." He laughed. "That's why I thin."

His tiny apartment was on the third floor of the building. The space had been cleared out for living purposes. Sparsely furnished, it was nonetheless clean and attractive with one very long brown couch against one wall. On the far wall, she saw a bed, with another some distance away against another wall. A dining table and chairs and a coffee table completed the furniture scheme in this room; beyond that were another small room and a tiny kitchen.

"Sit down, Cindy. I make you sandwich."

"Here, you take my roses, okay? Do you have a vase?"

He placed the bunch in an empty milk bottle, watering and spreading them artistically before centering them on the table. "How that?"

Smiling with appreciation, Cindy sank back into the huge, soft couch and waited. Being here seemed strange, but no stranger than anything else in her life lately. Nick worked in the kitchen, humming a tune. He served the food on dainty plates on the small table and invited Cindy to dine. The food was good, a well-seasoned large salad with romaine lettuce and many other vegetables, accompanied by grilled cheese sandwiches. He ate fast and then watched her while she finished her food. His eyes, half closed, were beautiful but disturbing. His gaze touched something deep within her, like the notes of a familiar song or a long-forgotten passage of poetry.

Feeling a little self-conscious under his adoring stare, she pushed her plate back and said, "Nick, what are you thinking?"

"Just you, Cindy. Just you. I want to touch you, hold you."

She hadn't expected this, not so soon anyway. "I'd better get back to school, now. The food was great, thank you."

"No! I don't mean to make you go. Don't go. Please stay with me awhile."

"Do you have a girlfriend?" she asked.

"No, not here. And I been here quite many months."

"Someone back there?"

He laughed. "No. Why you care?"

"I'm just curious. I'm curious about your country, too. What was life like back there, Nick?"

"Not like here." He took her hand and turned it over in his. "Here everyone free. I thought we were free there, too. Not true. I see that, now I in America. I like to stay here forever. Especially now." He gave her a look whose meaning was obvious. It made her feel warm and desirable. Then he looked away. "Yugoslavia is beautiful country. I want you to see it someday. My home close to Italy on Mediterranean. Beautiful *voda*—water. I take you there. *Da.*"

They both leaned back against the couch. She wanted to know more about him. Now, he looked down at his hands folded upon his knees. Again, he looked incredibly sad.

"What's wrong, Nick? You look unhappy." She had the strangest urge to help him. He wasn't like anyone she'd ever met before.

"Because I like here. I like you. I want to stay in America."

She spread her palms shoulder height and shrugged. "Then stay. Why not? You have a good job with your uncle. Why wouldn't you stay?"

"I can't, Cindy. No papers."

Uh-oh! She paused for a long moment. "Well, what kind of papers do you need?"

"What do you call it—a green card."

Half-kidding she said, "Why don't you marry some American girl? Then you could stay."

His eyes opened wide. A broad smile spread across his face. "That a good idea. Will you marry me, beautiful Cindy?"

"Hey, wait a minute, Nick. I didn't say me." She laughed at the suggestion. She saw his eyes grow melancholy once more. She said, "There are lots of girls around." *This guy can't be serious. Does he actually expect me to drop everything and marry him? How crazy.*

"I not want lots of girls. I want you."

He's kidding, she told herself. "Really, can't you get your green card any other way?"

He shook his head. "My uncle try. New friends try. But time running out."

It must be awful to be forced out of a country you love. Cindy thought of how devastated she had felt when she left Jericho High School and that was just a school. But to have to leave America . . . She'd done a great deal of traveling with her family as a child, but she had always been glad to come home when it was over. She tried to think of some answer that would be helpful to this interesting new person sitting next to her. "I'm sorry, Nick," was all she managed to say.

He turned those breathtaking eyes on her. *Wow, his*

eyelashes are long, she thought. *I wish I could help him. No, I won't even think about that, I've just met this guy. I certainly haven't fallen in love with him or anything like that. I'm not sure I've ever really fallen for anybody. When will I ever be in love—true love? I don't really understand the real love of a man and a woman. I've never seen Mommy and Daddy hug or kiss or even hold hands. And Mommy never had a chance to talk to me about such things. Some books describe love as if it were almost sacred, but I can't even imagine such a feeling. Why? What is wrong with me? What is missing inside me?*

"I would take good care of you, Cindy," Nick said, interrupting her musing.

Geez, he really is serious! She felt almost hypnotized, wanting to help him but not knowing how to do so except by marrying him. "Nick, I couldn't. I don't even know you."

"I'll let you know me right now." Gently he reached for her. "Beautiful Cindy. I not hurt you. I want to show you how I feel about you." He kissed her gently.

She felt as if she were trembling all over. He wasn't like any other boy she'd ever been with. He wasn't hitting on her, he was adoring her, worshiping her with his lips. Nothing like this had ever happened to her before. So innocent, so caring, and . . . *He must love her; he really must.* She was unable to tell him to stop.

They lay back on the couch, lips locked, arms around each other, yet there was no urgency, no demand—only Nick's lips telling her he cared. It felt so good to forget the life she was living and to forget the tragedy that had caused her suffering. She clung to Nick as if she'd found a life raft floating in the sea after a shipwreck.

When they finally broke apart, it was getting dark

outside. She sat up, dazed, and glanced at her watch. They'd been kissing—just kissing—for almost four hours. She'd completely missed her afternoon class. *What,* she thought, *is the matter with me? Am I grasping at anything, anyone, to keep from sinking into the unthinkable part of my life?*

His hand stroked her hair. "I love you, Cindy. I want to marry you with all my heart. Please stay with me tonight. I'll be good to you. You'll see."

Maybe it will be okay to spend just one night, she thought. *Where else am I going, anyway? But if I do, will he take that for acceptance of his proposal? I can't marry some stranger. This is crazy; I'm too mixed up already. Instead, I need to think of some concrete way to help Nick . . . and myself.*

"Well . . ." she began, then her voice trailed off. She wished she knew what to do. Suddenly Cindy felt young, confused and very impressionable.

"I won't—how you say it—press you. I have to go back to my uncle's store. Please stay till I come back, beautiful Cindy."

She watched him leave. Inside she was all mixed up. She thought, *What if I do marry him? He could get his green card. At least I'd be helping someone. And he would be helping me. I'd have a safe place to live where I could try to heal from this . . . this mess my life has become.*

She went back and forth in her confusion. She needed a sign—something to let her know if what she was considering was right. *Please, please, can't there be some kind of sign,* she thought.

Suddenly she saw something—a slight movement— in the darkening room. A warm flush crept over her. At the far end of the room where the one bed was pushed against the wall, there seemed to be a figure of a woman in a pale blue nightgown. *An apparition,* she told herself, *or could it be . . . Mommy.*

She blinked her eyes and peered at it. It amazed but really didn't frighten her. Was this the sign she had asked for? Perhaps this meant that the marriage would be all right. She closed her eyes and held them shut for a minute, then opened them. The figure was still there against the wall. She couldn't see a face nor did the apparition have feet, but she badly wanted to believe that this vision was her mother watching over her, trying to tell her all was well. The sight lasted another few seconds, then it was gone. Cindy fell back onto the couch, wondering if she'd had some kind of spiritual contact with her dead mother. She began to believe she had.

Am I getting a sign, because it would be better to stay here with this man who seems to need me so much, than to go back with Daddy who tried to kill me? Wouldn't this be better than the craziness of Liz's house with all its instabilities?

Cindy shook her head, trying to clear the confusion. She was like Nick in a way, she decided. They both needed help. *Would it be worse to marry Nick to help him remain in the United States than it would be to stay with my Dad and live with evil? This can be a way for both of us to survive,* she thought.

Cindy got up, splashed water on her face and finger-combed her hair. *All right,* she thought, *I'll spend the night and, if I still feel the same way tomorrow, I'll tell Nick that I'll marry him.*

After dinner that night, they lay down on the couch to sleep, both wearing their clothes. The apartment was dark except for the glow of streetlights from Avenue of the Americas, three stories below their window. He held her chastely in his muscular arms as he might have held a baby. The next thing she knew, it was morning. Nick was talking to her softly.

"Dear Cindy, I must leave. Go on route. But please don't leave me. I want to marry you. Please marry me. Please."

A clean smell clung to him, a good body scent. Sleep had not marred his handsome, chiseled features. She took a deep breath. "All right, Nick. I'll marry you and help you get your green card." What she neglected to tell him was that she, too, needed a safe haven.

"Cindy, you'd do that? Oh, beautiful, beautiful Cindy, you would?"

Thoughts of what her father would say flashed through her mind, but she pushed them away. He wouldn't be able to hurt her anymore. She'd be a married woman with her very own apartment. A safe place. She'd never have to live at the house on Horseshoe Road again.

Then fear overtook her. *Daddy will come after me,* she thought. *I can't marry Nick! No, the idea is too weird even to contemplate.*

"Well," she said, unable to meet his eyes, "sure I would, but I'm not eighteen yet, you see, I can't. You'll have to get an older girl to help you with the immigration problem."

"When you be eighteen, beautiful Cindy?"

"Uh . . . in about a month, actually."

"That not too late." His face lit up with hope. "We could go on—what is word? The trip for bride? Ah, honeymoon?"

She hadn't really thought further about being married to Nick beyond the idea that they were saving, sheltering each other. The word "honeymoon" brought her up short.

Nick pulled her to her feet and started dancing

around the room with her. Finally, breathless, they both fell back on the couch laughing. "You've made me very happy. And I be good husband. I make you want to stay with me, Cindy."

Chapter 22

Fractured Wedding Bells

T he next weekend when Cindy drove to the house on Horseshoe Road to pick up her mail, Jack Sharkey was waiting at the top of the long driveway.

"Nevalda said you'd be home shortly, so I waited."

"Hi," she said, rolling down the driver's window as she pulled her Honda in beside him and parked. She knew that he couldn't go in the house to speak to Howard or Liz; their lawyer would claim harassment. She also knew that Sharkey often went to the Diamond home on Briarcliff Circle. Sometimes he told Cindy; sometimes Liz mentioned it.

"How are you doing, kid?" He escorted her to the patio entrance, stopping to pet the two dogs that were wagging their tails in the enclosure in back.

"Okay, but there's something I need to tell you." She took a deep breath and then rushed on. "I'm going to get married," she said in a shaky voice.

The detective raised his eyebrows. "Really? That's a surprise. Have I met him?"

Cindy looked away from the detective. "No. He works in the flower district where Grandpa's main office is. He's Yugoslavian. He's here on a temporary visa."

"Well, congratulations, Cindy." Sharkey looked as if he wanted to say more but didn't.

Sharkey never, ever said discouraging or derogatory things to her and she wanted to be completely honest with him, for she thought of him as a good friend. But she didn't want to give him excuses to start saying "fatherly" things to her.

"I was hoping you were here to give me some news about my mother's case," Cindy said quickly changing the subject.

"And I was hoping you might have seen or found out something new," Sharkey replied.

"There is one thing," Cindy said, her face becoming pensive. "My father's talking about moving."

"Oh, really? Where?"

"Well, you know, of course, that he's no longer working with Grandpa. But he wants to go down near where Grandpa goes in the winter, Delray Beach, Florida. He's going to invest in some beauty shops."

"Has he purchased a house down there?" Sharkey asked.

"No, but he and Liz recently went down to Florida to look for one." She bit her lip. "Will that foul up the investigation?"

Sharkey shook his head. "Don't worry, kid. There are telephones and planes. You just need to hang in there, okay? Uh, have you told your dad yet? You know, about the marriage?"

"No, not yet, but I will soon." She thought she saw a cloud cross the detective's face.

"Look, Cindy, if you need me for anything, day or night, call."

"Okay," she said softly. "I appreciate all you've done, Jack."

* * *

Cindy turned eighteen on a chilly sixth of November. The restraining order had expired and her father told her, "You better come home. You've got some mail here."

An official-looking envelope was waiting for her on the kitchen table when she arrived. She went upstairs to her room and quickly tore open the envelope. It contained a check, the inheritance from her mother's school insurance program. She assumed Paula, who was away at college, shared equally as a beneficiary and had already gotten hers.

At the dinner table that evening, she turned toward her father who was sitting next to Liz. "Thanks," she said softly.

"So you got it," he responded.

"Yes."

"How much?"

She couldn't suppress a big smile. "Six thousand dollars, Daddy."

"Well, well, isn't that nice," he mocked "Okay, Cindy, let's see how fast you can spend it."

"Now Daddy, I'm only planning to spend a little of it."

"Sure, of course." He rolled his eyes.

"I do have something to tell you though, Daddy and Liz." She cleared her throat and looked at an invisible spot on the wall just above their heads. "Uh—I'm going to get married."

"You what?" Her father grabbed her arm. "So that's where you've been keeping yourself." His face reddened alarmingly. "When and where?"

"Oh, we'll probably just go to City Hall sometime in the next few weeks."

He shook his head from side to side. His lip curled. "Who is he? Do I know him? I suppose it's that Mark guy. You know, if I've told you once, I've told you a thousand times that . . ."

"No, Daddy, not Mark. I doubt if you know him. He works in his uncle's wholesale flower business, which is near the Saffer building in Manhattan. He's Yugoslavian and here on a temporary visa. He wants to stay."

"And you're the ticket." Howard rose to his feet. "Leave it to you to do something really dumb like that. You'll regret it, Cindy." He walked through the doorway heading towards the staircase in the foyer, yelling back over his shoulder. "But I'm stupid, you're smart. I know nothing; you know everything. Just don't expect me to come to the wedding."

Liz reached over and squeezed Cindy's hand. "You're sure, honey?"

"Yes, I'm sure. He needs me, Liz." She paused and added, "And I really need him."

Although Howard Band continued to be obsessed with Liz Diamond, he was also getting meaner and more violent toward her Cindy observed . . . and reported to Sharkey.

When Cindy came to the house the next weekend, Howard and Liz were in the midst of a violent argument. Even though Cindy was standing outside the house, she could hear them through the closed door— not well enough to comprehend what they were saying, but well enough to know how angry her father was. She hid behind a clump of trees and listened.

Finally, Liz rushed out of the door and attempted to open her car, which was parked at the very top of the driveway. But her car was so similar to Howard's that she accidentally went to his instead. Realizing her mistake, she ran to her own car, opened the door and climbed behind the wheel. Directly behind her was her husband, shaking his fist and trying to get into the car on the passenger's side, which Liz had locked.

"You are NOT going to Briarcliff Circle today, woman. You are NOT!" Howard Band screamed, pounding on the car door. "How would you like to end up like Florence?"

Liz tried to start the car, but in her agitation flooded the engine. "Leave me alone," she was yelling.

Cindy watched, horrified, as her father got down on the ground behind the car's back tires. Liz had managed to start the car, but seeing where her husband was, she slammed on the brakes and became hysterical.

"Howard, get out of the way. I don't want to run over you," she screamed. In back of the house, the dogs in their pens were barking and racing back and forth. It appeared to Cindy that Liz was pressing both the accelerator and the brakes at the same time. She was also shrieking at the top of her lungs.

Even so, Liz was no louder than Howard as he bellowed, "Get out of that car Liz Band. Do you hear me? You're not leaving this house!"

As Cindy stared wide-eyed, the noise—screaming, yelling, barking—continued. Little by little, inch by inch, Liz finally maneuvered the car forward in the small space at the top of the driveway and at last was able to turn around to drive past her husband. Liz was still screaming as her tires screeched down the long drive and the car spun onto Horseshoe Road.

Staying out of sight, Cindy watched her father get up, brush himself off and go in the house. She was relieved that neither her father nor stepmother had seen her watching. And now she knew for sure that she had to marry Nick . . . and quickly. She had to get away from these two crazy people.

* * *

The morning after FIT dismissed classes for the Thanksgiving holiday Cindy, dressed in a bone-colored suit with tan accessories, and Nick, in a light blue shirt and dark slacks, said "I do" in front of a justice of the peace and a witness at City Hall.

As soon as the ceremony was over, Nick kissed Cindy with the same fire he'd shown that first night together. "Mmm," he said, *"Dober!"*

"What does that word 'dobra' mean?" Cindy asked, speaking phonetically. She noticed Nick's smile.

"Dober mean 'good' in my country. And *ženska* mean woman. You my *ženska,* now, beautiful Cindy." He lowered his long lashes over those sad, sexy brown eyes with a look so passionate and full of longing that, for a minute, at least, she'd have done absolutely anything for him.

But his words were double-edged, both pleasing and frightening. Did she want to "belong" to anyone? Especially someone she knew so slightly. Still, the most important thing was, she never had to live in her father's house again.

She and Nick celebrated their "marriage feast" in a small European-style bistro a few blocks away.

Afterwards, she met his friends and his family, including his Uncle Kris and his brother who had been waiting at Nick's apartment to congratulate them.

He introduced one man named Glenn Bingham as a manager in his uncle's floral business. She noticed he was wearing a cross around his neck.

Moments later, two men about Nick's age kissed her and clapped Nick on his back. "Cindy, these are my best friends, Paul and Greg. His family famous. Have connections. My good friends, good *dober* people."

Later, Nick took her to the home of Paul's mother. Before the food was served, there were many toasts and many congratulations. It gave Cindy little time to agonize over the big step she'd taken. Sometimes the group spoke in their native language, which she soon learned was called *Slovene*. The house was crowded and Nick, with his arm around her, introduced her to everyone.

At that moment, the women, who had refused to allow the bride to help in the kitchen, called the group to dinner. Everyone sat down at a long table full of platters and bowls filled with interesting but unfamiliar food.

During a brief lull between the main course and dessert, Nick stood up and grasped Cindy by the arm. "Come," he commanded.

"What?" she asked, wondering whether she'd done something wrong.

He seemed serious as he tugged at her arm. "Cindy, come with me."

She left the side of the table, slightly embarrassed to be interrupting the big dinner, but no one paid attention. "What do you want, Nick?"

He led her into one of the bedrooms, picked her up and put her on the bed. "Cindy, you're my wife now."

"But Nick, right in the middle of the dinner? We can't . . ." His lips were on hers, coaxing, demanding. His hands peeled off her clothes, tossing them to the floor. His slacks followed quickly.

At that point, the full import of what she had done dawned on her for the first time. And she began to shake, afraid for the first time that, in trying to escape one problem, she had merely traded it for another.

Soon after their marriage, Cindy and Nick went to see George Nash, the immigration attorney whom Nick's uncle had recommended. The man's office was near Central Park. Cindy was pleased to learn that

Uncle Kris had not only paid for the lawyer, but also for all the expenses of getting Nick's papers. Nash schooled Cindy and Nick on how they must answer the hour or so of questioning they would undergo before Nick could receive his papers.

A few days later, they drove to the Immigration Bureau in Manhattan. Nick, of course, had already finished all the preliminary work in the months before meeting Cindy. Now, it was up to her—or rather to the two of them. They were herded into separate rooms where people questioned both of them at length.

"And what does the bathroom look like?" The man questioning her was watching her carefully. She had never considered that they were doing something they shouldn't do; all she'd ever thought about was helping Nick, who loved America so much.

"It just looks like a bathroom. It has a . . ."

"What color is the wallpaper?"

"Wallpaper?" she asked blankly. *Aha, they're trying to trick me in case we're not living together as husband and wife, in case I'm not really married to Nick. Well, I'm nnarried, all right.* "Our bathroom doesn't have wallpaper. It's painted." She was glad Mr. Nash had given her hints on what to expect.

The man smiled. "And how old is your husband?"

She smiled back, "Twenty-three."

The questions went on for what seemed like hours. She was sure she'd passed everything. If she hadn't been living in Nick's apartment she would not have known the answers to this lengthy interrogation. At last, it was over and she and Nick walked out hand in hand.

The papers, or at least the notice that the papers were on the way, arrived the following week. Apparently, both she and Nick had passed the exams with flying colors.

Chapter 23

Some Kind of Life

Once Nick had his papers, Cindy realized she had missed so many classes during the term that her grades again would suffer. She looked forward to doing better when FIT's spring quarter began in February.

During the interim, she used most of her energy trying to keep her husband happy. It took considerable time and effort to fix the eastern European dishes Nick liked.

"Dober! This *dober!"* Nick told her one evening after taking his first bite. She beamed knowing he appreciated her efforts. However, he spoiled the compliment by adding, "Your mother, she not teach you?"

"Teach me what, Nick?"

"Cook. She not teach you cook?"

Cindy shook her head. "She always loved cooking for my father and my sister and me. She spoiled us, I guess."

"She not teach you to sweep so good either." It was a statement, not a question. He got up and walked to the corner of the kitchen where Cindy had placed the broom behind the door. "Watch. I teach you." And he did. He carefully swept the room of every tiny piece of dirt.

Cindy was silent, not really watching him. Her thoughts had turned to her dead mother. It was the same every day of her life. Though she tried to look ahead, a smell or sight would catapult her back again.

"What be wrong, beautiful Cindy? Eat dinner," Nick said, returning to the table. His expression was concerned, as if he realized his mention of her mother upset her. She guessed he must have seen her swipe at her teary eyes.

Sometimes, the couple went out to restaurants rather than cook. While Nick spent his pay on groceries and had the use of the apartment rent-free from his uncle, Cindy paid for clothes, eating out and other "luxuries," knowing Nick didn't have spare cash.

One night, after she and Nick finished dining at a small restaurant on Long Island, she drove him to Old Westbury so he could see her family's home.

"Nobody's going to be there, Nick. When I spoke to Liz, she told me Daddy was going to take her dancing tonight, so this will be a good chance for me to show you where I grew up."

"You not wanting me to meet your family, Cindy? Why not?"

"Oh, you will some time, don't worry. We've only been married a short time, you know."

"Not so short. And your family didn't come to the wedding."

Cindy looked away. She certainly wasn't going to reveal to him the real reason. "Okay. But we have plenty of time later for your getting to know my dad and Liz."

As they drove into the posh *Stone Arches* community of Old Westbury, Cindy was amused to see her husband raise his eyebrows as he took in the opulence of the huge estates. He didn't make any comments until she drove up the long driveway of 9 Horseshoe Road and parked the car at the top of the hill behind the house.

"You live *here*?" His mouth and eyes were wide open with astonishment. He looked behind him at the hills and acres of trees and horse trails. He stared at the structures behind including the recreation room, the swimming pool and tennis court. "This your home, Cindy?"

"Yes, why?" She watched as he continued to absorb the scene—from the pedigreed dogs wagging their tails in their fancy enclosure, to the lush landscaping of the front lawn and huge dimensions of the custom-built, Tudor-style house.

"It—it's *dober*! Beautiful. Like a castle . . ."

"Let's go in, Nick. I'll show you around." They walked to the front door, where she rang the doorbell. Nevalda, who now lived-in, opened the door and they went in. After assuring Nevalda that they would only be there a short time and did not need her help, Cindy took Nick on a tour of the house. He "oohed and aahed" at everything from the vaulted cathedral ceilings to the magnificent fireplace with her mother's collection of antique beer steins on the mantel. His appreciation was very gratifying to Cindy, perhaps because he was so impressed with her mother's exquisite taste.

Afterwards, they settled in the den where they watched television for a while on her father's big screen. Nick was rapt as action filled the screen. "What a great TV."

"Are you ready to leave now?" she asked as soon as the program was over. She wasn't going to risk a confrontation when her father came home. She wasn't sure what her father's mood would be, especially upon meeting her new husband. She couldn't cope with a fight tonight. Reluctantly, Nick rose and followed her outside.

He didn't say much on the way home, but when they reached the apartment, he told her. "Your house, it's—how you say—magnificent. My apartment not much, but . . ." Nick gave her a soulful look and placed a chaste kiss on her cheek. "I do love you."

It was easy to care for him when his eyes spoke to her so eloquently. For a short while, lost in those deep coffee-colored eyes, she could forget everything bad that ever happened to her.

In the days that followed, Cindy tried to behave the way she believed a "good Yugoslavian wife" would behave. She catered to Nick, made him feel important. She and Nick entertained friends—his friends—frequently. It was a different identity for her, but for the first time since her mother's death, she felt safe from her father. Nevertheless, thoughts of that horrible night and her mother's death would not leave her.

One Wednesday, when Cindy came home alone to the apartment, she ran into a fortyish man with brown hair who seemed friendly in a nice sort of way. He was the manager of the floral shop downstairs. He had a small office on the fourth floor, just above the apartment she shared with Nick on the third floor. She recalled meeting him along with Nick's other friends right after their wedding. He'd been wearing the same gold cross. He reminded her that his name was Glenn Bingham.

As time went by, Cindy talked with him more and more when she came home from school, trying to drive away thoughts of the past. "How," she asked him one day, "do you always stay so cheerful, no matter how hard you work or whether the day is cloudy or bright?"

He smiled at her with a face that seemed to glow. "I

stay so cheerful because of the Lord. I study Jesus' words every day."

She hadn't expected that answer but found it interesting. "You're Christian then? Where I went to school last year, the kids were mostly all Christians, but I never went with them to church or anything."

"Jesus has answers for everything, Cindy. Sometimes you've looked so sad, I've wondered if something were bothering you. If so, lay it before Jesus. He'll help you." Glenn had a wonderfully kind face. He told her he was Catholic.

"I don't know how, Glenn," Cindy told him.

It seemed to be what he was waiting for, an invitation to tell her about his faith. He stopped working for several minutes and showed her the Bible he carried in his pants pocket. It was black and well-worn, but he opened it with reverence and began reading.

Whenever Cindy came to see him, Glenn read from both Old and New Testaments, explaining that Jesus was a Jew and had learned the old faith well, but carried it further. When he told her about Jesus dying on the cross, she saw tears in Glenn's eyes and felt like crying herself. It was obvious that Jesus was a personal savior to this man and that He had made a big impact in his life. The idea that her dad was an atheist, even though he outwardly professed the Jewish religion, crowded into her thoughts and made her feel ashamed.

"Jesus said, 'Whosoever believeth in me shalt never die,' " he told her.

Something strange stirred in her heart. She wanted to believe. Maybe if she prayed to Jesus for her mother, she would be assured that her mother would live forever. If anyone deserved to be in the heaven that Glenn had told her about, it was her mother.

Cindy frequently climbed upstairs to see Glenn and

each time became a little more certain that she wanted a faith like Glenn's. One day he told her the story of Jesus feeding the fish to a multitude of people. Then he told her about Mary Magdalene, the woman caught in adultery. "Jesus protected her when the crowd began to stone her. He told them, 'He that is without sin, let him cast the first stone.' And as each person lifted up his arm to throw, Jesus wrote that person's particular sin in the sand of the earth. In the end, all the people left and He told Mary Magdalene to 'go and sin no more.' And the woman was cleansed."

"You mean Jesus forgave her all the way? He cared for her just as much as anyone else?"

"Yes. She was perfectly cleansed from then on."

When Cindy left, she felt amazed. All this time she'd been feeling as if she were disgraced, because her father had murdered her mother, but now she thought Jesus in heaven would cleanse her. She felt tears dampen her eyes as she clung to that thought like a drowning person to a life preserver.

"Liz and I are going to Florida next week to see about the new house," her father told Cindy the next time she went to the house on Horseshoe Road to pick up her mail and try to get more information for Detective Sharkey. "We want you to come with us, toots." Then, emphasizing the word *husband* with the same vilifying twist he usually reserved for Liz's Briarcliff Circle, he added, "After all, once this *husband* of yours leaves you—and he will as soon as he gets what he wants—you'll be living in Florida, too. We'll get one house for Liz and me and then we'll look for one for you and Paula. How's that?"

She looked at her father in amazement, wondering if he was at all aware that she'd married to get away from him and that one day he might end up in prison. With him, it was just the same old insanity over and over again. Without another word, she picked up her things and left.

That night, she was glad to get back to the little apartment she shared with Nick. Over the next few weeks, however, Cindy noticed a gradual change in her husband. She remembered her father's words. No longer did Nick stay home with her as he had done in the past. Instead, he often went out. "I need my friends," he told her. He didn't return home early and when he did come into the apartment, usually smelling of beer, he never mentioned where he'd been.

He appeared to be hiding something, but Cindy didn't know what it could be and she was afraid to ask.

Chapter 24

Death and Other Losses

Cindy returned to school at the end of February, determined not to miss any more classes. Perhaps if it hadn't been for the psychology class she was taking, Cindy would have finished college and gotten her diploma. But the class had been studying how humans react to death and other losses. Jan Miner, the professor, was discussing the exact sort of emotional trauma Cindy had been experiencing for so long. The course became too graphic for her. Soon Cindy couldn't handle listening to the professor describe the same intense, excruciating feelings that she herself was suffering. It had been more than a year and a half since the night of her mother's death and she had thought she was recovering, but sitting in that class brought it all back with a slamming blow. Class after class, she found herself staring out of the window, blocking the words that stung so painfully.

"Miss Band. *Miss Band!*"

"Oh . . . yes ma'am?"

"I called on you. Didn't you hear my question?"

"Uh, no ma'am, I did not. What was it please?"

Everyone was looking at her. She felt her face redden and saw Dr. Miner shake her head. But Cindy couldn't help it. She tried to focus but found it impossible.

A few days later, the dean of students called her into his office. She liked him. They'd had talks before.

But, oh man, wish I were doing better in school, she thought. *Has my mother's death completely wiped out the brain I once had, turning me from a near-genius to a near-nothing? Somehow, I just have to try harder.*

"Sit down, Cindy." The dean tried to put the girl at ease by talking to her about the campus, her hobbies and her strong points in school. "Cindy, I know you're going through a dreadful ordeal. I've learned all about it. No doubt, it has been devastating. But Cindy, you have a wonderful background. You are a brilliant young lady. And your grades here at FIT are not reflections of your abilities."

He cares about me, she thought. She could feel and appreciate his concern. Choked up and unable to speak, she continued to listen as the dean explained that it wasn't fair to her that she remain in class when she couldn't keep her mind on the work.

"Perhaps it might be better for you to withdraw at present and return when you've had time to adjust to your loss."

She felt no criticism, only deep concern for her future. She was grateful for his attitude.

"But remember, Cindy, your records are here and we'll always welcome you back. Any time you feel more able to do the work, come back to us. We want you."

Cindy left FIT with mixed feelings. It seemed strange not to be going to school. Unfortunately, Cindy knew the dean was right—she wasn't able to concentrate on schoolwork. Maybe someday in the future when she pulled herself together, she would return to FIT. But for now, no. Too much had happened. Too much was going on. In leaving school, she felt she had failed her mother and herself, but she couldn't help it.

With more time on her hands, Cindy determined to concentrate on her marriage. She realized both her and Nick's emotional needs were too great to let the marriage fall apart as easily as she had let go of her career ambitions.

Yet her mother's death never left her mind, nor did her desire to bring her mother's killer to justice. Her two conflicting concerns, sustaining her marriage and avenging her mother, sapped all her energy.

The present, though, was such a contrast from her early childhood. She recalled wonderful camping trips where she rode horses; family vacations in the summer, visiting famous people who knew her parents and grandparents, cruises with great food . . .

She told herself there were good things in her life today, too. She worked at being a good person—worked at doing all the right things. She tried to keep in mind the good people she knew, like Jack Sharkey, her aunt and uncle, her husband Nick.

At the apartment one night, she cooked a tasty dinner that included steak, baked potatoes and a large salad of romaine lettuce, tomatoes and onions, which Nick loved. She expected him to settle back after dinner and relax, perhaps discuss his day and his plans for the future. Instead, he went into the bathroom, showered and came back wearing clean clothes. He gave her a peck on the cheek and started out the door.

"Wait, Nick, where are you going?" she cried, running after him all the way to the steps.

"I have to go out, Cindy. Why?"

"I thought we could uh—do something together tonight."

"Not tonight. I have plans."

"Plans?" she echoed.

"Yes. I go. Just me," he insisted.

"But Nick. Don't go. Please stay home." She told herself, *This can't be happening.*

Ignoring her, he quickly headed down the steps.

Why is he doing this? She tried to wait up for him, but he didn't come up the stairs until 2:00 A.M. By then, she was dozing.

"Where have you been?" She knew that wasn't the way to start the conversation. The question just slipped out.

"It not your business, Cindy." Without another word, he undressed, got into bed and quickly fell asleep.

A few days later, when Nick came home from work, she had already changed into a light blue, cotton pant-suit with matching purse and shoes.

"Nick, I'm taking you to dinner tonight. I drew out some cash and we can go to that restaurant you like where everybody knows you and . . ."

"Oh, sorry, Cindy. I got plans tonight. I meet Greg and Paul. They trying to help me."

Disappointed, puzzled and hurt, she said, "Help you what? They can come with us, if you like."

"No! I have something important to do," he said.

It soon became clear to Cindy that her husband really didn't care about her. No matter what she did, Nick continued to go out without her and he was drinking too much. It was driving her crazy.

"Don't go out," she begged him one night in late spring. "Kiss me."

"Cindy, please stop," he said, disgusted.

"Please, Nick," she whined, clinging to him, unwilling to let go.

Trying to get away, he shouted several words in Slovene, then backhanded her.

He hit me, she told herself in disbelief. *HE HIT ME!*

Not that it particularly hurt; he didn't swing hard. But the blow hurt her feelings. She couldn't believe it. She heard herself begging him, pleading with him—and suddenly she was hearing her poor mother beg her father. She must not fall into that trap. She wouldn't stay with a guy who smacked her. She had to speak now or lose herself.

"You don't have to go," she said. "I will."

He was silent for a minute watching her. Then he went into the bedroom. He came out with an envelope bearing a foreign postmark and stamps.

"What's that, Nick?" She reached for the letter and took it out of the envelope.

"It my orders, Cindy. I'm the one who has to leave. My uncle and friends have been trying to help me, but no one can. I have to go back to Yugoslavia." His eyes were so sad she reached out to touch him.

"What happens if you just decide to stay here, Nick? After all, you're a United States citizen now, or at least the husband of one. What could they do?"

"They hurt my family. They—how you say it—will persecute my father. And anyway, my parents need me. They write they have no money. I have to go. Maybe someday, I can come back. I come back to you, beautiful Cindy."

She hadn't expected his leaving to make her feel so lonely. Her voice choked as she asked him, "Will you write sometime?"

"Da, I write."

But somehow they both knew it was over. That night

they held each other tight. She felt a closeness that made her comfort him as best she could. Two nights later Nick left for Yugoslavia.

Cindy felt sad, wondering how it might have been if Nick had stayed. Then she put it out of her mind. The new situation—that she would have to go back to live with the person responsible for killing her mother—completely overshadowed the demise of her unconventional green-card marriage. All she could think of was that she would have to live in her father's house again.

Cindy continued to live at the apartment but knew it was only a matter of time until she would have to let it go. All she had done to get away from her father had been for nothing. During the next weeks, Cindy felt once again an indescribable emptiness. She needed something or someone in her life in which she could have faith and love, yet there was nothing that filled this void.

One afternoon she received a message from Jack Sharkey. He wanted to see her. Cindy called him back and told him, "I'm going over to Horseshoe Road now. Do you want to meet me?" Sharkey said he would.

At the house only a short time later, Cindy heard the front door slam. "Cindy," her Dad called as he trudged up the stairs. "I know you're here. I saw your car in the drive. I want to talk to you in my bedroom."

Shoving her mail under her pillow, she rose and went into the hall. "What, Daddy?"

"Can't you come to me once in a while? Must I always shout and make a complete ass of myself? Come in here."

She entered his bedroom. "Okay, I'm here." She tried to keep her voice light in an attempt to forestall the growing storm.

"Sit down here on the bed." She chose the chair. When she was seated, he paced back and forth across his bedroom waving an opened envelope. "Know what this is?" He shoved it towards her face. "A notice from FIT. You've quit. You've QUIT! Jesus Christ, Cindy. What's wrong with you? Goddammit, what's your problem?" He didn't wait for her answer. "I know what it is. Your mother spoiled you rotten; you don't even know the value of a penny!"

"But Daddy, I tried. I just couldn't keep my mind on school after everything that's happened. You should understand that."

She felt a hollow spot inside of her fill up with dread as her father's voice grew louder. "Couldn't keep my mind on school, couldn't keep my mind on school," he mimicked in a falsetto voice. "Of course not, it was on that dumb Yugoslavian you married . . . and that I support!" he said, balling up the envelope and tossing it into a nearby wastebasket. "Tell me, Cindy, what are you going to do now that he's gone? If I go to jail, then you're really stuck. Who is going to take care of you? Look at Paula. She's in college. She's got a future, you don't."

"Well, Paula's not going through this situation day to day. She's away from it."

His eyes blazed. He started swinging his arms around. "What exactly do you mean by that?"

Irritated at having her sister always thrown up to her, Cindy continued her diatribe. "It's so much easier for her and she gets money—her tuition paid for, new car, new clothes, everything."

"You could, too, but you won't. Instead, you talk to the police. *They're* your friends. That's who you call friends, the people who are trying to put me in jail for the rest of my life. How can my own flesh and blood turn on me? Just get out of my sight. Do you hear me? Get OUT! I can't stand the sight of you."

Weeping, Cindy went back to her room.

Scarcely a half-hour later, Detective Sharkey came to the door and was ushered in by the maid.

"How are you, Nevalda. Is Cindy here?"

"I'll call her, Mr. Sharkey."

The maid used the intercom. As soon as Cindy heard his name, she ran downstairs, two steps at a time. Sharkey was the one steady light in her life. He was like family. Better than family. "Hi, Jack. It's so good to see you."

Cindy's eyes were red and swollen. She knew Sharkey must suspect things weren't going well. Cindy was glad when he asked if she wanted to go outside. They trudged around the grounds and finally sat down on a marble bench beneath a maple tree whose gray branches were teeming with new green leaves. Buds were beginning to open. The air smelled fresh and sweet with spring.

"I'm going to have to move back in here with my father."

"Oh, Cindy, I'm really sorry to hear that," Sharkey said.

"My marriage is over. I know it. He's gone back to Yugoslavia. He has to serve in the army there. And I've quit—or been temporarily shoved out of—college. I just couldn't keep my mind on the work, Jack." She sighed and looked at him. "Is there something wrong with me?"

Sharkey shook his head. "Nothing that your father hasn't caused, that's for sure."

Although it was sunny, a chill breeze had blown in from somewhere and made them shiver. They left the bench and walked back towards the mansion. At the door, Cindy asked, "Do you work on my mother's case all the time, Jack?"

He looked at her for a moment, then shook his head. "No, I can't. They've assigned a lot of other cases to me. But I wanted you to know that we finally located a man who says your father tried to hire someone to kill your mother. The guy dropped out of sight for a while, but we found him. Just hang in a little longer, Cindy. We're going to get your mother's murderer."

The next time Cindy returned to the mansion on Horseshoe Road, Liz dashed into Cindy's room to get away from Howard's haranguing. It was obvious to Cindy that her stepmother wanted to talk and Cindy knew Sharkey was hoping Liz would say something that added to the case they were building against her father.

"What's happening, Liz?" Cindy asked to start the conversation. "Daddy giving you problems?"

"Of course," Liz said and flounced onto the bed. "You know what his latest deal is, don't you?"

Cindy, seated at her dresser, began to brush her long auburn hair. "What?" she asked.

"He's gotten a couple bids on the house."

Cindy sighed. She'd hoped against hope that the mansion would never be sold. Or at least not for a long, long time. "So then, you won't have two houses any more and you'll be moving to Florida for good, right?"

"We sure will. But I'll come back and forth, Cindy. I can't leave my kids, you know. They don't want to come to Florida." Liz got up and lingered in the doorway for a moment. "By the way, there's going to be an auction of stuff in the house. Do you want any of your mother's furniture?"

"No way. I can't even look at Mommy's things." It was next to impossible for her even to look at her mother's photos. It hurt too much and brought back all the horror of that night. *Will I ever get over it?* she asked herself. *I can't confide in, Liz; I still don't know if she is implicated in this or not.*

Although it wasn't a particularly good time for the Long Island real estate market, the mansion sold even more quickly than Cindy had imagined. The buyers began immediately to make plans to renovate the place. They were going to paint it "gunmetal indigo," which was actually a dark blue. They also planned to build a spiral staircase in the den and turn the basement into a recreation room.

Two sales were held to auction off the contents of the mansion, and both were very successful. Most of Cindy's bedroom furniture was sold. Her clothing and other small things she had wanted to keep were packed in suitcases and given to her father. He told her that, since her marriage was over and she had to give up the apartment, she would soon be homeless. He insisted she come to Florida the following month and attend college there. With no income and no prospects, Cindy had no choice but to agree.

After her father and stepmother left for Florida, Liz called Cindy. "There is just no living with Howie," she told Cindy. "I thought it would be better in Florida, in the new house, but our quarrels are just getting worse. So I'm going to go back to Long Island every time it gets too rough down here. How are you, Cindy?"

"I'm fine," she said, putting a smile into her voice. "I was hoping things would be better for you in Delray."

"Maybe they will be when you come down. You act as a buffer between us."

Thoughts of living with her father plunged Cindy into despair. That night she was unable to sleep; she remained awake, fearful and apprehensive. Finally, she realized she had to pull herself together and decided a brisk walk might help. After walking for two hours, she grew so tired she didn't think she could take another step. She figured she'd walked miles. She wasn't sure she had enough energy to make her way back. Her feet hurt, she was exhausted, discouraged, cold and damp from a light rain.

Suddenly, she noticed a church off the road to her right. It was not a big place, but somehow it looked inviting. The words her devout Catholic friend, Glenn, had recited from the Bible came back to her: *Ask and Thou Shalt Receive. Lo, I am with Ye Always.*

"Please," she said out loud, "if there is a Holy Spirit, please help me." *I want to have faith like Glenn's,* she thought. *Perhaps this is the time to commit.*

She walked up the front steps of the church. The door was open. Inside, stained glass windows cast a rainbow of lights onto the pews. She slipped onto one of the benches, then knelt in prayer. *If you're there, God, please, please help me. I need you. Please give me the strength to keep going.* Although this was something she'd never done before, it felt good and natural. She stayed there resting for five or ten minutes, then left.

When she went back out, she saw a phone booth by the side of the road that she hadn't noticed before. She fished in her pocket for coins and finally found enough to call Donny, Liz's son. The call went through and he picked up the telephone.

"I'm stranded, Donny." By checking the street signs on the nearby corner, she was able to tell him where she was.

"Okay, Cindy, don't be upset. I don't have my car; it's in the shop. But I'll tell you what. I'll call a cab for you and when the driver brings you to the house, I've got the cash to pay him. Okay?"

When the cab arrived ten minutes later, Cindy climbed in, wet and cold but full of a feeling of spirituality. That day, she made a decision that would affect her entire life. From then on, she would be a Christian.

Chapter 25

Tense Times

Before Cindy knew it her month-long grace period was over and she had to use the ticket her father had sent to join Liz and him in Delray Beach, Florida.

Sharkey had tried to reassure her. "He knows we're watching him. He won't dare touch you. Remember, keep your ears open. Maybe you'll overhear something we can use."

She awakened that first morning in Delray to the sounds of a fight. *Daddy and Liz. Familiar. Things haven't changed.* She heard her father's voice becoming more and more hoarse, but she couldn't understand the words he was screaming. Finally Liz screamed "Enough!" and her father stopped. She was sure he'd pay Liz back with a hard time as the day wore on; he always did.

Padding to the front door, Cindy almost tripped over Storm, her father's German shepherd. He liked big dogs, she knew. When she stepped outside, she was shocked at the brightness of the sun and the intense heat, not at all like New York. Still there was a light breeze. It flipped her long auburn hair against her cheeks.

Liz came up behind her, her face flushed, probably from the arguing. "I think you'll like it here, Cindy," she said.

"Yeah, but wow, it's really hot. Is it always this hot?"

"No, it was perfect until the last week or so. But this is good swimming weather. Do you want to go to the beach?"

Liz, Cindy could see, was even more independent here than she'd been on Long Island. The two of them had bagels and coffee by a table that looked out on the field next door; afterwards, they slipped into their bathing suits and drove ten minutes to the beach. It was a beautiful beach, a mile long, lined with colorful umbrellas and many people. There were enough breezes to temper the heat of the sun. However, the scorching sand made her don flip-flops in a hurry. The sea, perfectly still except for a few ripples, was a striking turquoise. She laughed as they both raced into the surf with much splashing and kicking. She felt the water close around her, temporarily soothing her cares.

They played and tanned for a long time until Liz said, "The sun down here can burn you pretty quick. We'd better go home."

They actually had a number of pleasant moments together that week. Cindy and Liz often arose early, before Howard, and slipped out to eat breakfast. One favorite spot was Ken and Hazel's, a popular restaurant by the railroad tracks in Delray Beach, which was frequented by everyone from bank presidents to janitors. Friendly service and gossip were plentiful and the fresh muffins were warm from the oven and delicious.

The following week, Cindy went to the pizza place in the mall across from Rainberry Lake and made a new friend of the young woman who worked there. Her name was Tory. Cindy asked if the two of them might go somewhere like a movie one evening, because she'd be starting college soon.

"Sure, that would be fine," Tory told her.

A week later, they got together and went to a movie. They had a fine time that night. They compared notes. Cindy learned that her new friend had a baby whom she worshipped. Tory brought her to her house and Cindy saw the love between her friend and her child. *The way my mother was with her daughters,* thought Cindy. "Michelle is a beautiful, perfect little girl," Cindy said.

Because they'd enjoyed each other's company, they got together as often as possible before school started. They became good friends. Tory came in one evening to wait for Cindy who'd been running an errand for Liz and was several minutes late. As she entered the kitchen from the garage, she heard her new friend talking to her stepmother in the living room. She wasn't trying to eavesdrop but she heard Liz say, "Cindy needs help, Tory. You see how excitable she gets. She needs help."

And then she heard Tory answer in a cool, firm tone, "I'm very sorry, Mrs. Band, but you're mistaken. It isn't Cindy who needs help, it's you." If Cindy hadn't loved Tory before, she loved her now. She was grateful for her new friend's kind expression of loyalty.

Cindy registered at Palm Beach Junior College in Lake Worth, less than a half hour from the house, and began school the last week in June. Her father bought her a car so she'd have no trouble getting there. Classes would last six weeks during this summer session, starting on a Wednesday and ending on a Wednesday. It would be over before the second week of August.

She found the atmosphere strange, of course. She wasn't used to palms and hibiscus on a campus or having open corridors outside the buildings. As a New Yorker, or more specifically a Long Islander, in a mob of mostly native Floridians, she again felt "different." They wore shorts; she wore dresses in an attempt to show respect for the school. To her surprise, it rained every afternoon. Most of the students, knowing it would soon stop, huddled under the overhangs. She braved the downpours as she'd done all her life. Still, determined to fit in and be as "normal" as any of the other students around her, she soon learned their ways.

Sometimes, from inside the buildings or her house, she spotted piles of white sand scattered along the landscape and for long moments would think it was snow. She wished it were snow; she'd never been anywhere before that was so hot and bright.

At home, the quarreling between Howard and Liz Band continued. When she was downstairs in her room with the door closed, she could only guess at the cause for the fights. After all, there was no "Briarcliff Circle" here in Florida to entice Liz away, but that didn't matter to her father. He blasted her anyway.

Sometime during the second week of school, Cindy was sitting at the dining room table studying. Suddenly, Liz came running down the stairs screaming, "Cindy, call 911."

Her heart pounding, Cindy grabbed the wall telephone, dialed and hurriedly asked the dispatcher to send the police. By the time she hung up, her father had run down the stairs and shoved his face right into Liz's. His voice was like a freight train bearing down on her.

"You're just grrr-eat, do you know that, woman? I'm out working my balls off to try to set up a new business and you're out tearing down everything I do. I dare you to leave. Try me and you'll be sorry." He had Liz backed up against the stairwell and was yelling at the top of his lungs. His face was purple with rage and twisted into that monster look he often wore. Cindy wrung her hands, wishing the police would hurry. "And your kids . . . You still send them money, don't you? DON'T YOU?"

"Quit it, Howie, just quit it!" Liz was becoming hysterical.

"Not until you answer. Aren't I right? Answer me woman, if you know what's good for you."

Cindy could see that Liz couldn't answer. Her stepmother was straining to get words out but nothing would come. It scared Cindy. What if Liz couldn't breathe?

"Answer me!" Howard Band screamed.

Liz whispered, "I have nothing to say. I didn't send them anything."

"You're full of shit. You're lying. Your kids are old enough to get along. They don't need you; I need you. Cut them off. They're spoiled bastards. Here, take the telephone, call them up. Do it. DO IT."

Suddenly Howard spotted Cindy. She moved behind the partition, afraid to leave for fear that he would kill Liz and afraid to stay. *Why can't he just leave us alone?* Finally, Cindy heard the police sirens coming down their street.

"You had Cindy call the cops?" Daddy was furious now. "Damn you, what's the matter with you?" He flung Liz away from him.

The police officer entered. Although the dog barked, he also wagged his tail at the uniformed man as if to show that he knew the cop was all right.

"Well, look, officer," Howard hurriedly offered, "we're just having a little disagreement. You know how that goes. It was nothing." He leaned over and kissed Liz's cheek. "Isn't that right, dear? Our daughter just gets a little hyper at times. She shouldn't have called you."

To Cindy's surprise and annoyance, Liz kissed him back. "Yes, he's right. We're okay."

The officer filled out a form, asked some more questions for his report, then left, stopping to pat Storm on his way out. He had scarcely gotten out of ear's range, however, before the fight began again in earnest. This time her father hit Liz. Cindy ran outside and didn't stop until she reached the beautiful, tropical lake at the end of their fenced-in yard. Her stomach hurt; her head pounded. She was glad there was somewhere to go to get away. She sank down beside the lake and idly tossed pebbles into the water, thinking, *Should I have fought Daddy? How could I? Last time I stood up to him, I ended up in the hospital. Besides, Liz is as wacko as Daddy. Just a crazy house, a crazy family, that's what it is.*

A couple of days later, Cindy was standing at her car preparing to leave for school, when Liz, her father and Storm came out of the house. Liz and her dad waved goodbye and began taking Storm for a walk. While Cindy was rearranging some of the books and papers in her car, she heard Liz and her father arguing again. Usually they didn't quarrel in places where neighbors might hear them, but this time they ignored the workmen building new houses across the street and became louder and louder. She looked up just as Storm lunged at Liz, knocking her down, apparently believing he was protecting his master—as if her father needed protection. This ended the fight, at least temporarily. Her father helped Liz up. She brushed herself off, looking aggrieved, while Howard continued on his walk. He laughed, adding insult to Liz's injury.

Liz ran back to Cindy as she stood by her car. "That's it," she roared. "I'm going back to Long Island. Come on, Cindy, you have to go along."

"But, Liz, my school . . ."

"Hang your school. This is important and I don't like to fly alone. You can make up today's classes. It's Friday. We'll be back by Monday."

"Well, okay, if it means that much." *Life is truly insane here,* Cindy told herself. She shut her car door and followed her stepmother into the house. Liz rushed to the telephone and called a travel agent who got both of them reservations on a plane leaving for New York that afternoon.

Some time later at Briarcliff Circle, Cindy had dinner with Liz and her kids. Although it seemed like forever since she'd seen them, Donny, Shelley and Bart were just the same. Afterwards, the group went out to a nightclub, but Cindy left early. She was tired and depressed, feeling somewhat like a displaced person. Returning to Florida was an even more confusing and scary thought. She had nowhere to go where she could feel safe.

Although it was obvious that Liz wanted to stay, she kept her word and returned on Monday so Cindy could attend afternoon classes at the college. But the quarrels between Howard and Liz continued to boil over and the police had to be called again. This time Liz flounced off to New York by herself, leaving Cindy, who felt she had to remain in school, to contend with her father's rages. Cindy managed to be away from the house as often as she could. And her father was busy, too. He was investigating the purchase of a group of beauty salons, although, he told her, the "price wasn't right, yet."

*   *   *

Whenever Liz was in Florida, the quarrels between her and Howard became more and more violent. It seemed as if Liz had Cindy calling the police at least twice a week. It didn't stop Cindy's father. If anything, it incited him. Cindy was glad she had Tory to talk to.

On Wednesday, July 15, Cindy parked her car in front of the house after driving home from school. As she entered the house, she was congratulating herself that she had only two and a half more weeks to go in the summer session at PBJC and she was doing better with her grades, when Liz walked past her and out the kitchen door into the garage, her face red and angry. "My son Bart, you know, is now at the University of Miami and he wants me to come down. And I'm going." She watched her stepmother get into her car.

"Damn," Liz said, "I've got the wrong keys. These are Howie's. Why did he have to buy us the same color cars!" She went back inside and up to her room. The quarreling began immediately. "Yes, Howie, I AM going," Liz was screaming. A few minutes later, she called down to Cindy, "Call the police. Call the police, now, Cindy. This monster won't let me go see my own boy and I WILL go."

"You're not going anywhere." His voice was threatening. "You are not going. Do you hear me? Bitch! I'll stop you whatever way I have to."

Liz screamed at the top of her voice, "Cindy, call the police."

As usual, Cindy obeyed. "This is Cindy Band on Northwest Tenth Avenue in Rainberry Lake. Please come. My dad is threatening my stepmother." The dispatcher recognized her voice. That was embarrassing because she'd called for Liz so many times. Before long, even over the loud voices upstairs, she could hear the siren. She shuddered.

Her father charged down the stairs and out into the garage. She watched him from the kitchen door, making herself as invisible as was possible, not knowing what he was going to do. She saw him lift a screwdriver from the neat pegboard that held all their tools.

As the police approached the front door, she saw her father insert the screwdriver into the screws holding Liz's license plate onto her car. His face was distorted and determined.

Her stepmother opened the front door to let in the two police officers and, wiping tears from her cheeks, led them to the garage. "Get away from my car," she yelled at Daddy. "You can't take my license plate off."

"I can and will. Make no mistake." He kept on working.

"Officers, this isn't legal, is it?" Liz's tone was high, out of control. "He's taking off my plate so I can't drive anywhere and I need to go to Miami to see my baby."

"Mr. Band. Sir, would you please stop what you're doing and talk to me."

Liz sounded on the edge of hysteria again as she shrieked, "That is *my* car, Howie."

"And *I* bought it for you." He continued to work on the removal of the plate.

"Sir, I need to talk to you," said one of the men. "'Will you please stop and turn around, sir?"

Howard ignored him. The lawmen asked politely two more times, while the subject of their call went right on twisting on the screws, which were rusty and stubborn.

"Why don't you just let her go if she wants to see her son?" the taller cop asked.

"It's my car," Daddy growled, still struggling with the license. "And I've got her keys."

At last one of the officers leaned over and snapped a cuff to his wrist.

Cindy's hands flew to her mouth. *Now what will Daddy do?*

Howard Band jumped to his feet, enraged. The two policemen quickly pulled his other hand behind his back and finished cuffing him. "Can't a man even take care of his own car and family?" he roared.

"You have the right to remain silent . . ." the officer read him his rights.

"You're arresting *me*? What the hell for?" His jaw jutted; his brown eyes flashed with rage, but he kept himself under control.

"For obstructing justice, sir."

"Well, look what you did now," he sneered at Liz.

Liz was whimpering, her brilliant blue eyes wide.

"He's going to the county jail, Ma'am," one of the officers told Liz, who observed the scene with a look of dismay.

Cindy watched the men lead her father away. One of them held his hand over her father's head to keep him from bumping himself as he climbed into the back seat of the patrol car. They were being very polite. But Cindy knew her father would be furious about this when he came home and he'd probably take it out on her and Liz. He always did. She tried not to think about that right now.

"Are you going to get him out?" Cindy whispered to her stepmother.

"Do something, Cindy!" he yelled as the police shut his door and drove away.

As soon as the cruiser was out of sight, Liz went to get her keys. "I'm heading for Miami, loose license plate or not. Bartie's expecting me and he'll be leaving soon to go back to New York," she told Cindy. "Want to come, too?"

"I'd better not, Liz. I've got to study."

Cindy didn't hear Liz come back that night, but she

did hear her stepmother getting ready the next morning, apparently to go pick up her husband at the county jail in West Palm Beach, less than twenty miles north. When Liz returned with him and pulled back into the driveway, Cindy was just getting her books together to leave for school. She could hear their raised voices as they approached the front door. *They're fighting again already? What could they have to argue about now? Liz just rescued him from the county jail. You'd think Daddy would at least be grateful for that,* Cindy thought.

"We had to pay a fine," Liz told Cindy when they walked in the house.

"I'm going to take a shower," her father growled. He strode out of the room. The jail incident wasn't mentioned again.

But the fights did not diminish in frequency or intensity. Time and time again, the police were summoned to Rainberry Lake to intercede between Liz and Howard. One moment, Cindy wished she were on her own. The next moment, she felt too insecure and frightened to be anywhere by herself. People had told her she was like her mother. Did her mother feel this way—a captive in an insane world? Was that why she hadn't left her husband, even when he had been so cruel?

Chapter 26

Treacherous Tales

At last, Detective Jack Sharkey had the lead for which he had been searching. A man who used to be a parking attendant near Al Saffer's Floral Supply company had told a snitch, months after Florence Band's death, that he had information on the Howard Band case. The information had been taken and noted by the police department, but when Jack tried to follow up, he found that the attendant had moved out of the area and no one knew where he was. Now, he finally had located the man.

Ted Warren had been a parking attendant at Leland Garage, two buildings east of Al Saffer's building. He told Sharkey, "For two years, Howard Band was a regular customer." According to Warren, the summer before Florence Band died, Howard Band had come in one day at lunchtime and asked a favor of him. Did he know anyone interested in doing a job?

"I asked him to tell me the nature of the job and he said, 'to waste somebody,' " Warren said with a grimace. "I told him I didn't know anybody, but he said to think about it, that maybe I could come up with a name for him."

According to Warren, Band returned repeatedly, telling Warren there would be something in it for him if Warren could find someone to do the job.

Moreover, Warren said, when he had told Band that he was unable to come up with anyone, Band had muttered something about how he knew people at his office he could ask.

Going to Saffer's offices, Sharkey asked to see the records for all people employed by the company during the year before the death of Florence Band. This led him to question two other men.

The first man told a story that was even more treacherous than Warren's. Harry Michaels had been a traffic manager at the company. He told Sharkey, "I arrived early one morning as I usually did. I liked to get in and get some paper work done before everyone else arrived and things got hectic. Also, it gave Mr. Band and me an opportunity to sit together and discuss any problems or situations that had come up with distribution and deliveries.

"This one particular morning I entered Mr. Band's office and during the conversation he made a statement to the effect that he had a friend who was looking for somebody to rub out a person."

"What did you say in response to that?" asked Sharkey.

"I was speechless, sir," Michaels said, his eyes widening. "After a minute or so, I told him I didn't know anyone of that sort."

Sharkey rubbed his chin pensively. "Did you and Mr. Band have any further conversations on this topic?"

"No, sir," Michaels said, shaking his head firmly. "There wasn't anything else to say."

Next Sharkey located Frank Wallis, who had been a truck driver for Al Saffer's company. Wallis told a similarly chilling story. In the spring before Florence Band's death, Wallis had a conversation with his boss, Howard Band, in Band's office. Band told Wallis to close the door and Band closed the window and pulled down the shade.

"Then he sat down," Wallis said, "and told me in a voice that was just above a whisper, 'Frankie, I have a friend who wants to have somebody done away with. Can you help me?' I was surprised, but I said, 'Gee, I don't know, Mr. Band. I'll ask around.' Then I went back to work."

"Did you get back to him on the matter?" Sharkey asked.

"I was hoping he'd forgotten about it, but about two weeks later, I'm out loading my truck when Mr. Band calls me aside and asks if I came up with anybody for the matter we had discussed."

Wallis made eye contact with Sharkey and held it as he said, "I told Mr. Band, 'Sorry, but the guy I know is in jail for twenty years to life.' "

Sharkey chuckled and Wallis joined in. "I guess that stopped him, at least for the moment," Sharkey said, then added, "Unfortunately, not for good."

Sharkey felt elated by the break in the case he had sought for so long. However, he now found out that Marty Bracken, the Assistant District Attorney in charge of the case, was being promoted to ADA Bureau Chief of the rackets division. He was glad for Marty—it was a choice job—but Sharkey didn't want to see the Band case go down the drain.

Sharkey went to ADA Barry Grennan, who controlled prosecutorial assignments over all such cases, and explained his feelings.

"Okay then, Shark, you go find someone to take the Band case," Grennan told him.

"Are you serious? You'd trust me to do that? Okay, I *will* go find someone." The detective left Grennan's office smiling.

Not wanting to waste time, Sharkey made a list of four top prosecutors he believed could do the job. First on his list was ADA William Dempsey, III. His resume was excellent and he was very intelligent. Jack telephoned him first, then set up an appointment on March 22 to meet with him.

Entering Dempsey's office, he saw a nice-looking, slender, young man with brown hair, glasses and a friendly smile. "I'm Bill," the ADA said, rising from his desk chair to shake Sharkey's hand. His voice was impressive. Very deep, it held just the right touch of power and compassion. Sharkey had learned that Dempsey had taken courses in psychology; Sharkey thought that might help the ADA understand his own deep feelings of compassion for Cindy Band.

He's the one, Jack instinctively thought. The detective made his pitch, laid out some papers for Dempsey to study and asked him to consider taking the case.

It didn't take long for Bill Dempsey to decide whether or not he would take the Florence Band murder case. He read the material Sharkey had left with him, then called the detective and said he would prosecute the case.

"I have some promising new leads," Sharkey said and told him of interviewing the three men Band had approached about hiring a hit man.

"Good, good," Dempsey said. "But remember, the more evidence we have the better, if we're going to take this case back to the grand jury."

"I'm working on it," Sharkey assured him.

Jack Sharkey was not a man who gave up. His stubborn determination and his thoughts of Cindy, how she was caught in an impossible situation, prodded him.

One of these days, he would be ready to prove that Howard Band had murdered his wife. But whether the District Attorney would take the case back before a grand jury wasn't in his domain. Still, he had to gather all the evidence he could and let the ADA make that decision.

When not working on current cases, Sharkey continued to pursue the Band case. Several months passed. Then one weekend, after he had just tied up the loose ends on another homicide, Sharkey found himself free to devote some serious time to the Old Westbury case. Thus Sharkey was pleased to get a call from Bill Dempsey, the ADA he had handpicked to handle the case.

It was a cold Monday morning in February when, in answer to Dempsey's summons, Sharkey climbed to the second floor of the Nassau County Court House in Mineola and walked down the hall to the prosecutor's office. The former assistant district attorney's name had been removed from the door and replaced with *William J. Dempsey, III* in gold-leaf lettering.

Dempsey rose to shake Sharkey's hand across the desk.

"Hello, Bill," the detective said, accepting the armchair that the prosecutor pointed out. "You sent for me?"

"Good to see you again, Jack. Yes, I sent for you. It's about the Band case. I guess you thought I'd forgotten."

Sharkey didn't reply.

"You'll be glad to know the Saffers—Al, the father, and David, the son—have the same feelings that you and Cindy have. They've been pushing my boss to reopen the case. You, of course, worked with the Saffers during the investigation. They hold you in high regard."

"Thanks. Yes, I did. The Grand Jury presentation had its vote withdrawn, you remember."

"Exactly. When you came to me about my taking over the Band case, the whole thing was about to be dismissed, Jack, but the Saffers don't feel that Florence Band received justice. So my boss brought the Grand Jury transcript to me and had me read it. He asked me what I thought—because the Saffers had pressured him to reopen it. I told him I had met with you and had told you I would consider reopening the case. But naturally, we have to have new evidence and that's why I asked you here today. What have we got, Jack?"

"Well, actually, we've got a lot. It's circumstantial, though. Unfortunately, we don't have confessions, but I try to stick around enough so that Howard and Ms. Diamond—now Mrs. Band, of course—will know we're still on the case. I keep thinking that one of these days she'll crack. I'm sure she knows what happened; possibly she was right in the Horseshoe Road house while it was going down."

"If she didn't crack during the grand jury testimony, why do you think it will be any better at the next one?" Dempsey tapped lightly on his desk with a pencil.

"Yes, that's always a question. We really thought she'd give it up then, but she pops these pills, you see, and that gets her through such scenes, apparently. It's amazing. She must have had a little help from them when she testified at the grand jury hearing."

"Well, that's water under the bridge, now. Tell me what you've got so far, Jack, and let's talk about our next steps. Tell me who we've got on our side; that will help."

"Well, we've got the three men Band approached about hiring a hit man to rub out his wife, but I guess you could say the younger daughter, Cindy, is our best hope. She's been devastated by her mother's death, yet she's determined to get her mother justice."

"Is she stable?"

"Stable enough. Just having a hard time. She's only a kid and too much is happening, too fast. And the worst part of it is, she lives with the guy she knows murdered her mother—and it's her father. That would shake anyone's stability. But she's bright and she's willing."

"Star witness, right?"

"I'd say so. Of course, let's remember that although she wants to see the murderer punished, it's going to be awfully hard on her to testify against her father. I mean, think about it."

Dempsey nodded. He could see that Sharkey was concerned about the girl.

"I talk to Cindy often by phone, plus I see her when she comes back to New York, which is pretty often," Sharkey continued. "Right now, she's in Florida, Bill. I'll get her to come back up here and bring her in to see you. Problem is, she really doesn't have a place to stay up here. The old house is sold and she has no money."

"If she's that important to the trial, we can put her up in a hotel for a while. We'll want her up here soon. But first, let's go over what you've got now. Fill me in on the new stuff since I've read the transcript."

"Band tried to kill Cindy—that's new since the first grand jury. And I just interviewed three guys who say Band tried to hire a hit man to kill his wife.

"Well, I'd say that's pretty strong material. Tell me about these three guys. Will they be reliable witnesses?"

"I hope so."

"Okay then, we're closing in. What's next, Jack?"

Sharkey rubbed his neck. "I still want to work on his current wife, Liz. I think she's implicated in all this, but she seems to be having trouble with him since they married. Cindy's been keeping me informed."

"Trouble?"

"He's been abusive and Cindy's had to call the police several times. I'm hoping Liz gets sick of it and decides she wants to put him away where he belongs."

"I'll be hoping the same thing," Dempsey said with a smile. "And the sooner the better."

Chapter 27

Moving Things Along

While she knew Jack Sharkey hoped she would learn new information from her father and Liz and help tighten the web of evidence he had been patiently weaving, Cindy, though willing and able, was still frightened of her father's violent temper. She planned to head out early every morning to run and then swim in the ocean, because she was convinced that daily exercise helped her function and deal with stress. The combination of salty sea air and the caress of the sand under her feet when she kicked off her running sneakers helped her throw off the omnipresent depression threatening to engulf her.

But on one warm fall morning, as she tiptoed towards the front door to escape, she found her father waiting for her. He held out a cup of coffee, cinnamon-flavored, and said, "Let's talk." Obviously, he had planned to rise before she did and waylay her on her way out the door. Cindy took the coffee and sat down at the breakfast table. Storm was under the table and she leaned down to scratch the dog's ears. It was a distinct surprise to find her father seemingly in a good mood for a change. He began telling her his goals.

"I'm planning to buy a bunch of salons—beauty salons, you know, toots—and I'll need someone in the know to help make the business a success." He spooned two pancakes onto her plate that he'd removed from the griddle minutes before. He pushed the syrup towards her.

Geez, he's being so nice to me, she thought, wondering what he wanted.

"Well Cindy," he continued as he seated himself beside her, "you're real good with hair and makeup. You're beautiful, you know, little girl. It will come easily to you. I want you to sign up for a beauty course."

So that's it. She had been expecting to have to smooth over some kind of altercation or apologize for some kind of wrongdoing on her part, but this wasn't so bad; it was an easy way to keep him happy and communicating with her. His suggestion was unexpected, but she wasn't opposed to the idea. "You know, Daddy, I've actually heard of a beauty school around here. Romar. It's in a mall in Boynton Beach. About six miles north of here, I'd guess."

"Good. Don't waste time. Get on it. You'll do great. By the way, Butchie-girl, I spotted a nice little white Chrysler Cordova the other day. I'm going to buy it for you to replace that used-car I got you when you first arrived in Florida. This way you'll look sharp tooling around and going back and forth to school."

"Wow!" she said. "Thank you, Daddy. Say, this is a good breakfast."

"Eating together like this, doesn't it remind you of times I used to take you to restaurants in New York? Just you and I. Remember?"

"Oh, sure. Yes, I do." She thought back to when she was younger and her father would say to her, always unexpectedly, always out of a clear blue sky, "Let's go for a treat" and they'd go out together. "Usually you'd take me at a time when no other customers were in the restaurant. You were so well-known, Daddy, and seemed so powerful, so confident, and the waiters would hover around us and give us fantastic service. Those times were really fun for me."

"And remember, Cindy, how I'd look all around the restaurant and then tell you that you were the prettiest girl in the place. And you'd look all embarrassed and I'd say . . ."

"You'd say, 'No really, just look around you.' And you'd tell me I was so beautiful—that I had your lips, your smile . . ." Cindy laughed, recalling. He'd made her feel so special. So much had changed since then. It seemed a lifetime ago. Still, when he turned on the charm, like today, she understood how he had enticed so many women, including her poor mother. *Perhaps in his own way,* she thought, *he loves me.*

The sudden thought that she was dedicated to help put him in jail started the old agitation roiling through her again. This time though, she recovered quickly, reminding herself he had tried to kill her, too.

They continued to talk about everything from Liz and her kids to the beauty shop business to Delray Beach, their new hometown. She told him she would learn the beauty business if that was what he wanted.

Two days later, Cindy drove the short distance to Boynton Beach in her new car. She signed up at the Romar Beauty School in a shopping plaza off Federal Highway. She was immediately placed in a class with a group of young women all eager to get started dyeing, perming and cutting hair, as well as learning to do manicures, pedicures and facials. Most of them were talking to each other as if they were old friends.

One woman stood apart. Older than Cindy by at

least ten years, she was a sexy-looking, blonde Latina woman with an intriguing accent who had trouble at times communicating.

Feeling sorry for the woman, and remembering how her mother always went out of her way to help students for whom English was a second language, Cindy tried to make friends during the next break. "I'm Cindy Band. What's your name?"

"I'm Tequila Garcia," she said with an accent as thick as the gel they were learning to use on hair. "I'm from New York."

"Oh, me too," Cindy said, noting that the woman was attractive in a mini-skirted, flashy sort of way. "I'm from Long Island."

"I come from New York City, way uptown. I've got two boys. How about you? You got any kids?"

For a moment, Cindy was shocked that the woman would consider her old enough to have kids. Probably, however, Tequila had had her first child when she was as young as Cindy. Cindy shook her head.

"Married?" Tequila asked.

Cindy started to say yes, but considered that there would be a lot of explaining to do—the green card, Nick's being drafted in Yugoslavia and all. She shook her head again.

"Me neither," Tequila answered. She didn't mention whether or not she ever had been in the past. Cindy assumed the pretty woman was either separated or divorced.

At that moment, the teacher returned and turned the class discussion to theory and technique. Cindy noticed her new friend frowning and told herself she must try to help the woman later with the unfamiliar terms.

The students were told to bring their lunches to school, a fact which Cindy related to her father when she returned home that afternoon. "I think I'll eat in a nice, shady park a little way down Federal Highway from the school. It's on the waterway," she told him.

As time went by, she and Tequila went to the park together when the weather was nice—which, as Florida's mild winter season approached, was most days. Although they had very little in common except what they were learning in school, Cindy felt she was preventing her blonde classmate from eating by herself and being lonely.

Cindy told her father about the pretty woman with the cute accent she had met. "She's got about a size zero figure and she lives in a mobile home west of Delray Beach. Oh yes, and she comes from New York, too. She lived way uptown in the city, in Spanish Harlem."

When Liz returned from New York, the quarreling began again. Howard Band still appeared to be obsessed with Liz. He hadn't been that way with his first wife, Cindy's mother. With Liz, if he couldn't have her attention all the time, he'd be furious at her. He didn't want her even to *think* about other things—including her own children.

One morning Liz came downstairs in a long pink robe—early as always after a fight with Howard. Cindy was reviewing some facts in her school textbook at the breakfast table. She never thought of asking Liz to fix breakfast, but sometimes she remembered how her mother always made sure her daughters had a nourishing breakfast. Every morning. *Wonderful, old-fashioned breakfasts, sometimes with fresh biscuits and home fries. But that was then; this is now,* she reminded herself. *Liz isn't my mother.*

Suddenly, she noticed for the first time how tired and pale her stepmother looked, how she seemed unable to even make small talk as she prepared the morning coffee. A dollop of cinnamon, which Daddy insisted upon, soon scented the kitchen air. Liz took a seat at the table opposite Cindy, looking as if she'd aged overnight. When she finally spoke, it was in a hoarse whisper.

Liz seems so unhappy. Why doesn't she leave him? Cindy mulled it over in her mind. *Because she can't, of course. Daddy won't let her go. Or perhaps Liz is afraid Daddy will kill her, too.* Cindy shuddered.

Such thoughts only brought further anxiety to Cindy's confused mind. Had she suspected somehow that her father was going to kill her mother before he did it? Were there warning signs that she had overlooked or ignored? *Could I have stopped it from happening?* she wondered. *No, no, I never suspected for a minute. Now it is Liz who is suffering. Of course, unlike Mommy, Liz fights back. Plus she has her pills . . . way too many pills.* Cindy didn't know which was taking the greatest toll on her stepmother—the violent quarreling with her husband or the mood-altering pills she was popping.

Sighing, Cindy gathered her books and left for school.

Just before noon that same day, Howard appeared at the Romar School of Beauty. Cindy and Tequila were already on the sidewalk, ready to get into Cindy's car and drive to the park for lunch.

"Hey, Cinnamon, I've come to have lunch with you, honey," he said, holding a brown bag and a six-pack of Coke. He looked at Tequila and winked.

Cindy saw him scrutinizing her friend. *Uh-oh, here he goes, turning on the charm.* "Daddy! What a surprise. I want you to meet my friend, Tequila Garcia. Tequila, this is Howard Band, my father. I—we were just leaving to go eat lunch, Daddy, but . . ."

Tequila interrupted in her lilting, Spanish-tinged accent, "Oh, you two go ahead. I don't want to barge in on your lunch together." She pulled back and turned to reenter the school with her lunch.

Howard quickly grabbed her arm. "Not at all. I wouldn't think of it. You come with us, of course."

"Yes, Tequila, come with us," Cindy echoed, noting the heavy-lidded gaze her father fastened on her schoolmate.

Tequila smiled at him. "Well, if you're sure."

The three drove to the park in Howard Band's car. They found a table and spread out their sandwiches. Cindy's father added a container of potato salad to the meal and handed each of them a can of soda. The weather was dry and blue-skied. Chamber of Commerce weather, he called it with a chuckle.

Cindy was quick to see that her father was attracted to her blonde companion although there was probably a fifteen-year difference in their ages. Tequila didn't seem to mind. She flirted back at him, laughed at his jokes and told him little stories about herself to such an extent that Cindy was astounded.

"Your papa's pretty cute," Tequila told her after he drove the two of them back to school and deposited them at the entrance.

Cindy wasn't sure whether to be flattered or outraged. The picnic-*a-trois* was only the beginning. Her father began meeting them a couple of times a week for festive picnic lunches.

"You know," he told Cindy in private, "Latinas are very passionate."

Cindy thought she might gag.

A few days later, her father was sitting at the table by the front door reading the *Palm Beach Post* when Cindy came home from school. He glanced up at her, then back to his paper.

"I'm almost finished with the term," she told him.

He cleared his throat and didn't answer at once. "Okay. Fine. But—uh—I'm not sure I'm going ahead with the beauty salon chain. I'm considering a thriving transmission repair business down in Tamarac."

She sighed but said nothing.

"And where's Liz?" he growled, his arms flailing. "That woman's not back *yet*. She's gone up north to be with those miserable brats on Briarcliff Circle. And every time I call up there trying to reach her, that nasty little Bart hangs up on me. Why isn't she home yet?"

"I don't know, Daddy."

He whirled around to face her. "And you. Why do you always stick with Liz? I don't understand you. You are NOT going to be on her side when she comes back, you understand me? Because I'm your father. Why does she stay away from this home? *WHY*?"

"Because, Daddy, you yell and scream and . . ."

"LIAR! Double-crosser! I'll fix you." He rose and placed his face inches from hers as he yelled obscenities. She felt terror as she always did when he became angry, but this time she stood her ground. She was gaining strength. She could hold on. With what she'd learned about faith from Glenn Bingham, she would put herself in God's hands. And Sharkey would help her gain justice for her mother, if only she held on.

After his explosion, her father left the room. There on the table where he'd been sitting was an envelope addressed to her. Slightly rumpled and discolored, it bore stamps from overseas. Cindy snatched the envelope and tore it open. Inside was a long letter from Nick, which he'd written soon after his arrival in his native land. It had taken the mail a long time to reach her. The stationery, a soft, pale shade of yellow, was decorated in the background with a faint, tasteful silhouette of a man and woman. *Beautiful Cindy*, it began. The "beautiful" was misspelled. Touched, she could tell he'd labored endlessly over the writing.

She took the letter to her room, read it through once and then again twice more. It didn't say a lot, but she was glad he was all right. She put it away in her bedside drawer and felt tears sting her eyes. She wished him well. She had a strong feeling the letter would be the last contact she'd ever have with Nick.

The next time Detective Sharkey called, he told her, "Things are moving, kid. And Cindy, I've talked to our new ADA about you and all your help. His name is Bill Dempsey and he wants to talk to you. We're hoping to have enough evidence soon to reopen the case. You'll like Bill. He's a great guy and very intelligent, very sharp."

"Jack, I'm so glad I have you! I've got more to tell you and I'll be glad to meet Mr. Dempsey. You know how often Liz flies to New York? Well, next time she goes—I have a feeling it could be any day now—I'll come, too. I'll call you just as soon as I get there."

Cindy's intuition was right. Two days later, Liz and Howard got into an epic shouting match and she heard Liz say, "I'm leaving." Liz rushed down the stairs, flushed and angry, her blond hair bouncing.

"If you're going north, Liz, I'd like to go with you, okay?" Cindy said softly.

"Well, start packing," her stepmother answered.

The next morning, Cindy threw a few things into her suitcase and got ready to fly to Long Island with Liz. Her stepmother was always ready to make the trip, even though it enraged her husband.

Detective Sharkey had told her the District Attorney's office was going to set her up in a hotel as soon as she got there. Knowing she'd be staying longer than her usual weekend jaunts, she packed extra clothing.

As she headed out the front door behind Liz, she was carrying two bags instead of her usual one. Her father stopped her. "Cinnamon, where are you going with all that luggage?" She didn't answer, hoping to avoid a run-in with him. "Cindy Ruth Band, do you hear me? Where are you going?" He roared.

"I-I am going to a hotel, I . . ."

"What for? You're not staying with Liz?" He'd come up to her by the front door now and had one arm stretched against the wall, thus preventing her exit. "I'm talking to you, young lady." His face already was red and contorted.

I might as well tell him and get it over with, she thought. *I'm going to have to acquire some iron in my spine in order to go through with this.* "I'm going because Detective Jack Sharkey and Assistant District Attorney William Dempsey want to talk with me," Cindy said. "I'm going to be a witness in their case."

"You're going through with this? My own daughter! Are you crazy?"

For a moment, she thought her father was going to have a stroke. He sputtered. His red face turned purple with fury. Finally, he said with as much venom in his voice as he could muster, "Get out of my sight. You disgust me."

She left, feeling burned and raw, wondering if he realized that after she was placed in protective custody, he would be prevented from influencing her testimony in any way.

After the plane had landed and Cindy had retrieved her luggage, Jack Sharkey met her in the lobby of the

Hempstead Plaza Hotel and accompanied her to the room the DA's office had reserved for her. "We'll be checking on you every night, Cindy. Every night. So don't leave after ten unless you let us know, okay? Again, you can do what you wish in the day, although we'll be getting in touch with you to discuss the coming grand jury presentation."

"Okay, Jack." She felt small and somewhat scared.

"Another thing, once you're in for the night, lock your door and don't let *anyone* in, okay?"

"Okay." She watched him leave. She knew there were guards stationed in the hall watching over her through the night.

Then she looked around the room. It was attractively decorated and pleasant. Luxurious, even. At least she wouldn't have to hear any quarreling at night. She got undressed, took a shower and climbed under the fresh white sheets.

The following day, Sharkey contacted Liz. He asked her to come to the courthouse at ten. Without doubt, she'd been the biggest problem in the first grand jury presentation. They'd expected her to admit something or at least throw some doubt on Howard Band's story. But she had seemed spacey and didn't make much sense. They blamed it on those blasted pills.

When Liz Band arrived at ADA Dempsey's office, she was dressed like a movie star in a colorful top over sleek satin pants and high heels. A mink coat hung over her shoulders. The men offered her a chair and sat down when she did.

"Would you care for coffee?" Bill asked. He called for his secretary who brought in cups of steaming brew for each of them.

Liz toyed with hers but didn't drink. "What can I do

for you gentlemen?" she asked, showing a dazzling smile.

"Mrs. Band," Bill began. "We know you had a part in Florence Band's death." She started to protest. The ADA put up a hand to silence her. "We're here to offer you immunity if you will testify against your husband."

Her blue eyes opened wide. "A wife can't testify against a husband," she said demurely.

"Don't be too sure, Mrs. Band. Let's talk."

Chapter 28

Wired

The very first time Cindy met Assistant District Attorney William J. Dempsey III, she liked him. She looked at him across his desk in the Nassau County Courthouse and saw a serious, good-looking man, somewhere in his thirties, who seemed dedicated to his profession as well as to the people, such as herself, who were looking to him for justice. She quickly felt a sense of trust in him, just as she had in Sharkey. What's more, she immediately sensed a close bond between the ADA and the detective, which endeared him to her even more.

"This is Cindy Band, Bill," Jack Sharkey said, introducing them. "She's almost as much a victim in this case as her mother." For a moment, Cindy felt the protective touch of his hand on her shoulder.

Once the three were seated, Dempsey got right to the point of the meeting. "Cindy, Detective Sharkey tells me you want to bring the murderer of your mother to justice." At her nod, he continued, "You can help us now, Cindy. We're close to that goal. If you're willing to wear a Unitel for awhile, we can get the final evidence we need. Will you help us to do that?"

Hesitantly, Cindy nodded. "What's a Unitel?"

"A wire—a recording device," Sharkey explained. "You've probably seen some shows on television, haven't you, where an individual wears a small recorder somewhere on his or her body? As a rule, when the person talks to the man or woman who's under suspicion, the conversation is monitored by the police in a car outside or at headquarters. Do you know what I mean? Have you seen anything like this?"

"Yes, but . . ."

Bill Dempsey interrupted, "Your sister Paula is coming home from college soon, isn't she?"

"Yes. She'll be working for a judge in Queens, I understand."

"You must remember," continued Dempsey, "you can't tell anyone about the information you've been gathering—not Paula, not your aunt and uncle, not your grandfather."

Cindy looked sad for a moment. "My aunt and uncle haven't been close to me since I left my cousins' to go back to my dad's house. They think I went back to get things from him—like a new car. They don't know I did it for my mother." She sighed. "Jack told me early on I couldn't tell them or Paula or anyone else about my real reason for going back to live with my father."

"I know keeping this secret is hard for you, Cindy, and living with your father and his wife must be even more difficult," Dempsey said. "You've been terrific. Without your help, we couldn't have gotten this far. Detective Sharkey tells me Paula has sided against you and with her father, is that correct?"

"Yes, but I think it's because she finds it impossible to believe any of this could be true about him. Also, I think Daddy has persuaded her she'd be better off with him *out* of jail than *in* it."

"Cindy, here is our request. We want you to put this

gadget—the Unitel—under your clothes and wear it later on when you talk with your sister."

Cindy was taken aback. She said, "What could Paula say that would be beneficial to your case? After all, Paula had nothing whatsoever to do with the murder."

"Unfortunately, Cindy, Paula's been insinuating to some people with whom we have spoken that *you* might have had something to do with your mother's death," Sharkey told her.

"Me?" Cindy shook her head. "She just wants to divert you away from my dad. She doesn't believe I would have hurt my mother."

"I think you're right, Cindy," Sharkey said, "but we have to anticipate the kinds of problems we'll encounter when we arrest your father and we have to protect you."

"Well," Cindy said, "thank you for that." Pausing, she looked first at Sharkey, then Dempsey. "I trust you both, so if you think wearing a wire will help, I'll do it."

A few days later, Cindy reached her sister on the telephone. Immediately afterward, Cindy called Sharkey.

"She's still planning to testify on behalf of our father," Cindy reported.

"That's what we figured," said Sharkey.

"And she thinks I'm pretty terrible to be working with you and the district attorney's office. But I know my father *did* do it. She just simply ignores that fact."

"I know. Listen, Cindy, when your sister returns, could you set up lunch or something with her? We'll get you fitted with a Unitel on the day before you meet her. That way, if she tries to misconstrue your words in court or accuse you wrongly, we'll have proof of what was actually said." Sharkey paused. "And who knows, maybe she'll tell you something that we can use."

"I doubt if Paula knows anything, Jack. My father is very smart. He knows how to play innocent and persecuted with Paula and make me look like a fool—if not a lunatic. But okay. I'll do it. Paula's returning next Wednesday and starting her job the next day. I'll try to make it for then. Is that okay?"

"Perfect. Call me. And by the way, don't forget to wear something loose and heavy like a sweatshirt. That way, nobody will be able to spot that you're wearing a wire."

The next day, Cindy telephoned Paula and they arranged to meet the following Thursday on Paula's lunch break.

On the day she was to meet Paula for lunch, Sharkey and Dempsey sent Cindy, accompanied by two young officers, to the police station which was located in another building a short distance away from the Nassau County Courthouse in Mineola.

"Don't worry, Cindy, we've told the officers at the Queens courthouse who man the metal detector that you're coming to meet your sister, so they'll have their machine turned off while you go through the gate," Bill said.

"Good luck," they each told her as she walked out with the police duo.

Once at the station, the two officers turned her over to two policewomen who took her into a room and fitted her with the Unitel. They wrapped white surgical tape around her whole midsection. By the time she pulled her navy blue sweatshirt over the gadget, no one could see anything out of the ordinary.

When she was completely dressed, a third officer entered and explained to her exactly how the wire worked and told her all the do's and do not's of the operation.

"I just hope," she told the officers, "that I don't give away that I'm wearing this thing." She gave a small laugh. "Ooh, it feels cold." She tried to be nonchalant, but one question kept intruding on her thoughts. *Am I doing wrong to spy on my sister?*

"Now, after you meet with your subject," the third officer said, "you turn the Unitel on right here. It's not hard to do." He pointed and Cindy listened carefully, then tried it, turning it on and off. "You all set?" he asked. When she nodded, he, too, wished her good luck.

As the original officers drove to the courthouse in Queens where Paula was interning, they passed a small, private parking lot and told Cindy they would wait there for her after she had finished having lunch with her sister. "We'll sit here the entire time monitoring," they told her. "Nobody will think anything about it, because there's lots of law enforcement officers here all the time. When you're all finished, meet us here, okay? We'll run you back to the Nassau County PD to get that thing taken off." They continued driving another block and turned the corner to the courthouse where Paula had begun her summer job with Judge Mellon. They stopped and let Cindy out.

She entered the big stone building, passing through the gate just inside the door with no problem. As in many courthouses around the country, security personnel sat there, monitoring for guns and knives. This, she realized, was done to prevent someone with a grudge against a witness or defendant, from sneaking into a courtroom. Cindy went upstairs to find her sister. Standing outside the judge's chambers where she knew Paula worked, she took a deep breath to calm her nerves and almost ran into Paula coming out the door.

"You got here on time." Paula pretended to be shocked.

"I'm always on time." She showed Paula her watch. "See. Exactly noon."

"Give me a break. You were always late coming in from dates."

"That's different. Where do you want to eat, Paula?"

"Oh, I don't know. There are a couple of places down the street. Let's go outside and decide."

"Okay."

They took the elevator to the first floor then headed out the same door Cindy had entered a few minutes before.

At lunch, Cindy made small talk for a minute or two. She could tell by Paula's tone that her sister was wondering why Cindy had wanted to meet. It made Cindy feel even more self-conscious, as if she were doing something very, very wrong.

"Uh . . ." Cindy began. "How's your new job so far?" When there was no response, she added, "How do you really feel about all this, Paula?"

"About all what?" the older girl replied. "About what, Cindy? What are you talking about?"

"You know—the investigation and stuff."

"You're the one involved in all that. I think the cops are just out to get Daddy instead of investigating who *really* did it. And if they don't leave him alone, where will you and I be? Answer me that?"

Cindy sighed. It was always the same with Paula. Changing the subject, Cindy said, "This is nice, being together like this, Paula. We ought to do this more often."

"Why?" Paula asked flatly. "Don't tell me you're finally finding time for your sister?"

Cindy laughed. "Of course. I would always find time for my sister. I just thought we really need each other now."

Paula broke in, her face reddening. "We wouldn't be

in this situation if you weren't helping to prosecute our father. I'm not going to stand by while you do that, Cindy."

"I have to do what I have to do," Cindy said quietly.

Paula stood up, staring at her sister. "Then I'll have to do what I have to do," she said.

After their lunch meeting, Cindy met with Jack Sharkey and Bill Dempsey.

"I hated doing that," Cindy said. She sat down across from the two men.

Dempsey smiled at her. "We were just afraid that Paula might corner you later, ask you questions and turn the answers around. The wire was to protect you from having your sister undercut your testimony and falsely attribute statements to you or, worse, say that you'd confessed to being implicated in the crime. It was very important that we rule that out. And now we'll be able to."

"I'm just glad it's over," Cindy said.

Dempsey frowned. "Well, that part is, but there's something else."

"What?" Cindy asked, her heart starting to pound. Espionage was not to her liking.

"Now Cindy, we really want to know if your stepmother had her hand in this murder, too. We want you to wear the wire with her. I think you know that your hotel room is wired. You could ask her to visit you at the hotel a couple of nights from now. That's when we'll give her the subpoena for an appearance before the grand jury."

"She isn't going to like it," Cindy warned.

"We're counting on that," Sharkey said with a smile. "If she starts ranting and raving to you, maybe she'll let something slip."

Cindy sighed. "Okay. I'll call you after I set up a meeting with Liz."

"Good, Cindy. Meantime, just keep your eyes open," the prosecutor said.

Detective Sharkey walked her to her car. "Cindy, I know from what you've reported that your dad is still flying into fits of anger. That must frighten you."

She laughed, but there was no humor in the sound. "Yeah, every day. Liz is forever having me call the Delray Beach police. They're getting worse, those 'fits.' "

Sharkey shook his head in sympathy. "He's probably going to get even worse when the pressure on him increases. If everything works out at this grand jury presentation, he'll have to return to New York. When that happens, you be careful, Cindy. Don't do anything to aggravate him."

"I'll try not to," she said softly.

Early the next morning, Paula telephoned from her job at the courthouse. "Cindy," she asked, "why were you grilling me yesterday?"

Paula is really quick and smart, Cindy thought. Cindy knew she could have lied to her sister, but she didn't. "Paula, I have to tell you. I was wearing a wire."

"What?"

"A Unitel. I was taping you."

Cindy heard Paula's shocked gasp and wondered if she should have kept quiet. "You were taping ME? Why?"

"So you wouldn't 'undermine' my credibility."

"That is asinine! Spying on me for the prosecution. Goodbye, Cindy." Paula hung up.

Chapter 29

The Grand Jury Reconvenes

On August 31, the Grand Jury convened. The set-up was much the same as at the earlier hearing on the Florence Band murder case; there were twenty-three jury members. This time, however, the prosecution's case had been expanded. Twenty-five witnesses had been subpoenaed. In addition to Cindy, this list included both Paula and Liz. And there were several additional pieces of evidence that had encouraged the district attorney to go ahead with this second grand jury presentation.

The most telling piece of new information was Cindy's testimony about her father's violence and his attempt to kill her. In addition, there was new testimony concerning the murder-for-hire plot—the three men who claimed Band had wanted them to find a hit man for "his friend." Also, there was additional testimony from the Westchester County Medical Examiner's Office in which Dr. Roh concurred with the findings of the Nassau County medical examiner. The testimony went on for nine chilling days, while Cindy prayed that this time her mother would receive the justice so long denied her. In the end, Cindy's testimony and the additional new evidence made the difference. The second grand jury indicted Howard Band for "murder in the second degree."

"We did it, kid," Bill Dempsey exulted when he telephoned Cindy at the hotel with the results. "Maybe that will make you feel better. Jack will be flying down to Florida to pick up your dad. First, he has to get the warrant. But we don't want you down in Florida when we bring your father in. That wouldn't be wise."

Cindy couldn't keep the admiration and joy from her voice. "You did just great, Bill! I know Jack Sharkey must be happy, too."

Within days of the grand jury indictment, Sharkey called the Delray Beach Police Department. He spoke to Sergeant Rick Lincoln who agreed to execute the warrant and make the arrest. By this time, Liz had returned to Florida.

"Our department is familiar with Mr. Band," the Florida police sergeant said. "We've had a number of calls to the Rainberry Lake home for domestic violence."

Sharkey felt an immediate bond with Lincoln. They talked for a while, enjoying the communication. "I'll be coming down with one of my men soon, Rick," Sharkey said, passing on the intelligence he'd collected on the suspect. "He has a new auto parts and transmission shop in a place called Tamarac and is supposed to be doing well." He gave the Delray cop the address exactly as he'd gotten it from Liz.

"Oh, yes. Tamarac is down near Ft. Lauderdale, not very far south of here and west. Can you tele-type me the warrant? We'll do a little surveillance and go pick him up. Is he dangerous?" Lincoln asked.

"Could be. He often packs a pistol."

"Okay, Jack. We'll take care of it. A pleasure talking to you."

At the Nassau County Police Department on September 13, Sharkey answered a call from Sergeant Lincoln in Delray. "Mr. Band came peacefully, Jack," Lincoln told him. "He's in the Broward County jail until you and your men get here. Tamarac's in Broward."

"Thanks, Rick," Sharkey answered. He called Cindy and told her about the arrest.

The next day, the story was plastered across the front pages of newspapers.

Cindy found that her father's arrest filled her with mixed emotions. She felt triumphant—she and the law enforcement officers had finally begun the process of getting justice for her mother. She also felt miserable—he *was* her father, after all, and she'd been the star witness that put him in jail. Still, she knew deep inside that she'd done the right thing. He'd killed her mother—her kind, wonderful mother.

That evening, Cindy telephoned the Broward County, Florida jail and asked to speak to her father. "My father has just been arrested and he's in jail," she told them. The people in charge told her they would have Howard Band make a collect call to her at her hotel.

When he returned the call an hour later, Cindy asked, "Are you okay, Daddy?" Then she told him slowly and carefully, "Daddy, the truth will set you free." She wept, sad for him at a very deep, spiritual place in her being. "Please understand, Daddy. I'm sorry, but I had to do it."

"But Cindy, I didn't do it. I didn't."

He can sound so very convincing. "I just don't believe you; I can't and I want the person who killed Mommy to pay. And I truly believe that person is you. And I want you to remember *this,* Daddy. *Remember,* the truth will set you free."

The next day, the assistant district attorney called her. "Hi, Cindy, it's Bill Dempsey. Your father will be brought back to New York tomorrow. I didn't want you to read it in the papers first. Yesterday, Jack and Lt. Shaun Spillane flew down to Florida to pick him up. They're there as we speak and will be catching the plane with him in the morning. If you need me, Cindy, you call. For anything."

The churning began in her stomach again. She was still afraid of her father, arrested or not. "Thanks, Bill, I appreciate your telling me." They talked a few more minutes, then hung up. Cindy didn't mention that she had spoken with her father on the telephone.

Sharkey, Spillane and Howard Band made the trip north together. The plane landed at La Guardia in perfect weather after a calm flight. They had discussed all sorts of mundane things, which the detective couldn't remember afterwards. Howard's career had been in sales and he could be a pleasant conversationalist. Somehow, the detective had a feeling that Howard was not sorry to be caught. "He acted almost relieved, as if he were hoping to get it over with," he said to Cindy when he called to tell her that her father had arrived back in New York.

Howard Band was arraigned the next day on a charge of second-degree murder, appearing before Judge Richard C. Delin. Band had made Paula his executor, giving her full control over the approximately one million dollars he had in his bank account. Liz, who had a generous mother and still received insurance money from her dead husband's estate, was not in a bad situation, financially. Cindy didn't know whether or not she was surprised when Liz immediately bailed Howard out of jail on a $100,000 bond, refusing to speak with the reporters who followed them around after his release. She managed to whisk him back to Florida until the trial, which was set for the following March, nearly six months in the future.

Cindy asked herself what was going to happen to her in the meantime. She certainly couldn't go back to Delray Beach, although that was supposed to be her home. Her father would be furious with her; there was no telling what he would do. Nick, of course, was gone. Cindy no longer had contact with her aunt and uncle or even her grandfather, whose second wife didn't like Cindy. Paula was angry with her for siding against their father—so where *was* Cindy to go? She decided to talk to Bill Dempsey. He'd told Cindy the DA's money was running out, but he would try to find a place for her to stay.

Bill Dempsey's boss, ADA Barry Grennan, called the Saffers and other relatives together to discuss the upcoming trial. The district attorney's office had naturally assumed Cindy's family would be taking care of her now that the grand jury presentation was over.

"Bill, we've got lots of work to do before the trial in early March," Grennan told Dempsey after Howard and Liz Band had left for Florida. "Let's get Sharkey in here along with the family members and have another talk."

When the day and time for this conference arrived, Dempsey walked into Grennan's office and said, "Okay, Al Saffer is in the waiting room with his wife, as is Cindy's uncle and some other family members. Sharkey's there, too. Let's go out there now and speak to them."

The two men went out to meet the group, first shaking hands and making a strong attempt to put everyone at ease. Her uncle and his father, Al Saffer, praised the prosecutors for their success with the second grand jury and for giving them, at last, a chance for a trial. They also were generous with compliments to Detective Jack Sharkey.

"Okay," Dempsey said and called for everyone's attention. "Let's get this bit of business out of the way first. You folks know we've been keeping Cindy in a sort of protective custody while the grand jury presentation was going on. But look, we can't keep this young lady in the hotel any longer. One of you will have to take her."

The relatives looked at each other. Sharkey raised his eyebrows and glanced at Dempsey. There was a murmur. No one came forward. The prosecutors waited. Finally, one of the family members asked a question about a different matter, completely changing the subject.

The three lawmen were puzzled. Sharkey, stunned, wondered what they could do. Her family wasn't going to take her in—perhaps, as Cindy had once told him, because she'd gone back to live with Howard Band, whom they obviously detested. What could he suggest? Cindy was between the precipice and the canyon. After the family left, he turned to Dempsey. "This isn't right, Bill."

"Jack," Dempsey said to him in a low voice, "I don't care, I'm not turning that girl onto the streets. I've got to figure something out. Any ideas?"

When Cindy was called to the office of the Assistant District Attorney, she could see at once that Bill Dempsey was upset. He'd already told her that funds were low, but she had no doubt he'd find a place for her to stay. She was a little shocked at his next words, however.

"Cindy, we've got to get you on government assistance. Right away. I'm sure you can qualify."

"You mean welfare?" she blurted. She saw Bill bite

his lower lip and realized this was hard on him, too. She wasn't sure why the idea of welfare completely crushed her. She guessed it was the thought of the contrast between her life now and how it had been before her mother died. She felt a wave of embarrassment, followed by nausea, sweep through her body. She stared at him, swallowing again and again, not knowing what to say. She could tell by his eyes that he cared what happened to her and hated having to force her into this decision.

"It wouldn't be for long. After the trial, when your father goes to prison, I would imagine you can go back to the Florida house."

She didn't reply, unable to trust her voice, and continued to stare at him with some measure of disbelief. He gazed back at her with a look that was so full of empathy, shared frustration and compassion, she almost felt compensated for this newest disaster in her life.

"I don't want you to have to do this, Cindy, but I don't know what else to do," he continued. "At least try it. I'll be hunting every spare minute for an alternative place to put you up. I just wish . . . I really wish . . ." He stopped.

"All right, Bill," she said, running a hand through her hair. "I'll do it. I just won't tell anybody, because I feel completely humiliated."

He shook his head and chuckled. "Oh, Cindy," he said, smiling at her with soft eyes. "I'll do my best to get you set up and in a place tomorrow. Call me, okay?"

She left his office, confident that Bill would, indeed, have a place for her the next day. She'd find somewhere to stay tonight. Her old friend Mark, her sister Paula . . . someone, someplace. But she couldn't reach anyone. She just heard the endless ringing of telephones not picked up. Not knowing what else to do, she went into the city and began to walk around her old familiar haunts—the streets in the flower district where her grandfather had his business and where she'd met Nick almost two years ago.

Confusion filled her, as if all the good things she used to plan for her life were gone, vanished. As she trudged along the street, taking in the familiar scents of the profusion of flowers and plants in the shops and warehouses, she saw Harry, a long-time employee in the area, an old black man with a kind manner. "Hi, Harry," she said.

"Hello there, Miss Cindy. Are you headed for Mr. Saffer's building?"

"No, I'm not. My grandfather is in Florida most of the time." She didn't mention that his second wife didn't like her.

"Something wrong, Miss Cindy? Anything I can help you with?"

"Oh, Harry, so much is going on and so much is going wrong, that I just feel down."

"Yes, Miss, I've heard about your troubles. I'm sorry."

"It's really difficult. I just want some peace now; you know what I mean?"

"Yes, I feel that way sometimes. I understand."

"I don't have money. I don't even have a place to stay." She didn't know why she'd blurted out the words. He couldn't help her. She saw him studying her.

"It isn't much, Miss Cindy, but you can stay at my place tonight."

She turned to face him directly. His face was kind and he seemed serious. "Go to your place?"

"If that's what you need—a place to stay."

Tears sprang to her eyes. "That's so kind of you. I just want a place that's quiet and no one is asking me questions. I'm so tired."

"Come with me, Miss Cindy. I'm on my way home now."

His apartment was small but very clean and tidy. He made up the couch with sheets and gave her a blanket.

Just before she fell asleep, Cindy told him, "I think you're my guardian angel, Harry. I'll leave early in the morning. And I thank you."

Chapter 30

New and Old Dangers

Bill Dempsey quickly went through the paperwork for enrolling Cindy in the welfare system and hurried the process along. When Cindy returned to his office the next morning, he told her "You're all set up with DSS—a few forms to sign and you'll be back in the hotel."

Cindy didn't mention where she'd spent the night and Dempsey didn't ask.

She passed the next two weeks in the hotel, where she washed her clothes in the sink at night and hung them over the shower rod to dry. There were no guards on duty; they knew her father was in Florida. It was the same comfortable room and it was still wired, but it had lost its feeling of being her safe haven. She was paying part of the room rate with the government's degrading *"handout"* money; the other portion was still being paid through the special funds of the prosecutor's office.

She tried to accept it. She tried to pretend it wasn't welfare. But the thought that she had now hit rock bottom still lingered.

When Liz flew in on Wednesday evening, she called Cindy at the hotel.

"I need to see you," Cindy said and invited her up to the hotel room. When Liz hung up, Cindy telephoned the two lawmen to let them know her stepmother was on the way and the wire was in operation. She could tell they were pleased.

While she waited for her stepmother, Cindy felt her agitation grow by the minute. By the time the woman finally arrived and knocked on the door, Cindy's nervous tension was almost unbearable. Somehow, though, she managed to steady herself, reminding herself that she had to appear normal.

"Everything okay, Liz?" she said when her stepmother came in and sat down on the bed. She added, "You and Daddy been fighting again?"

"Don't we always?" Liz's blue eyes were fixed intently on hers. "You know?"

Cindy wasn't interested in games tonight. "What?" she asked.

"He plans to go away. He's still got the money from the Horseshoe Road house."

Cindy frowned. "Well, where is he planning to go with the money?" When Liz didn't reply, she asked again, "Where's Daddy planning to go? He's in Florida. Isn't that enough?"

"No, he wants to go to Spain."

"What? Why?"

"Yes, Spain. He's all set. And I can't go—not yet—I just can't leave my kids. So instead of me, he plans to take you."

"Me? Not Paula?"

"Not Paula. She's interning in a law office, remember? Anyway, he wants you. You're not in school at the present time and have nothing holding you here. The other day he went to see a plastic surgeon in Palm

Beach. He wants to be operated on so nobody will recognize him. He'll get that done very soon."

More insanity, Cindy thought. *Unbelievable! As if we're living in an* Alice in Wonderland *world, where everybody just accepts the craziness and goes on pretending.* Cindy tried to think through this new insanity. "Well, Liz, you have to have a passport to go overseas."

Liz shook her head. "Right. And he's got his. And yours is probably still good from when your family all went abroad a few years ago. If you recall, I did the booking for the trip for every one of you. I think your passport is still valid, too."

Cindy turned pale. She couldn't believe this. *And he is being stupid,* she thought. "What makes him think I'd go?" she asked.

"I don't think he cares what you want, Cindy. He says you'll go one way or the other."

How can he do that anyway? Cindy thought. *I understand his wanting to go, but what is he going to do to make me leave the country with him? Can he even leave the country after being indicted by a grand jury?*

"This is crazy," Cindy said. Maybe she wasn't understanding something, but what made her father think he could do that? She wondered if he planned to kidnap or drug her. And then what? Would he kill her for testifying against him before the grand jury? Even though the police were listening to this conversation through the bugs in the room, she decided to call Bill and Sharkey tomorrow. *First thing in the morning.*

Both men stood up when Cindy entered ADA Dempsey's office. She could see by their faces that they were having trouble keeping calm. Sharkey held a chair out for her, then began to pace. Dempsey sat back down at his desk and drummed a pencil against the blotter on his desk.

"We heard it, Cindy. We heard what Liz told you about your father," the detective said at last, seating himself across from her.

"Can someone who's supposed to be going to trial— can he leave the country? And how is he going to make me go with him? Drug me? He's already tried to kill me once."

"I'd like to see him try!" Sharkey's entire body tensed. "He really thinks he's going to split and take her with him," he said to Dempsey, staring hard at him. "What are we going to do about this, Bill?"

Dempsey cleared his throat. "It looks as if we'd better put some guards on you, again, Cindy. Money or no money, we can't let anything happen to you." He glanced at Sharkey.

"Exactly," the detective said. "We can't lose our best informant. We wouldn't have a very successful case without you, kid. But really, I don't think he can pull this one off. He's blowing smoke."

"He's very underhanded," Cindy said. "Didn't he try to hire someone to kill my mother?" A disturbing thought ran through her mind. "Do you think he's found someone this time—to take care of me, I mean?" She could see how alarmed the two men were. She caught the worried glances they exchanged.

Dempsey didn't reply to her question. "Here's what we're going to do," he said, his kind face grave. "We're going to put you up at a different hotel here in Mineola, The Holiday Inn. You'll have a guard at all times, but you're free to come and go as you like during the day. Stay in at night. We'll have people watching you and we'll be in touch every day, okay?"

She nodded.

"Then," he went on, "we'll be able to step in if Band tries to make you do anything."

"Well, my father isn't here in New York. You know that. He's in Florida, but he's liable to show up anywhere."

"I think when we tell Mr. Band we're onto his scheme and have guards watching you, he'll realize how difficult it would be to take you anywhere. If you decide to see him, have him come to the hotel. It will be safer for you."

After Cindy left, Dempsey turned to Sharkey. "I'm worried about Cindy. She's our primary informant. So much of our case rests on information she's given us and can confirm." The two men sipped from their cups of coffee, both deep in thought. "We're building our case around her, Jack, but with all she's been through, I don't know how she's going to handle this crazy, new scheme of her father's. I'm also a little concerned about her testifying at the trial. Her father will be right there glaring at her, intimidating her."

"Bill, is there any way we can get more protection for Cindy? Something to make it easier on the kid?" Jack Sharkey looked out the window. The tree outside was ablaze in autumn reds and yellows, but he barely noticed. "She's suffered so much." He knew how much the girl trusted both him and Bill. Now she was virtually homeless. "It's over two years since her mother's death—two years of hell for her." Sharkey sighed. "But Cindy hasn't wavered from her quest to have her mother's killer punished. She always strives to be upbeat. Nevertheless, the strain on her is a terrible. I wish there was more we could do for her. What do you think, Bill?"

"She's coping the best way she can," Dempsey said, turning a serious face towards the detective. "And this

latest deal—Band's planning to take her to Spain—
must be tearing that girl in two."

"We have to keep her safe, Bill." Sharkey locked
eyes with the assistant district attorney.

Bill Dempsey nodded. "We're going to do our best."

When Liz telephoned Cindy in late September and
told her that she and Howard were leaving for a cruise
to the islands, Cindy welcomed their excursion as an
opportunity for her own relaxation. She figured that
their little trip was probably unknown to the authorities,
but she decided she wouldn't mention it to Dempsey or
Sharkey. She didn't want anyone to stop her father and
Liz. It felt too good to know she'd be separated from
her father by a several hour plane ride.

Before leaving, her stepmother told Cindy that if
she needed somewhere to stay, in case the hotel was
getting too costly, she could stay with one of Liz's
friends, a nurse at the Meadowlark Medical complex.
Although Cindy said it wasn't necessary, Liz gave her
the address and the woman's name. "She doesn't have
her own telephone there," Liz said. "So just stop by and
see her."

"Well, I will if I ever need a room. Right now, I'm
set," Cindy replied.

She felt really good about how Sharkey and Dempsey
were looking after her. How, she wondered, would she
have existed without the two men? So when Bill, who
regularly kept in touch, called and asked her to come to
his courthouse office the next morning, she was eager
to see him again.

"Cindy," Bill said as soon as she seated herself in
front of his desk. "I know we've been keeping you in
our protection, but the district attorney's budget is running so low. Our money fund, to put it bluntly, is almost

gone and, unfortunately, what you're receiving from DSS isn't enough to cover your hotel expenses."

"Yes." Aware of that fact, she waited to hear what he would suggest. She wasn't worried. She had complete confidence in him.

"I don't know what to say—or suggest," he said, not meeting her eyes.

After a minute or two of racing thoughts, Cindy offered, "Liz has a friend—a nurse—and Liz said she could put me up."

Dempsey smiled with relief. "That sounds great. Meanwhile, we'll be looking for some sort of housing for you."

"I guess that's what I'll do then," she answered. "I'll contact Liz's friend. If *you* think it's okay."

"Yeah, I do. Let me have the address and phone number of where you'll be staying."

Cindy fumbled in her purse. "She doesn't have a phone and I must have left the address at the hotel. I'll get it and go over there to see this friend of Liz's to be sure it's alright for me to stay there. Then I'll call you with the info."

"Just don't talk to anyone there about the case, Cindy. They wouldn't understand. And remember, we don't want you anywhere near your father at all."

Back at the hotel, she called Detective Sharkey from her room. "I have to leave here," she told him. "There's no more money left in the ADA's budget for me and the welfare money won't cover the bill."

"Damn," muttered Sharkey into the telephone.

"Bill doesn't want me to see my father at all."

"Well, Cindy, you know what he's threatened and how he flares up. You've seen how bad it can get," Sharkey told her. "I think he realizes the plastic surgery bit is out, now that we know. In other words, he won't chance grabbing you and trying to go to Spain. On the other hand, the trial is coming up in late February or early March. He's probably feeling the pressure." He sighed and his voice became more somber. "Thinking about the trial could make him do something desperate. We don't want you around him."

They only spoke for a couple of minutes. Cindy didn't mention that she was heading for the Meadowlark Hospital complex. She merely gave Sharkey a condensed version of what she had told Dempsey, leaving him with the impression that she was bunking in a nurse's apartment and would call Dempsey once she knew it was set. When they hung up, Cindy gathered her belongings and caught a cab. It wasn't a long drive.

The Meadowlark complex, as its name implied, contained more than several buildings. She was familiar with the ER because she'd been there once, but that was all. The taxi driver drove her round and round as she searched for her destination. Finally, aware that the meter tab was becoming exorbitant, Cindy had the driver let her off at a dignified looking old brick building with shrubbery in front. As the cab disappeared, she went in to inquire the exact location of the nurses' residence so she could meet Hannah Burrows, Liz's friend.

Cindy felt a bit confused as she opened the first door she came to and looked around for someone who could give her directions. The only person in sight was a janitor, who promptly left the building before she had the chance to speak to him. Now there was no one to ask. As she turned a corner she spotted a fifty-ish woman with a brown bun, a cardigan, a print skirt and round glasses walking away from her with a fast gait.

"Excuse me," Cindy called out as she trotted after the woman. "Can you tell me where the nurses' residence is?" She looked to Cindy as if *she* knew exactly where she was.

The bespectacled woman whirled around to face

Cindy. "Mmm," the woman answered, looking her over. "Tell me what you're looking for and who you are." She motioned to a nearby waiting room. "Why don't we just go in there and talk about it."

It never occurred to Cindy to be suspicious of her. She had always been very trusting and naïve, perhaps from being so sheltered during her childhood. "Yes, ma'am," she said, following the woman.

"Now then," said the woman, "what's this all about?" She sat down in one of the chairs lining the walls and patted the seat beside her.

Cindy took the seat beside her. "I'm Cindy Band and I'm here because my stepmother, Liz Band, said I could stay with her friend. Hannah Burrows."

She saw the woman's eyebrows lift. "Oh?"

Cindy wondered if the woman wanted verification of why she needed a room. She didn't want the woman to think she was a random homeless person just in off the street. "Well, you see, my mother was murdered and my father did it. He has tried to kill me, too, and so I need to stay here so he can't harm me."

Don't talk to anybody. They won't understand. She recalled Bill and Sharkey's words too late, but the woman seemed to be waiting for her to say more. Cindy made the story longer and more explicit, going into her inability to study and how she had married a man who wanted a green card and on and on . . . It surprised her that this woman kept asking for more and more details. *Before she even tells me where the residence is . . . ? This is weird.*

"I see. And do you ever *see* your mother?" The brown eyes peering at her behind the round glasses seemed to be very understandng.

What does she want me to say? Cindy asked herself. *Is she asking about the time I saw a vision of Mommy?*

"Yes, actually I did," Cindy finally said. "At first she'd be in my dreams. Then, one time, I saw her on the wall of Nick's apartment and . . ."

"This was a ghost, then?"

"Well, I guess you could call it that," Cindy told her. She explained exactly how the apparition had occurred and how it had helped, not frightened her.

The woman nodded and stood, then motioned for Cindy to follow. *Where on earth can Miss Brown Bun be taking me?* They walked through endless corridors for what seemed miles.

Finally, they passed through two automatic doors with no handles on the inside into an area with the tallest desk she had ever seen. There were office chairs all around. Cindy watched as the woman smiled at the Asian man behind the desk. He appeared to be a doctor.

"This is Cindy Band. Her guardian was here yesterday. She's all yours," the woman said as she turned and left the room.

Since the doctor wouldn't acknowledge Cindy, she sat down next to a middle-aged black woman.

"I'm just here to be psychiatrically evaluated," the woman told Cindy.

Why are they doing an evaluation in a nurses' residence? Cindy thought. "You have to take a test or something?" Cindy asked.

"If I pass, I get to go home," the woman said. At that moment, an attendant opened a door and called the woman in.

"Good luck," Cindy said, assuming she wouldn't see her again.

Since no one was paying attention to her, Cindy settled back in her chair and waited, expecting Liz's friend to come at any minute to welcome her. Instead, the time went by and she was ignored. Finally, the same door opened and the black woman came out. She waved at Cindy as she left the building.

Cindy checked her watch. *Geez, I've been waiting almost two hours!* She approached the black-haired doctor, "Excuse me, what am I doing here?" He answered her curtly and suggested that she be quiet.

More time passed. *This is crazy.* She tried again to get an answer from the doctor, this time raising her voice. He looked at her severely. "I said . . ."

The events that happened next were like something out of a horror movie. Four uniformed attendants grabbed Cindy and put her on a gurney. They tied her hands and feet with what seemed to be pieces of sheets and put her in a glass-encased room. When she protested, they injected her with some drug. As she tried to speak, they raised and locked the sides of the bed. In another second, Cindy lost consciousness.

When Cindy came to—she had no idea how long she'd been out—she was still tied to the bed with sheets. Not knowing how else to get loose, Cindy began gnawing at the strips, but got nowhere. *Who are these people and what do they want with me? Liz told me to come here. Is Daddy behind this? He tried to kill me once . . . he surely wouldn't have any qualms about railroading me into a place from which I couldn't escape until after his trial. Are Daddy and Liz trying to keep me from testifying?* She had no answers for the many questions that ricocheted through her mind.

An older, gray-haired man dressed in white entered the room and came up to her gurney. "I'm Dr. Tomlin. You don't have to bite the sheets." He untied her. "We're sending you up to the psychiatric ward."

Two uniformed attendants motioned her to come with them. They escorted her to the elevator and rode it to the sixth floor. The attendants marched her up to a desk there.

"Where's my purse?" she asked one of them dazedly. She was still affected by the drug they had given her.

"You'll get it," was the terse reply.

A nurse came back to the desk and brought Cindy into what she called the day room. She saw a young man there, about her age and nice looking. He was snacking on a bag of chips.

"What time is it?" she asked him. "Where are we?" Grabbing some cookies that were on a dish on the table and a four-ounce carton of chocolate milk, she sat and talked with the guy. The setting—and his responses— made her think of the movie *One Flew Over the Cuckoo's Nest*. Everything seemed surreal. Fuzzy. It was like being in a dream—a bad dream.

Someone said, "Here's your bed."

"This floor's low security," the man she'd been talking to told her. "They'll evaluate you tomorrow, you know, and give you some pills. Everyone here is on medication."

I don't WANT any medication, she thought. *Why am I here?*

Cindy found a phone in the corridor and grabbed it as if it were a lifeline. She was thankful she always kept coins in her pocket. Knowing she couldn't reach Liz, because she was with her father in the islands, she first called Bill Dempsey's office but couldn't get through. Next, she tried her grandfather. He'd help her. Her step-grandmother answered. "Shirley, may I speak to Grandpa, please?"

"What's wrong?"

"I just need to talk to him."

"Well, you can't. Your grandfather isn't well." Shirley hung up with a bang.

Shocked and outraged, she tried to call her sister Paula. She couldn't reach her either.

A short time later, she tried the assistant district attorney's office again and breathed a sigh of relief when the secretary put her through to Bill Dempsey. "Bill, Bill. I think my father's used his influence to put me in a loony bin. They're drugging me. It's horrible. Please, can you do something? Please, please." She told him what she'd been through.

"My God!" She could hear both concern and shock in his voice. "We'll get you out of there, Cindy, don't you worry. We'll have to go through channels, because that monster is still listed as your guardian." The relief she felt at Bill's promise was so intense, it made the experience bearable. Exhausted and drugged with who-knew-what, Cindy went to her bed and fell asleep.

The next morning, she was ushered into a doctor's office. He was balding and middle-aged. "Now look Cindy, don't worry. Your family feels you need help."

The interview with the doctor was a blur to Cindy. She heard little of what he said and instead concentrated on Bill Dempsey's comforting words.

It was difficult to be patient, but she had no doubt that Bill would get her out as soon as he possibly could. Meanwhile, she spent the rest of the day doing what the staff asked her to do, trying not to make waves. She found that individuals were labeled as being on certain "levels"—the lower the level, the worse they considered you—and that to move ahead to a higher or better level, one had to pass various question-and-answer sessions, games and tests. She didn't want to say or do anything that would cause her to be pushed down to the lower level.

Four nights passed and she still hadn't heard from Bill Dempsey. She was sleeping in a room with three or four other females. She awakened to pain. Three men in white staff uniforms were slapping and shaking her. "What—what . . . ?" She tried to become fully awake.

"Look," one of the men said in an angry voice, "the district attorney's office called about you. They were screaming at us. Now, we know your father's accused of killing your mother. And there's a girl lying in the bathroom unconscious. We think you did something to her." The orderly grasped her arm. Another attendant took her other arm. She couldn't move.

"What's going on? What girl in the bathroom? I don't know what you're talking about!" she cried out.

"You don't have to know anything," one man spat.

As she struggled to free herself from their grasps, the other orderly held her tighter, saying, "Oh, you're getting mean, now, are you?" A blow caught Cindy on the head and knocked her out.

Again, she couldn't tell how long she'd been unconscious. When she came to, it was the next day and a nurse told her she was being released.

"I'm getting out of this madhouse," she told the people at the desk as she left.

Late that afternoon, as she walked downtown, she stopped at the hotel she'd stayed at before and phoned Bill Dempsey. He wasn't in his office and she left a message for him. She also called the doctor at Meadowlark. Perhaps it was because of the effects of the medication, for she still wasn't thinking clearly, or perhaps it was merely the rebel in her wanting to say *nyaa, nyaa,* but when he answered, she said, "I'm back at the hotel and I'm never coming back."

"Come back and sign yourself in voluntarily," he coaxed. "That's what will be best for you. We have dinner waiting for you."

She felt like laughing. "I don't need your dinner. I'm having dinner right here at the Hempstead Plaza."

She walked into the dining room and sat down. As

she was waiting for her meal, a man came in and sat down at the next table. He began chatting with her and said he was a doctor. He seemed quite nice and they conversed quietly about the weather, politics and current movies. He'd only been sitting there a few moments when two men in uniforms—they appeared to be police officers—came up to her and took her arms. They hurried her out to a car parked in front of the hotel, saying "Come with us. Everything is going to be okay."

The man she'd been talking to said, "Don't worry, I'll follow right behind." Hearing that—and knowing she had a friend—calmed her momentarily.

Out on the street, the men bustled Cindy into the back seat of the car. Suddenly, she realized they weren't police officers at all. They were wearing some kind of security company uniforms. Panicking, she turned to the kindly doctor who had followed her from the hotel, but he merely smiled and gave a small wave as the car pulled out with a lurch. *Of course,* Cindy thought bitterly, *he's one of them.*

When they reached the Meadowlark Hospital Center, the men took her to the sixth floor. To her disgust, the same group of orderlies who had beaten her in the night was waiting for her when the elevator doors opened. The security men escorted Cindy right up to the orderlies, then left.

"Hi, Cindy," the doctor greeted her in a sarcastic, nasty tone. "I hear that you told people I hit you." He stepped forward, lip curled, eyes glaring.

Cindy shouted, "I can't believe this, you bastard!" She was so incensed she felt like hitting someone. They immediately grabbed Cindy and put her in a wheelchair. Then they held her down and injected her with medication. Again, she passed out.

When she woke up this time, Cindy was in a pink

metal cage next to a woman in a similar cage. "Where am I? What's going on?" She rubbed the site where they'd given her the shot. *Bunch of sadists!*

"You're in the criminally insane ward, girl," the woman told her.

She heard loud crashes and screams, people ranting and singing at the top of their lungs. There was a fierce din in the place that never seemed to stop. She turned pale when she saw a man with his ear partly hanging off.

The doctor came to her shortly after with a form. "If you sign yourself in, we'll put you on a better floor."

"No. I'm not signing anything. I'm especially not signing myself into this loony bin."

He left but returned three times more to try to persuade her to sign. Each time she refused. The fourth time, he yelled at her that she could be there forever if she didn't cooperate. Determined and angry, he growled, "You HAVE to sign." One of his attendants grabbed her. She didn't want another shot. Dazed and feeling nauseated, she finally succumbed to their demands. She signed.

"Good," the doctor said. "Take her to medium security."

They half-carried Cindy into a pink day-room full of other women. Too hazy to concentrate, she pulled two chairs together and went to sleep. *What drug did they give me?* she thought before passing out. *A sedative of some kind, but something even stronger than what they gave me the first time I was here.* Because she was so petite, it didn't take much to knock her out.

She woke up later, needing to go to the bathroom, and was directed to a small room with no door. She felt as if everyone were looking at her. Later on, a woman with short black hair in a Dutch-boy cut, wearing a flannel robe persisted in banging over and over on a door. The next day, the same woman flung her tray across the room. *How much longer,* she asked herself, *can I stand this?* When she questioned an orderly, he told her she couldn't be released until someone came to sign her out.

Later that day when the drugs wore off enough that she could think, Cindy called Paula again. "Cindy," her sister said, "you need help, but we're trying to get you transferred out of there. You must be patient." Though they had their differences, Cindy was truly hurt to hear her sister actually believed Cindy really belonged in a place like Meadowlark.

Not knowing who to turn to, Cindy phoned Sharkey.

"Tell them I'm coming for you at eight tomorrow morning. You can count on it, Cindy!"

He was as good as his word.

Later, when Dempsey asked if she wanted to sue the hospital, Cindy replied that she would be satisfied if the people who had beaten her were fired. "I don't want to sue with my father's trial coming up. I'm not in this for money and it will just be more bad publicity for my family."

A few days later, she learned that everyone involved in her treatment at the hospital was either transferred or fired. *Now they can't hurt anybody else.* For Cindy, it had been ten long days of hell.

When she saw her medical records, the diagnostic words were: "Not delusional. Do not medicate." *At least,* she thought, *my sanity has been documented.*

But Cindy's hospitalization had Dempsey and Sharkey worried.

"Your father is one hell of a conniver," Dempsey

told Cindy angrily. "He's cunning. Obviously, he feels your ten-day stay in the mental hospital will discredit your testimony." He watched her. She appeared very shook-up and highly anxious. "And he may be right. He may have won this round."

"You mean I might not testify?" Cindy asked, taken aback by the ADA's words.

Dempsey shook his head. "I'm just not sure yet. He knows it was your testimony before the grand jury that caused his indictment. It may be just as effective for us to have him see you in the prosecutor's corner every day. That may be enough to shake him."

Cindy nodded thoughtfully. She hoped he was right.

"Anyway, Cindy," the assistant district attorney told her, "we've gotten some additional funds for you. You can stay at the Hampstead Plaza for now, but we'll be putting you up at a different hotel while the trial is going on. It's slated for March, as you know, and I want you in protected surroundings." He smiled at her, a warm protective smile that made her feel safe. She knew how hard he'd tried on her behalf and her feelings towards him were good ones. She truly worshipped Sharkey for rescuing her from the mental hospital.

"When the trial starts you'll be in a hotel closer to the courthouse," Dempsey continued. "You'll have twenty-four hour guards. I don't want anything to happen to you, Cindy."

"Whatever you say, Bill," Cindy said, "as long as my mother's murderer is punished."

Soon Dempsey let Cindy know it was time to move back to Long Island. Her room was on the second floor of the Raceway Hotel. There were guards posted outside.

When she arose after her first night there and walked

to the café near the courthouse to eat breakfast, she ran into her father and Liz. Somehow her father had found out where she was and he wanted to let her know he knew. The awkwardness of the situation made conversation difficult.

"Hello, Cinnamon. Come sit at our table," Howard told her. Liz smiled, but there was caution on her face. She was glancing around to see if anyone was watching.

How can I possibly eat with them? Cindy asked herself. *Don't they know I'm the informant the prosecutor is guarding so zealously?* Old habits of obedience, however, die hard. "Uh—all right," she said, following them to a table.

"And how are you, Cindy?" Liz asked at last.

"Fine, and you? How was the trip?"

"It was okay," her father answered, his eyes intent on hers. "We have a very tough lawyer. His name is Robert Efrem. He's excellent and he knows I'm innocent."

As her father continued to stare at her, it was all she could do to keep from fainting. Cindy kept looking away or down at the plate of scrambled eggs he'd ordered for her. She didn't feel like eating. She felt nauseous. Finally she murmured, "Uh—look, I'm sorry. I'm not very hungry. I have to go back to my room."

"Well," Howard said, "we'll see you in court. Just be sure to meet us for breakfast tomorrow."

Cindy called both Bill and Sharkey that night. She needed reassurance. Each of them, separately, gave it to her over the phone. They told her she'd do just right, that guards were watching her and that no one would hurt her. The pep talks helped.

"I know that after all this time, this is what we've all been working towards. This is the big moment and I'll do whatever you need me to do," she promised.

After she hung up, she lay down on the bed. Dark

thoughts and memories ricocheted through her mind. *Does Daddy really think I'll get too scared to testify against him? The way he was staring at me . . . It reminded me of when I was in high school and used to carry my telephone into the closet late at night to call my friends. Daddy didn't like me to talk on the phone on school nights, but all the kids did and I just wanted to fit in. One time when I was talking to a friend, Paula came into my room and caught me. She said, "Uh-oh, I'm going to tell Daddy." She did tattle, too, for Daddy called me to his bedroom the next day. "You think I don't know? Well, I know." His face had taken on that grotesquely savage appearance I was to see so often during the next few years. He was almost breathing fire. "I know everything. If you don't believe me, just try me. If I ever hear of you disobeying me again, you'll be very, very sorry. DO YOU HEAR ME?" He never said what he planned to do, but I never wanted to "try" him. That day, I ran back to my room in tears.*

Just as she cried now.

Chapter 31

On Trial

After three days of jury selection, the trial began on March 8. The morning dawned brisk and gray-skied. Though it was cold, Cindy slipped out of her hotel room and went running for twenty minutes. The exercise, as always, helped calm the agitation that had shaken her awake with thoughts of the courtroom drama about to enfold. After showering, Cindy donned a neat beige suit. She summoned her guarding officer to her room and accompanied him to a black sedan parked at the curb in front of the hotel.

"Good morning, Cindy," the driver said as she got in the car. The drivers were different from day to day. Sometimes they were detectives on duty, sometimes not. But they all worked for the government and they all wore badges. The other officer opened the back door for her and she climbed into the car.

"Hi." She smiled, but did not start a conversation. The agitation was beginning again. She felt as if a motor were running somewhere under her skin. She was sure that once she began to talk, she wouldn't be able to stop. Today was so important for her and her mother. She opened the window to get a fresh breath of air, but closed it quickly. It was icy outside.

During the short drive to the Mineola Courthouse, Cindy pulled her coat snugly around her and took several deep breaths. Howard and Liz went in a different car. Although they had insisted she meet them for breakfast at the nearby café each morning, she should have said "No." Instead, she acquiesced. Maybe she had agreed to breakfast to show them she wasn't afraid and they hadn't succeeded in bullying her. To show them that they hadn't won.

Liz looked different when she greeted Cindy at the café that morning. Most likely, the able defense lawyer had told her to dress primly, but in Cindy's eyes, her stepmother had overdone it. Liz's blonde hair, which she usually wore in a long flip, was pulled back starkly into a ponytail, making Cindy think of George Washington's wig. Unlike her usual flamboyant attire, Liz wore a simple, two-piece ivory suit. Her gold chains and other jewelry had been left behind. Plain beige pumps accessorized the outfit. Still, Liz looked very attractive, Cindy acknowledged.

As she sat across from her father and Liz, Cindy barely touched her food. Staring at Liz, she tried to ascertain what her role had been in the crime, knowing that the man across from her at the breakfast table was on trial for the murder of her mother, in large part because of Cindy herself. She wondered why her father had insisted so strongly that the three of them have breakfast together every morning. Was this a strategy suggested by his attorney to show Howard Band to be a family man still loved by his daughter? Or was it merely another way for Howard to demean her?

Pale and shaky, Cindy hadn't felt this distraught since the night her mother had died so tragically. They finished their breakfast quickly and, once at the courthouse, the three went their separate ways. Her father was whisked away by a man Cindy hadn't met. She didn't know where Liz went.

As soon as she walked through the crowded hall into the courtroom, where the notice on the door annotated the high-profile Band case, Cindy could see that the benches were filled with spectators. The first two rows, however, were saved for family members and the press. She took a seat in row one. A television camera had been set up in row two. Several reporters, recognizable by their turned-back steno pads and pens at-the-ready, were hunched into spots on the benches, taking notes as they questioned people in the seats all around them.

Bill Dempsey approached her. "Good morning, Cindy. In a few minutes I'll be making opening statements." He smiled reassuringly. For a moment, she felt more secure.

She watched the ADA walk away, then stop at another man's signal. The two men—she thought the other one was her father's defense attorney—appeared to be engaged in a heated discussion. She thought she heard her name spoken by one of them. Bill was frowning and looking in her direction. She wondered what might be wrong.

A few moments later, she heard Jack Sharkey's voice above the chatter of the crowd and turned to see him in the aisle standing by her row. He leaned down to speak to her. "Okay, Cindy?"

"I feel nervous, Jack," she whispered. "Isn't it about time the trial gets started?"

"It won't be long, kid. Trials are notoriously late in starting. Always some last minute addition or something."

"I get to stay in the courtroom and see the whole thing, don't I?"

"You sure do. It's not like the grand jury presentation when you had to sit in the hall. Today—every day, you'll be able to see all of the proceedings. And remember, if it wasn't for your input about what your dad did to you and your mother, none of us would be here today. As you can see, Cindy, some witnesses have to sit outside or up in the jury room until they're called. We have to require that to keep their answers from being influenced by what someone else says from the witness stand."

"Well, I won't change my testimony if you call on me!" She thought of how encouraging both he and Bill had always been to her. It helped so much.

"I know you won't. But remember what we told you. Bill may not call upon you to testify, Cindy, because of the stunt your father just pulled. You know, the mental hospital thing. But since Bill may still put you on the stand, your viewing of other witnesses will be slightly restricted. You can see everyone testify except for your stepmother, sister and me. When each of us takes the stand, Bill wants you to go up to the jury room on the second floor and wait."

"Whatever you feel is necessary."

"You're sure you're okay? You look a little pale."

"I'm just a little cold." She could see he was looking at the way she was shaking. She didn't want him to know how nervous she was. They shouldn't worry. If they needed her to testify, she'd do it even if she were on her deathbed. Deep within herself, she had long ago made that decision. It was the right thing to do.

"I've got a jacket right here. It will warm you right up." He started to remove his suit coat.

"No, no, Jack. No, I'm fine, really. You keep your coat." She could hear herself talking too fast. She took a deep breath trying to calm down.

"Cindy, don't worry. You've done so well all this time. It's almost over. This is it and you're still our star.

Just keep your chin up and don't let them rattle you. Having you on our side during this trial is a powerful signal to your father—and the jury. And a great incentive to those of us who have been committed to achieving the justice both you and your mother deserve." Sharkey lifted his head as the bailiff moved to the front of the podium, then turned back to her. "Okay, we're about to begin, Cindy. See you later." Sharkey gave her a comforting pat and moved to the back of the large room just as Dempsey reentered the courtroom. She saw the ADA say something to Sharkey, who raised his eyebrows. For a moment, they both looked at her. Then Sharkey nodded and Dempsey walked forward and took his place at the right-hand table in front.

"All rise." The uniformed bailiff announced the entrance of the judge, Nassau County Court Judge Richard C. Delin. The crowded audience stood up and remained standing until the judge, dressed in his black robes, motioned for them to sit. Cindy noted animated conversation between Judge Delin—termed *The Court*—and the lawyers, although she couldn't understand what they were saying. Later, she was to read in the newspaper that the judge agreed to admit evidence taken from the Band house the night of the murder even though it had been acquired without a warrant. This was permitted because the police had been called to the house at the defendant's request.

Five minutes inched by, then the bailiff made another announcement that heralded the entrance of the twelve jurors and three alternates—the people who held justice for her mother in their hands. Again, the courtroom spectators stood in respect to these citizens.

The clerk said, "People versus Howard Band. People ready?"

Bill Dempsey answered in the firm, decisive tone of

voice Cindy had come to know and respect. "People ready."

"Defendant ready?"

Her father's attorney, Robert Efrem responded, "Defendant ready." And the trial began.

After opening statements from both lawyers, Dempsey called his first witness, Old Westbury Police Officer Dennis McCavera. He had been on duty when a call came asking him "to respond to 9 Horseshoe Road at around 0019 hours," or, in civilian terminology, nineteen minutes past midnight.

After describing the well-to-do residence, the officer detailed his first steps that night. "Upon arrival, I pulled my car into the driveway, which is on the left-hand side of the house as you look at it. I exited my car. As soon as I got out, a voice summoned me to the front door. The person at the front door was Dr. Sultan. He instructed me that Mrs. Band was lying at the bottom of the stairs and that it was bad."

ADA Dempsey's voice deepened as he asked, "What, if anything, did you do at that point, Officer McCavera?"

"I entered the house, opened the cellar door and went immediately downstairs and checked the body."

Dempsey asked for the "geography" of the grounds surrounding the Band household.

"The grounds of the property facing the street is a partly wooded area, rising up on a hill. The driveway is on an incline. The backyard is leveled out with a swimming pool for backyard use. But it's a semi-wooded area where this house is."

Continuing to question the officer, Dempsey ferreted out that McCavera had entered by the front door and went right to the cellar stairs just off the kitchen, which is in the rear of the house. The door to the cellar was on an interior wall, directly opposite to the rear entrance of the house.

The prosecutor showed photos of the house, which the officer identified the Band residence. Interrupting, the defense attorney asked for a *voir dire* to establish the fact that the house *had been* the Band residence but didn't belong to them today.

"Officer McCavera," Dempsey continued, "you had mentioned during the course of your testimony that there was some food spillage within the basement; is that correct?"

"Yes sir."

"Can you tell us what spillage or what food there was in close proximity to Mrs. Band's body?"

"There was a turkey carcass covered with aluminum foil, with a pan lying on the floor. It would be slightly to the left of the head. Beyond that was a container of spaghetti with a spill of sauce on the floor."

"Can you tell us what the condition of Mrs. Band's nightgown was at the time that you observed the body?"

"Yes, sir, it was intact. It wasn't ruffled by any means."

As Dempsey questioned the officer further on what he had done that night, McCavera elaborated. "Mr. Band was upstairs at the time, making a wailing noise." Then, rushing on, he added an afterthought. "It appeared to be an insincere cry."

Defense Attorney Efrem objected. The Court sustained the objection. "Jurors are ordered to disregard that last remark."

When the prosecutor told the officer not to characterize but simply tell what Mr. Band was doing, the officer said, "He was wailing." McCavera said he had put his hand on the defendant and found that his body was "soaking wet. I assume it was from perspiration."

Efrem objected again. Dempsey reworded the question and got the same results.

The witness then told how he and another Old Westbury police officer had found guns belonging to Mr. Band. The other officer had wanted them removed.

"I object," said Efrem, "That's not relevant. He had a permit for those guns."

After some argument, the questioning resumed. Dempsey eventually brought to light the evidence that had caused Sharkey to view Florence Band's death with suspicion. Mrs. Band had ligature marks on her wrists and ankles. The ADA held up crime scene photos showing the indentations, which McCavera recognized. Dempsey then led the officer through the next few hours, asking him to repeat what the defendant had told him about what happened. His next question referred to the arrival of other officers at the mansion and whether McCavera had observed either of the Band children arriving at the scene.

"Sometime before the arrival of the Crime Scene Unit, Cindy Band came home."

"Can you tell us what, if anything, you observed when you did, in fact, see Cindy Band in the house?"

"She was very upset and she was crying very heavily, hysterically, when she found out about her mother."

"Can you tell us what you next observed her do?"

"She was constantly crying and moving through the house. She tried to go down to see her mother at that point, but we wouldn't let her."

Dempsey continued to walk McCavera through that fateful morning, his words painting a picture for the jury. The jurors leaned forward in their chairs.

When Dempsey thanked the officer and ended by saying "no further questions," Defense Attorney Robert Efrem began his cross-examination. He led the officer through his arrival at the Band house, then asked him if his desk officer, Sergeant Cross, had ordered an ambulance that night. Dempsey objected: "Hearsay."

Judge Delin replied, "Sustained."

Thwarted in his attempt to bring out information about the ambulance, Efrem moved on to other questions. Cindy listened, her heart stuck in her throat. The defense lawyer pounded away at the officer on many points: how McCavera had answered questions at the earlier grand jury presentation regarding whether her father "wailed" or "cried," whether he heard the dogs barking and the appearance of the spilled food in the basement. Finally, he asked McCavera what Dr. Sultan had said to him when he first found the body.

"Dr. Sultan said to me, 'Stay with him, stay very close to him,' Mr. Band was in a—he was in a state. It was very, very hectic. He was screaming and wailing . . . I kept asking Mr. Band what happened, with no answer, he kept on crying or wailing, making a wailing noise. He was crying." McCavera insisted that he gave those same answers during the Grand Jury testimony.

Dempsey's next witness was Sergeant Arthur French, the officer who first interviewed Cindy in her room. At the time of the murder, he was working as a detective assigned to the third squad. He had arrived at the house with Detective Meyers. Dempsey's questions for the witness concerned what the detective had observed at the crime scene.

Although she had heard it before, tears rose in Cindy's eyes as French described the ligature marks found on the victim's wrists and ankles. He went on to describe how he found bits of rope and BX cable around the body. These were then admitted into evidence. Sergeant French then described the condition of the basement, including the spilled food on the floor and how he had examined the defendant's shoes. French revealed that Howard Band's shoes appeared clean even though Band told French he had stepped in the spaghetti sauce.

French's testimony was interrupted by the clock,

which signaled 4:00 P.M. The first day came to a close and the jury was instructed not to talk about the case or read news items about it during their evening hours.

"Now, as of this morning," Judge Delin told the jury, "The weather report states that a great deal of snow is expected overnight. I would suggest to you that you listen to the appropriate radio stations tomorrow morning to find out if the Court will be open, if there is a heavy snowfall. If not, see you tomorrow."

As it turned out, the weather on the following day—Friday—was too severe to continue. The trial resumed after the weekend on Monday, March 12.

During the re-cross-examination, Sergeant French gave an answer that made the listeners chuckle.

Defense lawyer Robert Efrem asked: "You said on redirect that you examined the bottom of these steps for evidence of food. Can you tell us what training you have in distinguishing particles as to whether or not they are food substances or something else?"

"I would object," said Dempsey.

Judge Delin stepped in. "I would overrule your objection."

French frowned, "I know what food is."

"What training have you had, Sergeant?" Efrem asked with a shrug.

Again, French frowned. Deeper this time. "Forty-five years of seeing food."

Efrem took another shot. "That's it, forty-five years of seeing food?"

French smiled wryly. "That's a lot of food."

Efrem's mood was serious. "Have you had any formal training?"

Efrem matched him. "Forty-five years, growing up, seeing food."

The defense attorney ignored the laughter that broke out in the courtroom and asked if the witness were a "chemist" or "lab technician" or even a member of the Crime Scene Unit. The answer was no.

Changing the subject, Efrem then objected to the sergeant's questioning of Mr. Band on August 25th and asked the officer if he'd read the defendant his rights. To that, the police officer said no.

Dempsey countered by asking, "Isn't it correct that Mr. Band was not under arrest when you asked him questions. Wasn't he free to go?"

Sergeant French nodded. "Yes."

Cindy watched with admiration as Dempsey questioned another witness, Dr. Armando Deschamps, a general surgeon who'd been practicing medicine for thirty years and had, at one time, worked on behalf of the Nassau County Medical Examiner's Office.

From time to time, her father's lawyer objected to certain questions, although she really couldn't see to what he was objecting. At one point, Efrem claimed Dr. Deschamps was not qualified to give his opinion that Florence Band had not died from a fall down the stairs even though the doctor said he'd visited around "7000 scenes of death."

On the other hand, Dempsey had also objected at times during Efrem's cross-examination. It was a game, sort of, Cindy decided, but with very serious results at stake.

Cindy's uncle, Florence's brother, was the next witness to take the stand. After establishing that he had gotten in touch with his sister about once every month, Dempsey asked, "Did there come a point in time, prior to the death of your sister, when you spoke to your brother-in-law about the status of his marriage to your sister, Florence?"

There was an objection which was quickly overruled.

Florence Band's brother's answers revealed that he

had spoken with Howard Band five or six times over a four- or five-year period.

Efrem was up again. "I object, your Honor." The two counsels were called to the bench. "That's over four or five years."

Judge Delin looked at Dempsey. "Will you be able to pinpoint these dates?"

Dempsey shook his head. "How can I pinpoint the dates?"

Even though the prosecutor said they weren't four or five years ago, but over a four to five year period, the judge ruled this too remote.

Dempsey said, "Thank you, your Honor."

Cindy could see that the confrontation between the two attorneys was drawing the spectators' attention. Every seat was taken at the high-profile trial and all heads were turned toward the witness stand.

"When you spoke to Howard Band about the marriage this past July," Dempsey asked, "what, if anything, did he say to you?"

Efrem was on his feet again. "I object." When the judge overruled him, he asked to approach the bench. "I know your Honor has been tolerant."

Delin glared at him. "Intolerant?"

"No, no. Tolerant."

The judge scratched his chin. "I thought I was tolerant. Come up." More conversation occurred at the bench, then more argument between the attorneys. Finally, the judge told the witness he could answer.

Cindy's uncle looked weary, but his voice was firm. "Mr. Band complained to me." When the defense attorney objected to these words, he changed his answer. "Mr. Band said that my sister, her spending habits had gotten to the point where he found it intolerable. That she had insisted on some large renovations to the house, including a patio and landscaping, which he felt—he said it was choking him financially. He talked to me about the rearing practices that were going on in the family and his difficulties understanding my sister and what was going on with the younger child, Cindy. Mr. Band said his bags were packed and he was going to be out of the house one way or the other, whether it be that day, the next day or within a short period of time. He said that he had been looking into renting an apartment in Port Chester and was not sure when he would leave. I asked him to keep me informed, so that I could continue to discuss things with my sister as to what would happen."

Bill Dempsey next asked about the status of the marriage itself. Robert Efrem wasn't about to let such broad questioning go unchallenged. He said "Your honor, to go back over this with leading questions is improper."

Delin, who was obviously weary of the quibbling between the two lawyers, said, "If it's repetitious, I will not permit it . . . Go ahead."

"Mr. Band indicated to me that he would ask my sister for a divorce," Cindy's uncle said, "but he didn't want to pay the $11,000 in legal costs he estimated it would take to pay for the divorce. He said he had requested my sister to use a divorce kit, which she refused to do."

A few minutes later, when Bill Dempsey called Cindy's sister to the stand, he looked over in Cindy's direction. She knew she was expected to leave. She trudged upstairs to the jury selection room and waited. No one else was there. She wondered what her sister was saying.

The prosecutor led Paula, looking attractive and professional in a navy suit, through his opening questions. Though Paula's voice was soft, it carried well in the courtroom. In due time, she told the court that she was twenty-two, that she was at Lake George at the time of her mother's death, that she was a law student at St. John's and that she'd gone for a ride with her father when she first arrived home. She answered that she did not remember where they drove. When he asked her about the autopsy, Defense Attorney Efrem objected, saying Dempsey was cross-examining his own witness. The prosecutor was again accused of "cross-examining" Paula when he asked her if she recalled making a statement to Detective Sharkey.

"Was the statement accurate to the best of your recollection?"

Though Paula's hostility was evident, she answered the next questions with an aplomb that spoke favorably of her future as an attorney.

"I was pushed. Detective Sharkey said to me, many times, that if you don't cooperate, your father is going to walk."

"Judge," Dempsey said, "I object to this."

Delin nodded. "Sustained. Not responsive."

Dempsey continued. "You were pushed, Paula?"

"Yes. Yes, I was."

A discussion followed between the two lawyers and the Court regarding the prosecutor again cross-examining his own witness. After arguments and objections at the bench, Dempsey resumed, asking Paula if her father had spoken to her about the "physical makeup of the mother." More objections followed.

Dempsey prodded, asking, "Did your father say anything about the physical composition or makeup of your mother?"

"What do you mean?" Paula asked.

Dempsey went on. "Did he tell you that your mother—"

Efrem rose. "I object. Counsel is doing something improper."

The judge was growing short-tempered. "If you don't keep quiet, we are going to have a problem here."

Although Dempsey was glad the judge had stepped in, he could not help admiring Efrem's searing performance. He had shown himself to be a powerful adversary who was unwilling to yield anything in defense of his client. And he was not about to be cowed by the judge's words.

"I object to that procedure," Efrem said.

Delin pounded his gavel. "Be seated, Counselor. I sustain the objection."

Paula was also showing herself to be both intelligent and able. She asked questions of her own to the prosecutor. Dempsey let her refresh her memory by glancing at her original statement. Finally, in response to the question about her mother's physical qualities, she answered, "That she was soft and light in weight."

Dempsey said, "And anything else?"

Paula quickly replied, "And that if she fell, she wouldn't make any noise." There was a soft murmur in the courtroom. It had come out in prior testimony that on the night of Florence Band's death, Howard Band had told one of the officers that he'd heard what sounded like someone falling.

Questioning further, Dempsey brought out that Paula had known Liz Diamond and Howard Band were having an affair before Florence Band's death.

The prosecutor then amended his statement to say that Liz and Howard were having an affair and that Ms. Diamond had extended Mr. Band a loan before the murder. Dempsey was on a roll now and couldn't resist playing to the jury. "You put that together with the statements of Howard Band to his brother-in-law, 'my wife is choking me financially—I can't keep up the payments'—and add in the fact that he is getting $64,000 double indemnity after his wife dies."

Objecting in a booming voice, Efrem said, "We are throwing facts, none of which are related to the case. You are trying to put in everything that is not necessarily really germane to the issue." At the defense table, Howard Band had grown pale. He sat rigidly, as though any movement might betray him.

Dempsey's voice had a steel edge. "I would submit, Judge, it's relative on the financial motive-to-kill. It's relevant."

In the jury box, heads swiveled back and forth from the prosecutor to the defense attorney.

Later, during Robert Efrem's cross-examination of Paula, he said: "It's the prosecution's theory that no one else could have entered that house except Howard Band because, one, as a result of their perimeter check, the place was not broken into. And, two, because they had two vicious dogs."

"Objection," Dempsey said, rising from his chair.

Judge Delin rapped his gavel. "Sustained. There is no testimony as to the viciousness of those dogs."

Efrem wasn't going to accept this, however. "But it is coming."

Delin wouldn't give an inch. "But it's not here now. I sustain the objection."

Efrem told the Court that the witness would testify that Cindy had often stepped up on the garbage can and climbed into her bedroom window when she was out late.

Dempsey objected. "He is asking this witness to testify on the habits of another witness."

It was then that Efrem dropped what he hoped was a bombshell. Fortunately, the prosecutor had anticipated it.

"Cindy is a possible defendant," Efrem stated. "She has no alibi. She came in the house ten minutes after the murder. And she had a way to get into that house."

Delin seemed surprised at this line of questioning. "Well, if it's your theory that she committed this homicide and did it by entering the house on that circumstance . . ."

Dempsey was furious now. "It's not admissible, your Honor. This witness was not present. She was up in Lake George. I think you might be able to elicit it from Cindy, but not from this witness."

Efrem sparred. "I can ask this witness if she saw her do it."

Judge Delin broke in. "What happened on this occasion, Counselor."

Efrem began, "We are trying to show that the opportunity . . ."

Delin rebuked him. "Too speculative."

Efrem glared at him and continued. ". . . that someone else entered that house existed. He is going to argue in summation that no one else could have gotten into the house. It was sealed off. The only testimony is with respect to the first floor. Now I have to establish that it's meaningful that they didn't go up to the second floor . . ."

Dempsey interrupted. "There is going to be testimony by another witness that all the windows were checked for forcible entry. I think it was Detective Buchan. But, my basis for the objection as to this particular point is that it's asking this witness to establish the habits of another witness."

Efrem didn't give up, his own voice harsh with authority. "It's her sister."

After a discussion, the court said that if the defense lawyer were merely trying to show that there was an opportunity to enter the house in that manner, he would allow it.

Efrem, whose patience had all but run out, said, "Can you tell us what the habit was with Cindy upon her arrival home and her entry in the house, other than the doors?"

After a long moment, Paula, her own voice sounding harsh, said, "If she wanted to get in, the doors were locked, she didn't have a key—she would climb on top of the garbage cans and climb up on top of the rain gutter and she had a window extending out from the house. She climbed up to the rain gutter and walked in the window."

On redirect, Bill Dempsey asked, "Did you see your sister Cindy when you came back to the house?"

"No."

"Did you see her at any time on August 25?"

Paula looked into his eyes and said, "Yes."

"What was her emotional state?" Dempsey asked.

Paula had him and she knew it. "Bananas, as usual."

A look of surprise and disgust came over Dempsey's face. "It was bananas as usual," he echoed.

After a moment of pained silence, Paula looked straight ahead and said, "Yes."

Next, the prosecutor asked about the nature of the family dogs.

"They were like mice," Paula responded, adding "they rarely, if ever, barked when strangers came to the house."

At lunch, when Cindy learned of Paula's statement about the family's pets, she disagreed and said, "My testimony would have been the opposite. Those dogs would not only have barked, they would have eaten them up."

Learning of Paula's comment about her distraught

emotional state the day after their mother's death, Cindy said nothing. But she wondered why her sister had felt Cindy was acting strangely. After all, their mother's body had just been found. Who would not have been agitated?

Chapter 32

Conquests and Betrayals

When the session broke for the afternoon around 4:30 P.M., Dempsey, upset now over Paula's testimony late in the day, rushed out of the courtroom. Jack Sharkey spoke to him in the hall for a few minutes about the case. They both felt anger at the low points made during Paula's testimony. "Can you believe that? They tried to blame it on Cindy!" Sharkey exclaimed in disbelief.

As Dempsey hurried towards the elevator, he saw Paula walking down the hall. He caught up to her and said, "Are you so jealous of your sister that you had to go on the stand and say what you did?" Without waiting for an answer, he walked away.

A few minutes later in the upstairs room, Cindy was happy to see Dempsey approach. "I'm furious," he said frowning. "The defense stooped to a new low by trying to make it appear that you and your friends could have done the deed." He passed along what he'd said to Paula in the hall.

Dempsey saw Cindy turn pale and realized he was upsetting her. He stopped and took a few deep breaths to calm himself. Then he patted her arm and gave a small smile. "Cindy, I don't think we're going to have you testify," he said. "It's apparent your father will stop at nothing to get off. After all, look at what your father has already done to you. Especially his latest stunt, trying to discredit your testimony by having you committed to a mental hospital. You can bet the defense will use that to try and make you appear unstable, if not crazy."

Cindy was silent as she dealt with her mixed emotions. Deep down she felt relieved that she wouldn't have to testify against her father, yet at the same time deprived of her final role in achieving justice for her mother. "But I want to be sure my mother's killer doesn't get off, Bill. And after all, he tried to kill me, too."

"He won't walk, Cindy, I promise you. You've made it possible for us to see to that. In fact, you've lived through hell to ensure that goal. And we won't fail you . . . or your mother," he said emotionally.

"I know you won't," Cindy said softly. "And I believe somehow my mother knows it too."

The following day when Cindy arrived at court, Detective Sharkey approached her before the trial began. Despite her firm convictions about her role in all this, Cindy had suffered through an old nightmare the previous night and had woken up crying. Her eyes and nose were still red.

Noticing how upset she seemed, Sharkey gave her a big hug. "I need to ask you something. Have you seen Liz?" he asked.

"No. I haven't seen her since the first day. Maybe she's at her old house on Briarcliff Circle instead of the hotel."

"No, not there nor at the hotel. It's strange; we didn't subpoena her before the trial began and now that our process servers are trying to do that, we can't find Liz anywhere. Nobody seems to know where she is."

Cindy thought a moment, realizing instantly that this was very important. "Well, it's possible she went to California. She has a cousin, Ben, there and I recall her saying she wanted to visit him and his wife."

Sharkey let out his breath through pursed lips. "Damn! Well, it's our error for waiting. If she's not subpoenaed, she has no legal obligation to be here."

"But she's supposed to testify, right?"

"Yes, she is. That's why we've granted her immunity. We need her. We've been telling the jury about this girlfriend who became his second wife and they want to see her. If you know the cousin's last name and where he lives, I'll call and see if I can get her back here."

He said a quick goodbye, because he needed to talk to Bill Dempsey and work on trying to reach Liz before the trial reconvened. *Probably impossible,* Cindy thought. *If she is in California, the time is different and she's probably asleep. If Daddy had skipped town, that might have made sense. But Liz—who would expect that? What is she afraid of? She's been given immunity.*

Dark thoughts plagued Cindy as the day's testimony began. First came Police Officer Bradford Davis, then Helen Gund (who had spoken to Florence Band around nine on the murder night), then Officer Dennis J. Dougherty (who had taken fingerprints) and, finally, Detective Jack Sharkey. When the detective got up to take the witness stand, Cindy went to the jury selection room.

As Jack Sharkey was sworn in, his resolve was firm. He knew basically what Dempsey would be asking him. Both men hated what Band had done not only to his wife but also to Cindy. They longed for this case to end with a conviction.

At Dempsey's request, Sharkey identified himself, stating that this was his seventeenth year with the Nassau County Police Department, thirteen of which he'd served as a detective. Next, he was asked questions that covered his actions on August 25 from 2:00 A.M. to late that evening. After that, Dempsey queried him on Howard Band's demeanor when Sharkey and Sergeant Mangan questioned him at the Old Westbury Police Department.

Quietly but firmly, Sharkey told the jury, "Mr. Band said he was looking for his wife and went to the bottom of the stairs and saw his wife, Florence. He said he went down the stairs. He said he passed and stepped in some spaghetti sauce. He said he saw something wrapped in some tin foil. He walked around his wife, put his hand underneath her neck to cradle it and cried out, "Florence, Florence." He said he put her head back down then ran back up the stairs and out into the garage. He got into his car and drove across the street to Dr. Sultan's house, pounding on the door, screaming, "It's Florence, it's Florence."

The testimony continued with Detective Sharkey repeating what Howard Band had told him about the rest of the night of his wife's death: how Dr. Sultan had returned with him and shook his head after examining the body as if to suggest there was no hope.

Sharkey's voice took on a harder edge and seemed to fill the courtroom. "I asked him why, while he was lying in bed and then went to go looking for his wife, why would he get dressed? He said, 'Are you trying to say I killed my wife?' I said, 'By no means. I'm trying to get the facts.' At which time he said to me, 'Are you?' "

As Sharkey told of how he had asked Mr. Band about the events of the night, Efrem rose to his feet and said, "Your honor, the witness is raising his voice."

Delin motioned to Sharkey with his hand. "Go ahead."

Efrem shot a quick glance at Dempsey, then back to the judge. "I would like the record to indicate, your Honor, the witness is raising his voice."

Delin sighed, frustration showing in his face. "I don't feel it's reached that level where the Court must admonish the witness. Go ahead, Detective Sharkey."

Sharkey continued to relate what had gone on. He told the court that, although Mr. Band told police that he had stepped in some pasta sauce when he found his wife's body at the bottom of those stairs, he did not have any sauce on his shoes. That was one of several inconsistencies Sharkey had found in Mr. Band's account of that evening.

The detective testified that he couldn't understand why Mr. Band had dressed himself fully to go down to the kitchen to look for his wife or why he hadn't called 911 for help rather than driving to the home of a neighboring doctor.

Then Sharkey told the rapt jurors how he had escorted Mr. Band to the Old Westbury police station at five o'clock in the morning and how Mr. Band repeated his story twice. When Sharkey had asked why he had dressed to go down to the kitchen, Band ended the interview by asking whether Sharkey was accusing him of murdering his wife and whether or not he was under arrest. When Sharkey told him 'no,' Band rushed out of the station. Sharkey related that despite Band running out, when he caught up with him, Band got into the detective's car and was driven home.

* * *

In reasonably quick succession, Dempsey called on Major Richard Childs, Richard Frischmann, Dr. John King, Dr. Leon Sultan, Officer Scott Wanlass and Neil Ferrick. Cindy had reentered the courtroom in time to hear her friend and classmate testify.

Answering the preliminary questions, Neil said he was twenty-three years old and lived in Jericho. He told the jury that he attended a party with other people about his age on August 24 and he saw Cindy Band there. Asked when he left, he said it was "twelve or twelve fifteen." He didn't recall if Cindy had had anything alcoholic to drink.

Dempsey asked, "When you left, where, if anywhere, did you go?"

Neil replied, "Well, I was going to drop Cindy off at her home, but we stopped off at a drive-in movie in Westbury."

Dempsey wanted more clarification. "When you say you stopped off, did you go, actually go into the drive-in movie?"

"No, we were outside of it," Neil said, shaking his head. He continued to explain, saying they had stayed about fifteen minutes and he had thought Cindy dozed off. Since he didn't know the address of the Band house to tell the Court, he identified a photo he was shown. "That's the house," he confirmed, nodding his head.

Dempsey asked Neil what happened next and the young man described the police cars at the Band house. "I noticed Cindy got very excited. Curious to know what's going on, I drove up to the driveway and walked with her to the back of the house. Someone had told her that her mother had fallen down the stairs and she was dead. I believe it was a relative that told her."

"What did Cindy do at that point?" Dempsey asked quietly.

Neil replied, "She was very, very upset."

The next witnesses to come forward were Detective Sergeant Thomas Mangan, Michael Germane, Robert Eugene Ciri. They all testified to their findings on the night of Florence Band's death and their subsequent investigation.

Finally, the long day of testimony ended. That evening Cindy called Sharkey and gave him the name and phone number of Liz's cousin in California, which she had gotten from Donny. The following day, Cindy arrived at the courthouse and walked up to Sharkey, who was standing at the foot of the stairs. As they climbed the steps, Sharkey told her, "I reached Liz, but I couldn't get her to promise to return." They took the elevator and silently walked down the corridor toward the courtroom.

Suddenly, Cindy gasped and grabbed Sharkey's arm. There was Liz Diamond Band, right outside the courtroom door! "She must have taken the red-eye," Cindy whispered. "What did you say to her, Jack?"

"I told her how important she was." He gave a slight smile. "You keep her occupied, Cindy, and we'll serve her right here," Sharkey said and turned back toward the elevator.

Cindy nodded and walked over to her stepmother. She greeted Liz politely and began making small talk about Donny and the other kids. Within a few minutes, a process server walked up behind Liz, tapped her on the shoulder and shoved a subpoena into her hand. Sharkey stood right next to him. "We couldn't find you anywhere, Mrs. Band," the process server said with a smile.

Liz hissed that certain process servers hadn't searched far enough west. "Besides, I wouldn't have left California and come here today if I hadn't expected to testify." She looked at Cindy, then Sharkey. "I'm not stupid. Of course I know I'm supposed to testify. I'm a material witness for the prosecution."

Cindy felt like she might become sick to her stomach. She took a deep breath and asked, "Did you have a good time in California?" hoping the change in subject would calm her down.

"Well, it was a lot quieter than here or Florida," Liz said.

Shortly after, Liz was called to the stand. Demurely, she told the jury how she'd met Howard Band and how they had, indeed, had a relationship while his wife Florence was still alive.

Dempsey listed a number of places that he indicated she'd gone to with Mr. Band; she admitted to the places he mentioned. "Did Howard Band ever stop by a beauty parlor that you had occasion to be in and pay you a visit?"

Liz's eyes burned at the prosecutor as if she wanted to skewer him. "Yes, I would say so."

Dempsey met her eyes coolly, his tone of voice reasonable. "Did Howard Band attend a party that was held in your home on or about the first week of June of the past year?"

Liz sighed audibly. "Yes. He just stayed a very short time. It was a party to celebrate my daughter's birthday and graduation from high school. He stayed there a short time, because there was another party at his home for one of his friends."

Dempsey asked, "Were you sexually intimate with him on more than one occasion prior to the death of his wife?"

"Yes," Liz replied softly.

This response brought the gallery to life and Judge Delin had to rap his gavel lightly to put an end to the tittering.

Prodding, Dempsey asked, "Is it correct to say, Mrs. Band, that you had occasion to go to Holland with Mr. Band?"

Liz nodded. "Correct." She seemed to realize there was little she could do to save face.

"Do you recall whether or not you booked the tickets?" Dempsey asked.

"I booked the tickets," Liz replied firmly.

Dempsey continued, "Did you book the tickets in the name of Mr. and Mrs. Howard Band?"

"Correct."

Tears springing to her eyes, Cindy recalled that her mother had found those tickets and thought they were for her until Howard told her that he was taking a business associate instead.

"Did Mr. Band tell you that he wanted to divorce his wife?" the ADA went on.

Liz appeared unnerved and fidgeted in her seat. "Yes," she replied.

Noting her discomfort, the prosecutor wasn't about to cut short his opportunity to unearth the truth and he methodically led her through questions about the night of Florence Band's death. Liz conceded that Howard Band had been distraught that night and not making much sense. She denied being at the house and said they had spoken on the telephone.

Later, both Frank and Ellen Robertson took the stand in turn. Ellen Robertson described how she'd helped Florence clean up the kitchen on the afternoon of her death, a task that Band claimed to have done. Ellen wanted to relate how Florence had confided to her of marital misery during middle-of-the-night phone calls but the defense objected, so she testified mainly about the food.

As one after another of the prosecution's witnesses

testified, Cindy, for the most part, kept her eyes riveted on her father, who every once in a while looked at her, then quickly looked away.

Sharkey, sat in the rear of the courtroom and watched Cindy. *The girl has courage,* he thought. Even after her father's attempt to have her committed to a mental hospital, she wasn't broken. In a way, he was glad she wouldn't be testifying. Yes, she was very important to the case, but they had other good witnesses, specifically the three men Band had approached about hiring a hit man. Cindy had already served the most important purpose of being their eyes and ears in the Band household all this time. He looked over at Cindy and, catching her eye, gave her a broad smile. *You're something, kid,* he thought. Sharkey hoped Cindy knew how proud of her he was.

When Ted Warren began his testimony, the jury paid close attention. This witness, Cindy knew, was the man whom her father had approached to ask about hiring a killer. His testimony was one of the pieces of "new evidence" that, along with *her* reports, had enabled the district attorney finally to bring her father to justice.

Bill Dempsey, beginning slowly and methodically, asked the man his age—"thirty-six"—and what he currently did for a living—"a parking attendant"—and where he had worked before his present employment.

Warren answered that he previously worked at 140 West 28 Street, Manhattan, also as a parking attendant. He'd worked there for "almost fifteen years." He ran the place, he said.

Dempsey asked, "Can you tell us where your business was located with respect to Al Saffer's Floral Supply?"

Efrem objected. "He didn't say it was his business. He said he worked for them."

Dempsey shook his head. "I'm sorry, Mr. Warren. Let

me rephrase my question. With respect to the place where you worked, can you tell us where that was with respect to the Al Saffer Floral Company?"

"I would say two buildings apart from each other."

"That was in Manhattan, sir, is that correct?"

The prosecutor ferreted out that for two years, until Warren left that job, Howard Band had been a customer.

Dempsey asked, "Mr. Warren, I would like to invite your attention back to the summer months before Florence Band's death. Did there come a point in time when you had a conversation with Mr. Howard Band?"

"Yes."

Dempsey lowered his voice to a near whisper, as if sharing a dirty secret. "Did Mr. Band ask you to do him a favor?"

Warren answered thoughtfully that he had. "Mr. Band asked me if I knew anybody that was interested in doing a job."

"And then . . ." Dempsey encouraged.

Warren replied, "I asked 'What is the nature of the job?' He said, 'To waste somebody away.' I said I didn't know of anybody."

The ADA nodded at him. "Go on."

"Mr. Band told me to think about it. He came back a few days after, two or three days, and asked me the same thing again, and I said, 'No, I don't know of anybody,' and that I wasn't interested in this. So he said to me to think about it again and there would be something in it for me if I could find him somebody to do the job."

Dempsey put the finishing touches on the picture he was painting. "The first time that you saw him, was he alone or accompanied by someone?"

"He was with a lady, about 5'4", 5'5", blonde. Nice looking lady. Classy looking lady."

Dempsey paused, looked at the jury and continued. "What about the second time Mr. Band approached you? Was he alone then?"

"No. The same lady was with him."

Dempsey brought out that Warren had been close enough to the woman to identify her and that Mr. Band had come back a week later and discussed the woman with him. At that meeting, Warren told the defendant that he "didn't want to get involved in this sort of thing." He also testified that he saw the same woman frequently with Band after that time. Band told him that she was his travel agent. Warren told Dempsey that he had testified twice to that fact before the grand jury.

Efrem objected to this; the lawyers argued at the bench over Warren's apparent identification of Liz Diamond. Efrem asked for a mistrial due to "hearsay" and Warren's mentioning that he had gone before the grand jury. Eventually, Dempsey was given permission to have Warren identify a photo of Liz Diamond, which he did.

During cross-examination, Efrem revealed that Al Saffer, Florence Band's father, had once given Warren's fiancée a job.

After Warren's testimony, the prosecutor called to the stand the two other men who claimed Howard Band had also asked them to find him a hit man. One of the men caused the spectators to break into laughter. He said that after Band had queried him over and over again about a hitman, he told the defendant that the man he had been found guilty of murder and was sentenced to a jail term of twenty years to life. "That stopped his questions," the man quipped with a straight face.

*   *   *

Dempsey approached Cindy at the close of the day. He touched her arm lightly, to catch her attention.

She smiled. "You're doing just great, Bill. Thank you—from my mother and me."

He chewed on his lower lip for a moment. "Are you relieved or upset that we're not putting you on the stand?"

She stared at him. "I'm okay with it either way, aren't you?"

"Sure," he said. "I just don't want you to feel you haven't finished your part in this, because you have. Without you, we wouldn't have gotten to this point."

Cindy nodded. "I understand. Although . . ."

"It's because Efrem," he broke in, "is an excellent lawyer. If I put you on the stand, he would tear you apart because of the mental hospital business."

"I'm strong. I wouldn't break, Bill."

Dempsey waited a moment, took a deep breath and said, "Here's the catch. Cindy, you remember when they maneuvered to put you in the mental facility and, toward the end of your stay, you might not remember, but you signed a paper putting yourself in voluntarily? He has that information and he would crucify you with it."

"But they made me sign it, Bill. I wasn't wacko, and most of the people who mistreated me were fined, weren't they?"

"Yes," Dempsey said, "they were. But I won't have him tearing you up. You see, it's a matter of law that anything which could exculpate a witness must be made available to both sides. Remember before the trial started when Efrem and I were having a heated discussion?"

"I saw you. I thought I heard my name mentioned," Cindy said.

"You did," Dempsey went on. "He asked if I was going to put you on the stand. When I said 'yes,' he replied, 'I have some very interesting questions for her about being in a certain mental institution.' "

"I told him, 'Your client had a hand in that!' But he retorted, 'The young lady signed herself in, I believe.' "

"I'm not going to put you through a cross examination where they go for your jugular, Cindy. But don't worry. Thanks to you, we're going to get a conviction." He gave her a look that made her think again that he was her ultimate savior. She *knew,* if anyone could come through for her, it was him.

When it was the defense's turn, Robert Efrem produced his ace witness, a noted forensic scientist. Dr. Michael Baden was already well-known for his work as consultant to the House Select Committee on Assassinations. In addition, he had been called into cases involving the deaths of Nelson Rockefeller, John Belushi and Lee Harvey Oswald, as well as the case of Martha von Bulow. He would become even more famous in the future, when he played an integral part in the defense of O.J. Simpson as a member of the "Dream Team."

In the Band trial, Baden's testimony was pivotal for the defense. Earlier, the prosecution had presented Dr. Leslie Lukash, who, in his original autopsy report, said he couldn't identify what had killed Florence Band, but because of new technological tests, now claimed the victim had died of asphyxiation.

After Baden went on the witness stand, contesting Lukash's testimony, the trial turned for a time into an inflamed forensic battle between the two medical examiners. At one point, Baden brandished for the jury a jar containing a piece of the victim's spine.

Newspapers around the country covered the fireworks as Dr. Michael Baden contradicted every major conclusion of Nassau County's chief medical examiner, Dr. Leslie Lukash. Baden essentially said Dr. Leslie Lukash was wrong. Lukash had testified that Florence Band died of asphyxiation between 8:40 and 10:30 P.M. But Baden said that Mrs. Band died sometime around midnight and that the cause of her death could not be determined from the evidence available.

Lukash had testified that he had determined the time of Mrs. Band's death by evaluating and correlating five different tests. Body temperature alone would not be a reliable indicator, Lukash said, basing his assessment on his twenty-seven years of experience as medical examiner.

In his testimony, Baden said that in the Band case, body temperature alone was, in fact, a reliable indictor. Because her temperature had dropped at about a degree per hour, Baden concluded that Mrs. Band had died "shortly before midnight; that is shortly before the body was found . . ."

In a cross-examination by defense attorney Robert Efrem, Lukash testified that the bluish-red mottling or speckles on the side of Mrs. Band's face were petechiae and their presence indicated she died of asphyxiation. But Baden said that the mottling was not petechiae but liver mortis, or the settling of blood as it follows the force of gravity after death. Furthermore, Baden declared petechiae are not an indication of asphyxiation, because they accompany many other causes of death. He called the speckles "Tardieu spots", while Lukash had testified that they were not. "That's like comparing a blueberry with a watermelon," Lukash had said.

The day after Baden testified, headlines blazed "Pathologists' Court Battle Gets Hotter" because Michael Baden admitted he had once misdiagnosed two homicidal asphyxiations which then raised questions about Baden's skill in recognizing asphyxiation. Baden also admitted that in two cases he initially concluded, without autopsies, that two residents of a welfare hotel had died of chronic alcoholism. But after a man confessed to smothering them, he exhumed the body of one and found signs of asphyxiation . . . but he changed the cause of death primarily because of the confession.

Dempsey read Baden a passage from a well-known forensic pathology textbook. It said that, of the relevant cases, in half, the body temperature is unreliable for ascertaining time of death. Baden agreed that this was true, even though he had previously testified that, based on her body temperature, Mrs. Band died shortly before midnight.

After the battle of the pathologists, it was time for both the prosecution and the defense to make closing arguments. Knowing how critical the closing arguments can be, Bill Dempsey sequestered himself for eleven uninterrupted hours to write his final words to the jury.

On the day of closing arguments, Dempsey began his summation in the courtroom by immediately becoming confrontational. He recalled that the defense had suggested Mrs. Band died of undetermined causes and may have fallen on her way to put leftover pasta and turkey in the basement freezer.

"In your wildest imagination," the prosecutor said, his voice rising in his seventy-eight minute summation, "can you conceive of a person who falls down the stairs and ends up in this position?" He held up a police photo showing Florence Band's crumpled body at the bottom of the stairs.

In the quiet courtroom, one of the jurors could be heard to gasp.

Pointing to a container of spaghetti sauce in the picture, Dempsey paused and turned to the jury, taking in the length of both rows. Then he thundered, "How in the name of all that is good and holy did this container of pasta and sauce get all the way down the stairs and land in that upright position?"

Next, Dempsey showed the jury slides of marks on the victim's wrists and ankles which appeared to be rope burns, saying: "People who fall down a flight of stairs do not ordinarily have ligature marks . . . Who tied up Mrs. Band and who untied Mrs. Band?" Again, he paused, looking intently from juror to juror. He reminded them that Howard Band was the only one besides the victim who had been home that night. Dempsey also reminded the jury of the three men that Band had approached in an attempt to procure a murder-for-hire job. His next words produced a ripple of audible gasps from several members of the gallery. "This man went shopping for murderers the way that you may go shopping for vegetables in Pathmark. Does that not reflect an intent to kill? Does that not demonstrate proof beyond a reasonable doubt this defendant's intent to kill his wife?"

Finally, the prosecutor finished and it was the defense attorney's turn. In his summation, Efrem tried to discount the damaging testimony. "Even if he tried to hire a hit man, what does it prove?" Regarding the rope burns, the defense attorney asked, "Do people die as a result of compression marks on the wrist?" He pointed out that Dr. Baden's testimony was, in his belief, credible. In the end, Efrem said, "I submit to you that the evidence before you doesn't establish beyond a reasonable doubt that the death was homicidal or that my client killed his wife." He asked the jury to remember their responsibility. "Do not be misled. Do not draw inferences that are not bonded in solid granite. Do not draw inferences out of emotion based on speculation. I ask you to acquit my client. Thank you."

Around 3:30 P.M., the judge gave his last instructions to the jury. The courtroom, though full of spectators, was silent. The jury listened intently.

"Now the indictment accuses the defendant, Howard Band, of murder in the second degree.

"The defendant, Howard Band, in or about the twenty-fourth day of August . . ." the judge's voice droned on as he explained the charges.

"As it pertains to this court, the Penal law states, 'A person is guilty of murder in the second degree when, with intent to cause the death of another person, he causes the death of such person or a third person.'

"Members of the jury, murder is a specific intent crime . . . In order for you to find the defendant guilty of this crime, the People are required to prove from all the evidence in the case beyond a reasonable doubt each of the following elements. . . ."

The first element was simply a restatement of the time and place of the crime and the claim that the defendant asphyxiated Florence Band. Then the judge stated the other elements.

"And, two, that the defendant asphyxiated Florence Band with the intent to cause her death.

"And three, that the defendant's act caused the death of Florence Band . . .

"I'm going to send in the jury room a copy of the form of verdict which will be as follows: 'Murder in the second degree, guilty or not guilty.' "

After that, the jury was led out to begin their deliberations.

As they left the courtroom, Cindy felt a sudden

surge of elation. Bill Dempsey had done a spectacular job. She felt that her mother's cause would be upheld. But her emotions fluctuated up and down as the jury deliberated for over seventeen hours during a three-day period. Finally, the jury foreman sent a note to the judge saying they'd reached a verdict. The jurors were led back into the courtroom. The judge silently read the jury's words, then asked the clerk to ask for the verdict.

"How do you find as to the verdict of murder in the second degree," asked the clerk. "Guilty or not guilty?"

Cindy's heart raced. She gripped the sides of her chair.

The foreman answered, "Guilty."

Howard Band, standing with his lawyer, stared straight ahead when he heard the word "guilty." Then his knees appeared to weaken and he dropped back down in his chair.

Choking back sobs, Elizabeth Diamond Band, his second wife, left the courtroom. Both Paula and Cindy stared straight ahead, their emotions numbed in that moment.

The Clerk's voice droned on. "Harken to your verdict as it has been recorded. You and each of you say you find the defendant Howard Band guilty of murder in the second degree. This is your verdict, so say you all?" Each member of the jury answered in the affirmative. At the defense attorney's request, the jury was polled. The judge then thanked them and allowed them to leave the courtroom. The judge also thanked the lawyers and set April 26 as the date for sentencing.

Cindy watched wide-eyed as her father was led away in handcuffs. Howard Band was taken at once to the Nassau County jail. As Cindy got up to leave, she had conflicting feelings. On one hand, she felt triumphant. Justice had prevailed at last! Her mother's death had been avenged. On the other hand, she felt dispirited. Her own father was a murderer and she both hated and pitied him. To face a long imprisonment, to live with what he had done to a woman he had once loved, to know he took a mother from his own daughters must be unbearable.

At the sentencing hearing a month later, the judge looked directly at Howard Band and said, "Mr. Band, you have been convicted by a jury of your peers and it now becomes the obligation of this Court to fix an appropriate sentence.

"As the Judge who presided at the trial, I am fully familiar with the facts surrounding your crime. While it is indeed the horrendous murder of your wife of which you will be sentenced, yours was also a crime of theft. You stole from your wife her most precious gift, life itself. And it appears you did so for basic and selfish reasons."

His voice rose and took on a steely edge. "But you stole more than that. You robbed your own children of their mother at a time when she would be so important to them. These two young women who now must enter adulthood, make careers, marry and begin their own families without the love and guidance their mother could provide. Because of you they are now alone."

The judge looked out at the spectators gathered in the courtroom and then back to Howard Band as he pronounced the sentence: "Twenty five years to life."

Chapter 33

Aftermath

After the trial, Cindy's sister Paula unexpectedly offered to take her sister in. "Come to my place and you can help me study for my exams." Cindy understood this was Paula's way of making amends, of trying to dispel the enmity created not only by their mother's death but also by their division over their father's culpability throughout these years. Paula was now studying criminal law. She was so intelligent that she'd whipped through college in less than four years. Cindy admired her sister's ability to persevere even with all that had occurred.

Despite Paula's testimony about her, Cindy was very grateful that her sister offered to let her stay with her. She understood that, no matter how emotionally torn her sister might be, no matter what disagreements they might have had, they were still family. Cindy had been feeling so alone. Maybe staying at Paula's place would bring them close again. "Thank you, Paula. I appreciate it. I'm not sure I can help you, though. I don't know anything about the law."

"Nonsense. You always were smart, Cindy. You can

pick up enough to ask me questions just by looking in
my books, can't you?"

"Well, I guess so." Cindy laughed and for a moment
felt like a child again, following big sister wherever she
wished to go.

Soon after Cindy moved in with Paula, she found a
job as a floral designer in the Hilton Hotel across from
Madison Square Garden, which was near the wholesale
flower district. She traveled to work each day by sub-
way. She wanted to earn her way and not just live on
Paula's kindness.

Actually, that year turned out to be a surprisingly
"normal" time when compared to Cindy's life of the
previous four years. Although Cindy and Paula were
very different, with Paula being as matter-of-fact as
Cindy was emotional, they got along well. They followed
a routine of sleep, work, going out to eat, grocery shopping, studying and occasionally seeing movies. It was a
restorative time for Cindy, who was glad to have a sister again.

The first time her sister went to visit their father in
prison, Cindy didn't want to go with her. Truthfully,
she doubted he'd want to see her because she had
helped the prosecution. However, when Paula and Liz
came back from the prison at Fishkill, they told Cindy
that her father had asked for her.

Her feelings in turmoil, Cindy accompanied them
on the second visit. Visitors were transported into the
prison on a bus. The place was clean and modern, unlike what she'd expected. The three women saw Howard
Band, who was making guesses as to when and where
he'd be shipped next. He was going through various
routines such as physical exams, aptitude tests and psy-
chological tests.

That May, Paula received 60 percent of the Rainberry Lake house in Delray Beach, Florida; Liz received 40 percent of the house as per Howard Band's specifications. Cindy received nothing, but was given permission to live in the house.

Howard Band was moved from Fishkill to Green Haven Prison on August 13. Right from the beginning, he sent letters to the various authorities in charge. He was well-educated and wrote about any wrong that he wanted righted. He was appointed a counselor, who was there to help him and protect his rights within the prison system.

Cindy, Paula and Liz had very different feelings about visiting Howard Band in prison. For Cindy, it all revolved around what she had told her father after he was first imprisoned. *The truth will set you free.* She wanted, after all this time, to hear the truth from him, believing it would free not only him but also her. On that subject, however, Howard Band was silent.

"Girls," Howard Band told all three of them the next time they visited, "there's a guy here, Peter Black, who's my friend. He's a good fellow, but he never has any visitors. Not one. It's just pitiful. Nobody should have to live like that. Now, I want you to go to the desk and sign up as visitors for Peter. Go see him. I know it will cheer him up."

When the three women finished visiting with Howard, they obeyed his wishes. The clerk at the desk asked infinite questions and there was the usual red tape, but finally they were placed on the man's visiting list.

"What is Peter Black in for?" Cindy asked the clerk preparing their papers.

"Hold on," the woman said, opening a large book. "Let's see what his prison number is. Okay, I see it. Hmm . . ."

"Do you find it?"

"He's in for life. Murder One. He's an axe murderer. He killed his wife and child."

What! An axe murderer? "Did he really use an axe?"

"Oh no. That's just a term. He really killed them with a knife, it says here."

Cindy turned to Liz and Paula who were listening. "Wow, I guess that accounts for him not having any visitors. That's kind of ironic, isn't it? He killed the people who would have been his visitors."

Cindy didn't want to sign up for visiting privileges for Black, but she did. *This doesn't mean I actually have to visit him,* she thought. And she never did.

During the months that followed, Howard Band was placed on involuntary protection, because another convict had set fire to his cell while Howard was busy working in the transmission shop of the prison. Word got around that Band was a snitch, or was perceived to be, since he got along so well with the guards at Green Haven. No one knew who had done it or at least no one was *admitting* that he knew who had done it. Thus the guards had no choice but to protect Prisoner #84A3533 by isolating him, in spite of protests put up by Howard, himself.

Band wrote his counselor in late February asking if he could be placed back in E Block, 3 Company "due to my many friends there that will look out for me." He also asked to be reinstated for the "new visiting room as I was not placed in A Block for any disciplinary action." He told the counselor that he wanted back into "the vocational school of automatic transmission as well as my night class of typewriting." He specified that he have the "kosher diet" (he'd heard the kosher meals were much better) and participate in the upcoming Passover Family event. "See that I am rescheduled on the Family Reunion Program as I am scheduled to go on a trailer visit on February 23," he wrote.

When Liz visited him on a weekend in early April, Howard sent her to visit his friend Peter Black while Cindy and Paula stayed to talk to their father. None of the three had any idea until later what had transpired during that period in the courtyard in full view of guards and inmates. Five different inmates came to Howard soon afterwards and told him what they'd seen. In fact, the men agreed to write letters to the proper authorities detailing what they allegedly saw in the courtyard. The letters said basically the same thing and each was signed by a different inmate: "On Saturday morning, April 6, I saw Elizabeth Diamond Band engage in an act of sexual intercourse in the outside yard of the new visitors' room at Green Haven Correctional Facility with inmate Peter Black."

Howard Band now told his lawyer that he wanted to divorce Liz. However, when the letters were turned in to the superintendent of the prison, the man wrote back that, after an investigation, he found the allegation to be "quite suspect," and admonished Band: "You have used correctional staff for your own personal gain. This will not be tolerated and I would advise you not to do it again. Should you attempt this, disciplinary action will be instituted. If you have family problems, the proper avenue is to contact your counselor. Please keep this in mind."

However, shortly afterward, Howard Band did, indeed, divorce Liz. In the following weeks, Liz married Peter Black.

It puzzled Cindy and Paula since Peter, "the axe murderer," was in prison for life. Paula ignored the situation with Liz and continued to visit her father regularly. But Cindy ended her visits. She had grown weary of waiting for her father to tell her what really had happened the night of her mother's death. He was still denying his own guilt. That summer, Howard Band was transferred to Auburn Correctional Facility.

In July of that year, Howard requested that Darwin Garcia be put on his visiting list. Darwin, a teenager, was the son of Tequila, the woman who had attended beauty school with Cindy in Florida. Howard Band had been corresponding with her since he'd been sent to Green Haven. Shortly afterward, Howard turned in a correspondence form pertaining to the boy in which he requested "to correspond with a good friend of mine as well as being a friend of his family."

It would be another five years before Howard married the petite, blonde Puerto Rican woman.

The following year, Paula, still torn by her love for her father and her inability to believe he would commit murder, despite all the proof, attempted to have a new autopsy performed on her mother's body performed in an effort to find out whether her father was innocent. The Saffer family opposed the exhumation. Paula told the newspapers that Cindy had wanted the procedure, too, although in truth Cindy had made it clear she did not. In the end, Florence's grave was not disturbed.

Since the Florida house was sitting empty, Cindy decided to move down there and live. Paula now had her own place. She'd graduated from law school and was embarked on her law career. It seemed like a good idea for Cindy to make use of the Rainberry Lake house.

When Cindy arrived and entered the two-story home, however, she found to her horror that an upstairs pipe had burst and poured two inches of water onto the downstairs carpet. What's more, part of the ceiling had caved in. Paula flew down long enough to give Cindy power of attorney so that Cindy could get the wet carpeting removed along with the water. Eventually, the ceiling was fixed. There was still considerable damage to the floor upstairs, but Cindy felt she could live with that for awhile until she found a job.

She was glad that Tory, her calm, beautiful friend with the cute, little daughter, still remained close. From time to time, whenever they both weren't working or busy with other things, Cindy and Tory met for a movie, a double date or just spent time together. But there never seemed to be enough hours when they were both free at the same time.

Cindy heard from her father periodically, but he never disclosed the information for which she still waited, that which she longed to hear. She wanted the truth in her father's own words, a truth which she felt finally would heal her.

It amazed Cindy that her father was so often transferred from one prison to another. Cindy later discovered the reasons why when she went over his prison records. She managed to crack the codes listing his many infractions of the rules and the reasons for Band's many transfers to other high security prisons— most of them places where she'd gone to visit him. They included Clinton, Green Haven (he was sent to this facility more than once), Eastern, Sing Sing and Mohawk-Walsh. The codes revealed that the reasons for the transfers included sex, arson (having his cell burned twice), instigating trouble, going on a hunger strike, complaining about food and claiming that one of the correctional officers had a vendetta against him. The latter problem was the most serious and went on for some time. It had ended up in a shoving match and Howard was labeled as belligerent.

Meanwhile, the years passed.

One day, Detective Jack Sharkey, sitting at his desk busy with a myriad of details on the current homicide case he was working, couldn't figure out why he kept thinking about the long-closed case of Howard Band. It had been ages since the trial. Ten years, actually, almost to the day, he realized, looking up at the calendar on the wall. Perhaps he still thought of the case because Cindy phoned him periodically, just to check in. He appreciated that. It was good to know he'd made a difference in her life. Besides that, Cindy always updated him on her father's imprisonment and his many transfers.

When the telephone rang, startling him, he was pleased to hear her voice.

"Hi, Jack," she said. "Just thought I'd check and see how you were. And how's Jeanette and your daughters?"

He smiled to himself. She sounded just the same; her friendly, eager voice still like that of the sweet, confused sixteen-year-old he'd known so long ago. "Hello, yourself, Cindy. Everybody's fine, here. How are you, kid?"

"Great. Just wonderful. I'm working and doing well. But I wanted to tell you that my father's now up at Mohawk-Walsh Correctional Facility in Rome, New York. I think he may not be feeling too well, because that's supposed to be a medical place, isn't it?"

"Yes, it is. Say, are you married again, Cindy?"

"No," she laughed. "But I've got a boyfriend. He's really nice."

"Good, good. How's Liz doing?"

"Still married to Peter Black. Isn't that wild? Don't you wonder why she married him or at least why she stays with him?"

"Oh yeah, the 'axe murderer.' The guy that killed his wife and child with a knife."

"And then wondered why nobody came to see him," Cindy added, laughing at the irony.

"Are your dad and Tequila still okay together?"

"Oh, I thought you knew, Jack. Tequila divorced him." She asked him about Bill Dempsey and Sharkey told her Bill was very busy these days. They talked a little more before saying goodbye.

He wasn't sure why, but Cindy's words nudged him to make a call he'd thought about for a long while. After Sharkey had hung up, he dialed Mohawk-Walsh Correctional Facility and asked that Howard Band return his call. After leaving his telephone number, he put down the receiver and asked himself why he had phoned. Band had been in prison ten years. What could Sharkey hope to hear? Maybe Jack himself was still hoping to hear a confession first-hand so he could tell Cindy. He knew she still awaited that closure.

The call came later that day. Howard didn't seem surprised to hear from him. Sharkey said, "Are they treating you okay?" The prisoner answered yes, then detailed a long list of complaints, which the detective finally stopped with a laugh. "Whoa, Mr. Band!"

"You know, Detective Sharkey, I've written you a letter. I've listed a lot of things I think you might want to hear." Band stopped and coughed. "I'm going to send it to my lawyer in the city. Go get it from him, Sharkey, okay? I'll tell him I'm sending it for you."

Surprised and pleased, Sharkey told Band he would. He waited a week, then drove across the bridge into Manhattan and headed for the lawyer's office, full of optimism at what the letter might contain. A confession, he was pretty sure. He had the feeling that Howard Band knew his health was failing and, perhaps, wanted to make things right.

"Detective Jack Sharkey, Nassau County Police Department," he announced when he entered the lawyer's office. The two men shook hands and Sharkey sat in the chair opposite the attorney's desk.

"What can I do for you, detective?"

"Your client, Howard Band, says he sent a letter to me by way of you."

"A letter? What letter? I know nothing about that, detective. Sorry."

Uh-oh, now what's this? Sharkey thought. "Yes, sir, a letter. I talked to Mr. Band in prison last week. He said to come here and you would give me a letter he had written to me. May I have it, please?"

"No, no, I have no letter. Howard must have been pulling your leg. There's nothing here like that."

The two men talked a little longer. Because the attorney would not back down, Sharkey finally left, but he wasn't convinced the letter didn't exist. Of course, he couldn't be sure. Sharkey sighed getting into his car. *Maybe Band is pulling my leg.*

Driving back to the office, Jack Sharkey experienced a stab of disappointment. *That letter might have verified a great deal of my hypotheses and helped Cindy get on with her life.*

Chapter 34

Deadly Confessions

"Just keeping you informed," Paula said when she phoned Cindy late one afternoon in May. Cindy had returned to the Rainberry Lake house from work. "Daddy's in the hospital," her sister said. "Stomach problems."

They seldom talked for very long these days. Cindy knew her sister was busy with her law practice and recently had gotten married. Cindy thanked Paula for calling, wondering how sick their father really was. From everything she'd learned, his life at the different prisons had been as difficult as he once had made her mother's and her own. A passage from the Bible came back to her. *Vengeance is mine, saith the Lord.* "Amen," she said softly.

One night in the first week of July, Cindy came home around eight after a busy day at work. She lay down on her bed. The room was cool and Cindy snuggled back under the covers like a rabbit into its burrow. The air conditioner's hum in the deeply shadowed room lulled her to sleep. Hours later, she heard a ringing and thought it was the alarm going off. She bolted up in bed, startled to see total darkness through the uncovered windows. On a table by the bed, the clock cast a dim glow. Cindy squinted to make out the digital figures. Two o'clock. *Oh, for . . . !* She shivered. "What's wrong?" she said aloud, trying to brush away the cobwebs of sleep enveloping her mind. In another second, she realized it was the telephone ringing and picked it up.

It was her boss. He'd been out late and had just come home and picked up the messages from the answering machine at work. "Cindy, the prison called and left a message that your father's sick and has been taken to the hospital. They said it's important you call."

With a shaky hand, she wrote down the number he gave her. "Thanks, Don," she said and disconnected the call. When she heard a dial tone, she immediately called the prison.

It seemed forever before a voice answered; she was connected to someone else to whom she asked, "Can you tell me the condition of Howard Band, please?" Feeling herself trembling, she breathed deeply and tried to gain control. At this moment, her psyche regressed from a twenty-nine-year old working woman back to Cindy Band, the sixteen-year-old girl immersed in a nightmare world. She was afraid of what was happening to him—and afraid of what would happen to her.

"Yes, Miss Band, I'm so glad you called, my dear." The prison chaplain at the other end of the line sounded tired but compassionate. "You need to come here soon if you wish to see your father before he passes, child."

It took Cindy several moments before she fully absorbed the meaning of the words. "He's dying then?" she asked. "Must I come quickly or can I wait until after the weekend? I need to rearrange my work schedule and . . ."

"Well, I wouldn't wait, my dear," the man interrupted. "Mr. Band hasn't eaten for a long while and he's sinking. Whenever you get here, come to the front gate and tell them who you are. They'll let you in no matter how late it is. God be with you, Miss Band."

Cindy hung up, her thoughts wildly ricocheting. *Must call Paula. Must get in touch with my big sister, Paula. Paula will go with me.* Her hands felt like ice. She picked up her robe lying on a nearby chair and put it on. Her address book, which she took from the drawer in the bedside table, dropped to the floor. Shaking, she picked it up, looked up Paula's new number in New York state and dialed. But when Paula answered, she didn't seem surprised to know that their father was gravely ill.

"I was just there two weeks ago, Cindy," she said in a weary voice. "I can't go with you tomorrow. I've got to be in court. I'm trying a very important case right now. I have to be there. You go. Good night."

Cindy hung up, stung by her sister's attitude. Then she realized Paula must be having as difficult a time facing this event as she was. Cindy didn't want to cry. There was too much to do. Pack, get tickets, go to work, try to get time off, drive to the West Palm airport . . . She'd simply have to go alone.

Alone! A sharp pain stabbed her stomach. The thought of going to the prison alone scared her so much she thought she might throw up. She'd never gone alone to any of the prisons where her father had been held. *Another nightmare!*

When morning came, Cindy had decided she had no choice but to go immediately; she steeled herself. While throwing some clothes into a suitcase, she called her boss. He understood that she had a family emergency and she told him she would be gone for a few days. He wished her good luck. Then, wanting to express her feelings to someone, Cindy called her friend Tory, who immediately sympathized with her. Tory's friendship was always a comfort.

Though she tried to stay calm, by noon Cindy was fighting to control her emotions. She was trembling, dreading the trip and the confrontation. She wondered if she would become so distraught that she'd get lost when she switched planes in Pittsburgh. Suddenly the telephone rang and she jumped.

It was Tory. "I'm going with you," her friend said. "I'm coming right over. You can't go alone."

"But you can't do that. It's Fourth of July weekend. It will be impossible to get a ticket at this late hour."

"I've already gotten it. I had to buy first class. Paid fifteen hundred dollars."

"What! Oh, no, you can't afford that, Tory. Don't do it. I'll be okay. Honest."

Tory laughed. "Don't worry about it. I didn't pay for it. My boyfriend Sam did."

"Wow! That was great of him. What about Michelle, though?"

"No problem. Sam will baby-sit. I know this must be terrible for you. I'm not letting you go alone. Wait for me. I'm on my way. I'll be there in a few minutes. Look, Cindy, I know you'd do the same for me."

True to her word, Tory arrived at the Rainberry Lake home in less than ten minutes. The relief Cindy felt when she saw her friend brought tears to her eyes. She couldn't speak, all she could do was hug Tory. Her friend was not only an amazingly attractive woman, she was also a beautiful soul.

They took a cab to Palm Beach International Airport. It was sweltering, but Cindy was shivering. Both women carried their bags to the gate, hurrying because the holiday traffic had made them even later.

"What are you carrying there, Cindy? It looks like a cake?"

"It's Dad's favorite cake. Got it at a bakery near the house. See?" She pulled back the lid, letting Tory see that it was a marble chiffon cake, light and fluffy with a thick layer of chocolate. "He loves this kind of cake. I thought if he hasn't been eating, the cake might tempt him."

"Looks delicious." Tory smiled.

Seeing the time on the terminal's overhead clocks, they began to run. When they reached Gate 5, most of the passengers had already boarded. A loudspeaker was blaring out an announcement. The first leg of the trip—the segment to Pittsburgh—was overbooked, a voice bellowed through the public address system. A few people would have to "wait for another plane."

Breathless, Cindy and Tory rushed to the counter. Cindy had scheduled a "bereavement flight," so she was certain she wouldn't lose her seat. The agent, checking Tory's ticket first, checked her through at once. "You'd better hurry; the flight's boarded," the woman said. Then, glancing at Cindy's ticket, she asked, "Are you Cindy Band?"

"Yes, I am," she answered.

"I'm sorry, Miss Band," the woman answered in a sing-song voice, "there is no room for you on the plane. We'll have to rebook you."

"What? But you can't! I have to go. My father is dying."

"I'm sorry. We already have a full plane. Now we . . ."

Tory slammed her ticket on the counter but kept her voice calm. "Look, it's *her* father that's dying! If she doesn't go, I sure won't go and I'll want my fifteen hundred dollars back. Now."

The attendant bit her lip. "Mmm, well, hold on for a

moment, I'll see what I can do." She picked up a phone and dialed, then left the counter and trotted down the jetway into the waiting plane. The cake in Cindy's arms grew heavy and unwieldy. Behind the two women, the people in line for the next flight groused and fidgeted. At last, the counter agent returned. "It's okay. I went on the plane and called for volunteers. Someone else is getting off the plane—we're giving them a free trip. So *you* can make the flight." She validated their tickets without a smile.

Once aboard, the flight to Pittsburgh was routine. After they landed, the two young women had a lengthy stopover before changing to a commuter plane. It was late when Cindy and Tory arrived at Utica. There they changed to an even smaller plane, something Tory said looked like it had been built before World War II, all wings, struts and props. They landed at midnight at a small Oneida County Airport.

A taxi depot was just outside the nearly deserted terminal. The man in charge motioned to a cab parked a hundred yards away. In the few moments they waited, he questioned them. Obviously, he'd been through the routine before. "Visiting Mohawk-Walsh, girls?" he asked. They nodded, but didn't respond to his curiosity in the chitchat that followed.

The driver of the cab that pulled to the curb in front of them was a woman. She, too, was familiar with people arriving late to visit the prison. She drove them into Rome, the nearby town, pointing out the prison facility as they passed. The large, gray, somber-looking structure with high walls and barbed wire appeared absolutely impenetrable. Cindy shuddered, glad when the cab driver turned back the other way to let them off at a nearby motel. The city harboring Mohawk-Walsh was a small town, the sidewalks figuratively rolled up for the night except for a twenty-four-hour convenience store across from the motel. After paying the cab fare, Cindy and Tory went into the shop where, still carrying their bags and the cake, they purchased peanut butter crackers and a few other snacks. Arms loaded, they then crossed the street to register for their room.

Once inside, Cindy washed and applied lipstick, combing and recombing her hair until it shone. Even though it was now the middle of the night, she was going to the prison to see her father. That was what the chaplain had said she should do. "I need to look my best," she told Tory, who had phoned for a cab and was now lying back on one of the beds watching her. "My father always made a big deal about how I looked and what I wore."

"You look beautiful. It's been quite a while since you've seen him, hasn't it?"

"Yeah. A long time."

"Cindy, I'll just wait for you here at the motel if you don't mind. It might hold things up to have someone with you, even if I stayed in the lobby. And this meeting between you and your dad, it's too personal for anyone else to be there."

"Thanks, Tory. I'll always be grateful you came with me. I just feel as if I'm coming apart."

"You're okay. You'll make it. You're strong."

Cindy sighed. "I sure don't feel it. When I think of my past life . . ."

"Don't think of the past. You've come through so much. Just take one step at a time and you'll be fine." A knock at their motel door announced the arrival of the cab. "Now go. And don't forget your cake." Tory shoved the white box into Cindy's hands. "You look fine."

Cindy nodded her thanks and left the room. As the driver opened the taxi door for her, Cindy hesitated for a moment. It was cooler, of course, than in Florida, but dark and eerie. Oh, how she dreaded this visit. Her tears felt stored behind a dam, desperate for release and ready to break loose at any time. She turned back to Tory and waved "for luck," and saw pity in her friend's wide brown eyes. Finally, Cindy forced a wan smile and climbed into the cab, clutching the cake.

At the prison entrance, she paid the driver and got out, telling herself to put one foot in front of the other. The whole thing was agonizing and didn't seem to be getting any easier. Tonight, possibly, would be the worst. Sighing, Cindy pushed a button, uncertain as to whether she was at the right door. A buzzer announced her presence and a compact man in a neat sergeant's uniform took her name and said, "Follow me." Then he looked at the cake.

Oh Geez, maybe he thinks I'm bringing a file in it. "It's a c-c-cake," Cindy told the officer, so nervous she was stuttering. "It's for my dad. It's a chiffon cake. You can X-ray it, but that-that's all it is." By that time, she was trembling so much, she feared the cake would fall out of her hands. In a huge, glass-enclosed room, the sergeant took the cake and passed it through a detector, then told her again, "Come on, follow me." She followed, also going through the detector. When they were on the other side, the officer returned the cake to Cindy's hands.

The man was polite but not talkative. As they walked, Cindy felt the dank sadness of the facility, the stony impression of endless halls and lost souls completely sealed in by walls. As if descending into hell, they went deeper and deeper into the facility. She took full breaths to quiet her anxiety, but it only made her light-headed. At one place, she showed her ID to a woman in uniform. They proceeded to the next checkpoint and the next. She heard someone somewhere moaning and screaming in his sleep. In years past, her father had written that sometimes he couldn't sleep for the howling and screeching that went on in the prisons during the night. *Will we never get to our destination?* she wondered, breathing heavily. Whether from nerves or the long walk, she was having trouble catching her breath.

She followed the guard outside, through a patio where there were enormous floodlights, across a base-ball field, then back into another hall.

"Now we're in Walsh," the sergeant told her. "It's the medical part of Mohawk. They treat everything here from a rash to long-term nursing stuff. That section," he pointed to a long hall, "is for highly-contagious pa-tients. It's a hospice ward. Walsh has just been open for three years. It's not a bad place."

All in your viewpoint, Cindy thought with a shudder. *They probably have insane inmates here, too. Where is my father?* As it was very late, they saw very few peo-ple—a couple of guards in the hall and a prisoner being pushed in a wheel chair by another prisoner. Hearing moans from a nearby room, Cindy felt sick to her stomach. Someone was in deep pain. *Is that my father?*

Finally, after what seemed eons of walking, they ar-rived at the room housing prisoner 84a#3533. Howard Band. The sergeant said goodbye and left her. Taking a deep breath, she pulled herself together and entered, her mouth so dry she wasn't sure she could talk. The cake was threatening to jiggle out of her hands.

The small room was dimly lit. It smelled of sickness and disinfectant. A guard, sitting on a chair in the cor-ner, nodded to Cindy.

On the bed, hooked up to an oxygen tank, was her father. For a long, heart-stopping moment, she stared at him without speaking. He looked small and frail, as if he weighed about eighty pounds. Thoughts rushed to her mind. *Is this really my father, this drawn, shrunken man? How could he have changed so much? How could I have been so scared of him?*

He seemed to be half-asleep. Then he saw her. She saw his eyes light up. He smiled.

"Cindy, you came. I'm so glad you came." His voice was faint, but his delight was obvious. "Let me see how pretty you are! Isn't she beautiful, Rocky?" he asked the guard, who smiled and nodded.

She showed him the cake, still in good condition despite the long trip. "It's for you, Daddy, your favorite. I heard you weren't eating much and . . ."

Her father called to the guard who'd been sitting in the corner. "Come here, Rocky. Look at what my beautiful daughter made for me. Just look! I told you she's a smart girl."

The guard made appreciative noises and looked at Cindy with a smile. "I'll be right outside the door if you need me."

Daddy thinks I made the cake, she thought. She saw how happy it made him and didn't correct the error. "You want some, Daddy?" She held the cake out towards him in the bed.

He stretched out one pale hand and scooped into the marbled cake, taking small morsels and putting them into his mouth. "Mmmm, good, my favorite," he murmured as he reached for one bite after another. It didn't take long, however, for him to become full.

Exhausted, he lay back against the pillow.

Cindy washed off his hands and face with a damp cloth from a nearby bowl. She filled a paper cup with water, put a straw into it and held the cup to his lips while he sipped. He took only a sip or two. Trembling, he reached out toward her and she sat beside him, holding his hand as he rested.

"Cindy," he said hoarsely, "I want to tell you what

happened. I need to tell you. I need to confess to you, daughter. I need you to forgive me, Cinnamon."

Cindy was afraid she would not be able to speak without losing control of her emotions, yet she knew this was her last chance to know. Finally, she managed to say, "Yes, Daddy, please tell me what happened. Please tell me the truth about what happened to Mommy. The truth."

Howard Band sighed. His voice was so low when he spoke that Cindy had to strain to understand him. "I did it."

She tried to stifle the gasp that hearing those three words invoked. Finally. Finally, he was admitting the truth. Now she would never have to agonize over it again, never have to be afraid that she had done the wrong thing in helping the police and the prosecutor.

"How did you do it, Daddy?" She wanted to hear; she didn't want to hear. She wanted to run away; she wanted to stay. She felt sick; she felt elated. But most of all, now that he'd begun to tell her, she felt he had to finish. She simply had to know it all.

He didn't answer immediately. She held her breath, waiting. Finally he sighed again and said, "The day of . . . that afternoon . . . that was Liz that came to the door when everybody was outside in the pool. Liz wanted to do it right then, but she'd been taking Valium or Librium or something. I wasn't comfortable with it. So she left, then came back about nine. The Robertsons had gone home about eight. I opened the front door when Liz knocked and there she stood, all in black, black pants and a black turtleneck sweater. She even had on a black ski mask, which covered most of her face. And of course, her blonde hair was covered. So if you didn't *know* it was Liz, you wouldn't have recognized her. She had a gun pointed at me."

Her father took a shallow, rattling breath, then continued. "Mommy called down and said 'Who is it, Howard?' I looked at Liz and knew it was then or never—we had to go through with it. So I called up to Mommy and said 'We're being held up, Florence. Stay there.' Liz pushed the gun at me like she was a real burglar and we went up the stairs."

Her father stopped talking for a moment and appeared to be trying to catch his breath. Cindy could only imagine how frightened her mother must have been, seeing that burglar coming at her and her husband being held at gunpoint.

"And I already had the needle—a hypodermic—ready in the house, as Liz knew. I injected Mommy. It didn't work and we both panicked. We'd gotten the drug the year before when we did it to Carl Diamond."

Cindy gasped. *Would the madness never end?* "You killed Liz's husband, too? I thought Carl died of a heart attack."

"The stuff that was in the needle was supposed to bring on a heart attack in a way that nobody could tell the difference. It worked with Carl. What happened that night was that Liz and Carl went to see a sick friend and when they came back out to the parking garage, I was crouched in the back seat waiting, just like Liz and I had planned. I reached up, put a rope around his neck and twisted it while she gave him the shot. It brought on the attack and we put him in the back seat. Then I got in front and drove him to the hospital. We drove past two hospitals just to make sure he was dead. Then we pulled in the emergency room of one of them and called out for help. When the attendants came, we told them to hurry—that he was having a heart attack. They tried to revive him, but by that time, it was too late. The stuff was non-traceable. No one suspected a thing."

Cindy felt sick, hearing this second confession. It was

much more than she had expected to hear. She didn't speak but motioned for him to go on.

"So I'd held onto a vial of that drug ever since, just waiting for an opportunity," he continued, his voice a hoarse whisper. "We wanted to be together, you see, Liz and me. And besides, Liz got Carl's insurance, which was sizable. He was a clothes manufacturer on Broadway—very successful, lots of money. I used to bring clothes home to Mommy. Anyway, the drug worked quickly on him. But Mommy didn't die from the drug like she was supposed to. Liz held her at gun-point while I injected her, but she was too healthy and she was younger, of course, than Carl had been. Or maybe because we kept the medication for such a long time it had gotten stale and no longer worked. Well, we sort of freaked out then and put a pillowcase over Mommy's head. And while Liz held the gun on her, I ran down and got a trash bag and came up and put that over Mommy's head, too. It all happened so fast. I don't know . . . Oh, Cookie-baby, her last words were of you and Paula. She said, 'What's going to happen to my children?' Hearing that, I sort of woke up and real-ized what I was doing. I couldn't handle it. I jerked that bag off Mommy's head despite Liz screaming 'what are you doing?' At that point, Liz seemed larger than life, but I didn't want Mommy dead anymore. She loved you children more than life itself and I felt terri-ble. But it was too late. She was gone."

Cindy felt devastated. "Oh, Daddy," she said in a whisper.

"Then we didn't know what to do. We got some rope that I remembered was in the closet and tied Mommy up—hog-tied her, really, with her wrists fastened to her ankles. We decided to make it look like a burglar had come in and killed her. We knew you would be coming in before midnight and we were going to be gone and let you find Mommy and call the police. But, dammit, you were late, so I came home and there was Mommy still lying there dead and I didn't know what to do. The robbery bit wouldn't work anymore, so I dragged her down to the basement as fast as I could, then cut the ropes off of her and scattered food around. I was so scared at that point, I called Liz and we concocted the story about the Pepto Bismol. Then I rushed over to Dr. Sultan's house."

"What did you do with the gun, pillow case, hypodermic and everything?"

"When we drove away after—uh, after killing Mommy, we threw all the evidence over a fence in Brooklyn. Nobody ever found anything. I dropped Liz off where her car was parked, then I drove back thinking the worst would be over—that the police would be there and we'd be in the clear. I know it was wrong. I just loved Liz so much. We didn't want to hurt *you*, Cinnamon. Will you forgive me?"

Cindy turned her face away. "Daddy, I can't. I can't. But please, you've got to tell Paula." She realized her father was weeping—or maybe he was just putting on an act, she wasn't sure. Her chest felt so constricted, she thought she was the one who was dying.

"There isn't time for that. Cindy," he rasped. "Please, you have to forgive me. *Now!*"

Suddenly, she felt the urgency. She felt like dreamers do when they're trying to run but can't move a muscle. She felt as if she were strangling. "Daddy," she whispered, straining to speak. Finally the words came and she could say them. "Daddy, I forgive you. I do. Please hear me, Daddy. I forgive you."

For one brief moment, Howard Band opened his eyes. Out of that thin, skull-like face, he smiled at her. Again he shut his eyes, but the smile lingered on.

A few moments later sweat began pouring down his

face—copious sweat. She wasn't sure what to do. "Daddy," she cried out. The guard rushed back in the room and then hurried back into the hall to call a medic. Moments later, a male nurse came in and gave the gravely ill man a shot.

When her father seemed to have gotten past this episode and was resting comfortably, Cindy left. It would be the last time she saw her father alive. She returned to the motel and her friend Tory, who wisely asked no questions. The two women were back in Delray Beach the following day.

Afterward, when Cindy confronted her former stepmother, Liz denied everything. Two weeks later, on July 20, 1994, the chaplain phoned again. Prisoner Howard Band was dead.

Paula took care of everything. There was no service and Howard Band was cremated.

Epilogue

Gradually, Cindy began to feel as if a giant weight had been lifted from her chest. She was glad that she had managed to forgive her father, as her new faith counseled. It was as if her mother, too, was now content. Justice had finally been done and tempered with mercy.

Months passed and Cindy began to live her life again, this time with a lighter heart. A few years after their father's death, Cindy was visiting her sister in New York when Paula told her, "I'm deeding the Rainberry Lake house to you for a hundred dollars."

"It's yours now, Cindy," Paula went on. "All but the 40 percent belonging to dear Liz. Now you don't have to worry about being kicked out. No rent, no mortgage. All you have to do is pay the taxes each year. You *can* do that, can't you?"

"Of course I can." She smiled at her sister. "Thanks, Paula."

The next morning she said goodbye to Paula and her husband and hugged the two babies her sister now had.

Her sister's gift made her happy. She was now a homeowner. The year was 1998.

At the same time, one of the partners in a local nightclub needed extra help. Cindy had been at the club before. She knew Michael Connell and liked him. He asked her to be general manager of his club. Before long, however, the place had to shut down because of vandalism. Cindy handled the entire insurance claim.

Delighted with the way she'd taken care of it, Mike told her, "Cindy, you are an exemplary employee." As a result, he invited her to work with him in another company—an internet enterprise that traded computer chips.

She had met his other two partners. In fact, Franco, one of them, had driven her home a couple of times. When she joined the computer company, Franco trained her.

"It's a volatile business," he told her. "Suddenly stores say 'we want more.' But we don't have them. So people like me scramble around, find them and then charge whatever. It's very exciting. Some of the companies shut down in the summer, however, so we need to work hard the other months."

Cindy soon learned that their outfit traded with companies not only in the United States, but also in England, Germany and the Far East. A fast learner, Cindy was able to orient herself quickly to the trade. Each day, she called Asia first, as they operated on time that was twelve hours earlier. She called Europe about noon, then did domestic trading the rest of the day. As Franco had said, the work was exciting.

Telling Tory about the system soon after Franco had taught her, Cindy said, "I talk long distance to executives at these companies and find out what they need. I'm the middleman. I'm doing pretty well, I think. Already people have called and told Franco or Mike how helpful I am."

"I never doubted that you were smart and capable," Tory said She was always quick to bolster her friend's self-esteem.

"There's something else, Tory." Cindy grinned. "Franco's asked me out and I think I'm going to accept. He's so respectful of women I'm not used to that and it makes me feel great."

On their first date, Cindy learned what a delightful person Franco was. His caring attitude began to heal her wounded heart.

They began going out regularly and he continued to court her in a charming, European way. Often he brought flowers or cooked for her—wonderful omelets with cheese and other delicious creations. It made her feel cherished.

Unfortunately, months later the company had a change in partnership and closed. Ever since the time she had left the restaurant *La Vieille Maison,* one of her first jobs in Florida, Cindy had kept in touch with the owners. She called and told Carolyn Picot that her job at the computer company had ended abruptly.

"We have an opening in our office for an events manager," Carolyn said.

To Cindy's delight, everything worked out just right. Cindy was back to work the following week. She began booking and planning parties for the restaurant with clients from all over the world. She felt as if she'd come home.

Not long afterward, Franco became a partner in a newly formed computer-chip business. They spent more and more time together. She appreciated his patience and the love he was showing her. Her life was coming together so beautifully. And then Liz suddenly announced that she wanted to sell the house in Delray Beach, the house in which Cindy had been living. Turmoil seemed to have sought her out again.

* * *

The upshot of it all was that Cindy had to sue to try to retain the house that had been the home she so badly needed. Unfortunately, she lost her suit. On the day she found out, she rushed home to tell Franco, who was waiting for her. Fresh from work, she was wearing a chic blue suit that emphasized her fit, petite body. They went into the living room and sat down, but Cindy soon jumped up and nervously began pacing. Eventually, she stopped pacing and turned to the dark-haired, pony-tailed man watching her from the L-shaped sofa in her living room. Noticing her agitation, Franco reached up and took her hand.

"What am I going to do?" Her voice sounded agitated and she rushed on. "Dan Quai lost the case for me!" She bit her lip. "Liz has won again." She looked at Franco, misery in her hazel eyes.

"Cindy, I'll take care of you—always," her boyfriend, Italian, muscular and passionate, promised with a smile.

"But how can they sell my house out from under me just like that? It's my home. I've lived here since I was eighteen. I paid my lawyer a thousand dollars, money I barely scraped together and can ill afford to waste. He didn't do his job."

"Cindy, you have to calm down. You'll make yourself ill." Franco pulled her gently onto the sofa beside him and began stroking her hair.

Usually his touch comforted her. But today, as she stared through the sliding glass doors, the beauty of Rainberry Lake in her backyard made her ache already for this new loss. The scent, the colors, the click-clack sounds of all those feather-like Florida palms waving, the radiant blue sky which could become a riot of hues at sunset, the frogs with their syncopated chorus, the fragrance of gardenias and night-blooming jasmine—

they'd all been hers. She sensed the betrayal, which had begun so many years ago, even more than before.

What did Liz do to win the case? she asked herself. Liz might do anything. But one would think Liz had stolen enough from her over the years. Why would Liz take her stepdaughter's only home away, too?

This year, with her job and relationship with Franco going so well, Cindy had actually begun to feel her life was on the right track and she was headed for a happy future. *Now what?* Thoughts of past years of acquiescing, taking insults and barbs she knew she didn't deserve, accepting the lies of others, not making waves, trying to please those who had violated her life, ran through her mind. *I'm not going there again,* she promised herself. *No matter what I have to do.*

"Franco, I have to talk about it! I lost my temper at my own lawyer. Now he's furious and using what I told him in confidence to get back at me. It isn't right. There still is lawyer-client privilege, isn't there?"

"Tell me exactly what happened, Cindy." Franco stroked his neatly trimmed beard, as he often did while concentrating. "We'll work it out. After all, you own 60 percent of this house, don't you? They *can't* just kick you out."

"They're already doing it. If I only had the money to fight on . . ."

"C'mon, Cindy, we'll work it out. It'll be okay. Tell me the details."

"Well, you know that I hired Dan Quai to keep this from happening last month when my stepmother Liz threatened to sell the house. Remember, my father gave her 40 percent of the house. As I told you before, Dan agreed. He took the money and I thought he'd negotiated with Liz's attorney and everything was resolved. Today he tells me Liz and her lawyer had a hearing with the judge. Dan *never told* me beforehand about the hearing. He knew I had documents, and the judge wouldn't have ruled this way if I'd had the chance to show them to her.

"Dan called me this morning and said he went to the hearing with everybody and he lost the case. 'Sorry,' he said. And when I started to cry, he became all condescending: 'I feel sorry for you!' *Sorry?* And I'm without my home. Sure I was mad. Sure I lost my temper. I *trusted* him. Now he's telling me—and the judge—that I'm so upset because I have long term problems from all my past troubles. As if maybe I should see a shrink. Brushing me off like I was crazy or just a nothing."

Franco hugged her to him again. Tears ran down her face. "My life is coming apart again."

"Again, Cindy?" he echoed. "It's time you tell me about your past—all this stuff you've been holding in since your mother's death and not confiding in me. Losing your house is just a fraction of it, I know that much. It's time to stop the secrets. You've got lots of friends. You have me. You're a good person. People love you. Everyone at work, me . . ."

She pulled back and surveyed Franco through long dark lashes wet with tears. For so long, she'd been reluctant to trust anyone. *Once people closest to you betray you, it becomes impossible to trust anyone completely again.* Still, Franco had been so good to her. He was more than a boyfriend. He would never hurt her. And he was right; her friends at work—the wonderful owners, Carolyn and Leonce Picot, administrator Joyce Fix and all the rest—they gave her so much positive feedback, it had begun to raise her lost self-esteem.

"Darling," Franco's deep, slightly accented voice caressed her. His lips pressed hers in an attempt to drown out the worries.

Don't pull back, she told herself. It's Franco kissing me. Franco loves me. Relax. I love Franco. Why can't I overcome this aversion to being close? To any kind of intimacy? Cindy knew she must, if they were to have any sort of future.

"There's something I need to hear." Franco pulled away and looked at her.

She felt his sweetness and strength. *Why can't I forget the pain and trust him with my past? He will help me, I know he will. He must love me if he's willing to overlook all my hang-ups!*

"Cindy, please tell me what happened to you as a teenager. I know so little about those days and it's like a wall between us. You've told your lawyer everything, but not me."

"And look what happened. He used my words against me."

"But I'm *not* going to use it against you." Franco laughed, as if the idea were preposterous. "You have to trust me, Cindy. I want to help you, you know that."

She took a deep breath and let it out. "There are things in my past that I'd . . . well, I'd rather you didn't know about." She'd never told the whole story of her mother's death to anybody once she'd moved to Florida. She'd just kept it bottled up. It was too horrible.

She sighed, got up and went to the kitchen where she began to prepare him a drink. "What do you want? The usual?" she called out. She noted his nod through the pass-through window. She rarely drank herself. There was too much responsibility with her job at *La Vieille Maison* to risk making errors. She fixed his martini and took it to him, then sat down again on the couch.

Franco tasted the drink. "I really needed this." He sat the glass on the table beside the couch and looked into Cindy's eyes. "Cindy, it's time I knew." He touched her cheek. His dark brown eyes held her gaze. "I love you, Cindy. If I'm going to be part of your future, then I want to be part of your past as well."

My past! Her mind flashed back. She saw the horrific scene: the stairwell, her mother, her father, the police officers, the ambulance. They were jagged pictures randomly juxtaposed in her mind. Cindy shuddered.

I had such a privileged childhood. But in one split second on that hot August day, everything changed. Nothing has ever been the same since.

"Oh, God," she said aloud. A single tear ran down her cheek.

Franco was right, of course. It was time he knew the truth. Besides, maybe if she let it all pour out, she could finally move forward. Then again, maybe she never would. A chill, like a finger of ice, ran up and down her spine. But she sat him down and proceeded to reveal her soul.

From that time on, Cindy and Franco not only grew closer, Cindy grew stronger.

A few months later, Cindy received a call from Paula in New York telling her that their grandfather had died a week before. Paula had been away and since Al Saffer's wife, Shirley, had died a few years prior, no one had called to tell Cindy about it. She felt badly that she wasn't at his funeral, but she prayed for him every night.

Fortunately, her work kept her very busy. After a quiet summer, *La Vieille Maison* was gearing up for a big winter crowd. Cindy loved her job, the customers at the restaurant and her associates. And she had Franco. She began to realize that it wasn't the house but her life she now valued.

The following week, Cindy was off on Tuesday. That morning, she opened the front door of the Rainberry Lake home to let Franco enter. A wave of warm air blew in. It was a beautiful blue-skied day, the kind of southern fall day that makes a person want to reach out and hug the world.

While Cindy greeted Franco with a kiss, Charlotte, her black Labrador retriever, ran around the house wildly, wagging her tail to show their visitor that as the top dog of the house, she, too, was happy he had arrived on that morning.

"I have something to tell you," Cindy said with a wide smile. "I've finally accepted selling this house and, not only that, but despite my earlier shock, now I feel good about it. The realtors brought in several would-be buyers this week. Liz doesn't think they're offering enough, but I'm going to take one of those offers. I suddenly realized that when this house is sold, my last ties with Liz will be cut. People have said I should sue Liz in a civil suit for killing my mother; she wouldn't have immunity in a civil suit. But I won't do that. It will only prolong my torture. She's getting old and won't live forever. Daddy told me the truth and I'm leaving the rest in God's hands.

"You never have been a vengeful type, Cindy. That's something I admire about you."

"Oh, Franco," she said, hugging him. "I know now that my life can be in the present and the future, not the past. I'm so glad I have you to share it with."

He held her tight. His voice was low and husky. "I'm glad I've got you, too, my sweetheart. No matter what happens, we'll make it. Together."

Afterword

In 2001, the chairmen of Jericho High School's twentieth reunion sent Cindy a book about her old classmates with best wishes from everyone. They also sent her a photo of herself scanned from the 1981 yearbook.

Paula is a respected lawyer in New York. She is married and has two children.

Liz is still married to Peter Black. It is unlikely that he will ever be paroled. Her children are still close to their mother. Donny Diamond holds a good job; Bart is married.

Cindy is still in touch with Mark, the boy she dated in high school. He is now owner of an upscale gourmet shop in the New York City area.

Cindy and Franco are still friends. Cindy continues in her excellent position as events manager at *La Vieille Maison,* which maintains its position as one of the world's most prestigious restaurants. Fine people from all over the globe pass through the restaurant's doors. She remains "like family" to the owners Leonce and Carolyn Picot, as well as administrator Joyce Fix and the rest of the exceptional staff. One of her customers, Richard Feit, for whom she'd arranged a party in 2001, helped her and her co-author get this book to the right publisher.

Tory lives in a beautiful, oceanfront apartment about twenty minutes south of Cindy. She came by on Cindy's last birthday to help her celebrate. Also celebrating his birthday on that same day was Jack Sharkey.

Detective Sharkey, who retired from the force in 1999 with a big party given by the department, spends half the year on the west coast of Florida with his wife, Jeanette. In 2002, one of his daughters had her second baby. Jack received a prestigious award for his untiring work in the Band case. He was also given a huge surprise party by the Saffers and close friends of Florence Saffer Band for securing final justice for the murdered woman.

Assistant District Attorney William Dempsey is married and has a child. Bill told Sharkey he was glad God had given him a baby girl "born in November" because, as a Scorpio, she would always remind him of Cindy. Bill still works hard as an assistant district attorney in Mineola, New York, where he has an excellent reputation as an able and dedicated prosecutor.

Cindy has begun working to establish a support group for children and adults who have had family members murdered by other family members. She is dedicating this group in honor of her beloved mother, Florence Band.

SPECIAL UPDATE FOR THE PAPERBACK EDITION

Since the hardcover version of *Shattered Bonds* was released, authors Julie Malear, the writer, and Cindy Band, the heroine of the story, have stayed in touch. As this paperback edition went to press, the two women spent an evening noting how many things had changed.

"I saw for one that Cindy has grown up," Malear says after speaking with her. "Many times during the months I was interviewing her for the original book, I felt as if she was still sixteen, the age she was when the murder occurred. This was not surprising when you consider all the things she'd gone through. Probably a defense mechanism. What always surprised me is how she could be so sweet, generous and forgiving to people in the face of what had happened in her life."

Cindy has left the famous old restaurant, *La Vieille Maison,* which had been her work and her only family for the past ten years. She holds the owners and staff in the highest regard.

Cindy sold the house in Rainberry Lake and has moved several times in the same general area. There were many bad memories connected with the big home on the lake, and in selling, she severed the legal ties with her stepmother.

She is now involved in real estate with a neighbor friend, the father of two beautiful children. They live in a delightful home on a canal in Boynton Beach the next town north of Delray Beach. Here, she cooks to her heart's content and, as always, works out daily at a gym. Her black Labrador, Charlotte, is still with her and healthy despite having had a hip replacement last year.

Cindy has finally taken some Victims of Crime counseling to accept and better understand the happenings in her surreal life. "I now know the difference between people who care, and those who don't have my best interests at heart," she says. "And I realize that fear-based thoughts can change." She is doing fine. As someone who has gone through so much, she wants to reach out to others in trouble and that's what Cindy has done, after starting a foundation here in her mother's memory. She plans to do much more in the future with her "Shattered Bonds Foundation."

Liz still calls from time to time. One peaceful Sunday morning in 2005, two Boynton Beach policemen arrived at Cindy's residence. They asked her business partner to bring Cindy to the door and have her step outside. "There's been a death in the family, Miss," they told her. Since the only family member Cindy still had was her sister, she went into shock mode. "It's my sister," she cried.

"No, it's your mother."

"My mother's dead."

The officer said he'd call dispatch to make sure. "It's your mother. Here's the phone number." He was concerned that she was in bad shape and wanted her to make the call in front of him, perhaps thinking she might faint.

"No," she said, "It's my stepmother. I'm okay." However, with the lawman watching, she phoned. "Who's dead?" she asked her stepmother.

"Oh, no one. I just couldn't remember your number."

Cindy put the phone down and apologized to the policemen. She then finished her conversation with her stepmother, who, after the divorce from Howard Band, had married an axe murderer who was in prison on a life sentence. Cindy knew he had recently died leaving everything to her stepmother, an estate rumored to be worth millions. "You must be well off now," Cindy said. "You're the executor."

"Yes, that's what I was led to believe," the woman answered. "I was the executor, all right. Executor over what? Over *nothing*." Her stepmother told Cindy she'd be down in February. "And I have your cell phone."

Cindy now has a new cell phone number.

Cindy's sister and two children also arrived unexpectedly one day last year. She told Cindy's business partner who she was and that she wanted to see her sister. Although Cindy put her off that day, she became flooded with guilt when she heard her sister tell her boys, "See, I told you she might not want to see me." Cindy got in touch with her at the hotel and she and her partner spent the week taking them everywhere. She realizes that her sister, a successful career woman, has still blocked the tragedy from her mind.

The book has been responsible for Fox News flying Cindy up to New York twice, where Linda Vester featured her on *DaySide* because of the parallel between her parents' case and that of the Scott and Laci Peterson murder. Cindy also has been featured on a forty-city radio tour. The book was given a two-page spread in *The Globe*.

Both Cindy Band and Julie Malear have made frequent appearances at libraries, festivals, book stores, public television, and functions hosted by such organizations as Brandeis Chapter. Currently there is interest from abroad.

On a book tour in Tampa, Julie's family arranged a reunion between the authors and Detective Jack Sharkey and his family. Cindy was seeing her kind friend for the first time since her father's trial. It was a poignant meeting. She credits the detective with saving her life after her mother's murder. The case earned the detective several awards. Malear had gotten to know Sharkey and his wife by phone because of the many times she had called to interview him for the book.

When *Shattered Bonds* first came out in hardback, the detective had been drafted to speak at a country club on Long Island attended by many people in the area who had known of the controversial case. The Bands' neighbor who first broke the news to Cindy of her mother's death—was one of those interested in the book. Another was the famed Michael Baden, who took the book back from Ft. Lauderdale after meeting Julie at a SleuthFest convention there. While writing the book, Malear had phone-interviewed Baden who was involved in the controversial Band trial. Baden is star of his own forensic TV show and has written several books in addition to investigating the deaths of President Kennedy and Dr. Martin Luther King, Jr. He was also involved as an expert in many high profile cases such as Claus Von Bulow, O.J. Simpson, and the re-examination of the Lindbergh baby kidnapping.

Since writing *Shattered Bonds* with Cindy, some of Malear's short stories have come out in an anthology, *Tales from Below the Frost Line.* She has also written a novel, *More Precious Than Rubies.*

"Cindy has turned her life around, recovering from the past," says Malear. "She showed me some quotes she received during the counseling session, a paraphrase of a Bible passage with her name inserted. *I know the plans I have in mind for you, Cindy, plans for your peace, reserving a future full of hope for you. Jer. 29: 11-14.* The future is now."

Chapter 6

🙠

The next morning my aunt sought me out to accompany her to the meat market at the Shambles to procure sheep's suet for the Lord Keeper's poultice.

'Come, Ann. This is not a task I would do myself from habit,' she explained, 'and yet it will be a good lesson for you in how to go marketing when you have a household of your own.'

It was a fine, breezy day and my aunt decided that since it was dry and the mud in the streets would not sully our gowns, it would benefit our health to walk. I was happy. There was always so much to look at in this city of two hundred thousand souls, probably the busiest city in the whole world.

We first recognized the Shambles by its stench. Dozens of butchers' shops, cheek by jowl next to the slaughterhouses that fed them, scented the air with the ripe, rotting smell of discarded animal flesh. There were two rows of butchers' shops and another down the middle, each with a large window and wide sill, two feet deep, where the lumps of meat were on display to be poked and sniffed by fussy housewives